ṢŪFĪ MYSTICS OF THE NIGER DESERT

Arabic inscriptions on the graves, or meditation quarters, of the mystics of the *Maḥmūdiyya* or another Ṣūfī order within the ruined townlet of In Taduq

ṢŪFĪ MYSTICS OF THE NIGER DESERT

Sīdī Maḥmūd and the Hermits of Aïr

H. T. NORRIS

CLARENDON PRESS · OXFORD
1990

Oxford University Press, Walton Street, Oxford OX2 6DP
Oxford New York Toronto
Delhi Bombay Calcutta Madras Karachi
Petaling Jaya Singapore Hong Kong Tokyo
Nairobi Dar es Salaam Cape Town
Melbourne Auckland
and associated companies in
Berlin Ibadan

Oxford is a trade mark of Oxford University Press

Published in the United States
by Oxford University Press, New York

British Library Cataloguing in Publication Data
Norris, H. T. (Harry Thirlwall), 1926–
Sufi mystics of the Niger Desert.
1. Niger. Sufism. Sidi Mahmud al-Baghdadi
I. Title
297.4092
ISBN 0–19–826538–7

Library of Congress Cataloging in Publication Data
Norris, H. T.
Ṣūfī mystics of the Niger desert
Sīdī Maḥmūd and the hermits of Aïr/by H.T. Norris.
Includes bibliographical references.
1. Maḥmūd, al-Baghdādī. 16th cent. 2. Sufis—Niger—Biography.
I. Title.
BP80.M2845N67 1990 297'.4'092—dc20 90–30874
ISBN 0–19–826538–7

Set by Cambrian Typesetters, Frimley, Surrey
Printed in Great Britain by
Bookcraft (Bath) Ltd,
Midsomer Norton, Avon

To my parents,
Dora and Ernest

Whosoever obtains a Permission from the Guides enters into the Choir of the Saints, since all the saints are linked together hand in hand, and thus he enters into this company, and into the Chain of these Lords, as in a dance.

From *Fletore e Bektashiniet*, by Naim Frashëri, translated by F.W. and Margaret M. Hasluck, *Christianity and Islam under the Sultans* (Oxford, 1929), p. 558.

Preface

I HAVE to express my gratitude to a number of individuals and institutions in the United Kingdom, in France, and in the Niger Republic, the help of whom and the assistance of which have enabled me to complete this study, which, by its very nature, can only be an initial assessment of the contribution of the Ṣūfīs of Aïr to the history of Islam amongst the southern Tuareg and the adjacent peoples of Niger and Nigeria. Oxford University Press has generously agreed to finance the publication of this study, and I have also received essential financial help, in order to visit Niger on four occasions, from the British Academy, the School of Oriental and African Studies, and the Central Research Fund of London University. Nigériens of all communities, and all government departments, have co-operated with me, too many of them to name. However, I owe a special debt to Shaykh Muḥammad Ibrāhīm of Abalagh, Tahoua, who gave me permission to photograph his personal copy of the *Qudwa*, Ghubăyd ăgg-Ălăwjeli (Ghubayd) of ORTN Agades, who first introduced me to the Islamic history of Niger, Dr Djibou Hamani, formerly of the Institut de Recherche en Science Humaine and now head of the Department of History in the University of Niamey, Dr Aboubakar Adamou and Dr Maïkoréma Zakari and Dr Mary White Kaba, all of Niamey University, M. Diouldé Laya and M. Altinine agg Arias of the Centre pour l'Étude de l'Histoire par Tradition Orale, in Niamey, and Professor John Lavers of the Department of History in Bayero University, Kano. Professor al-Qāsim al-Bayhaqī of the Islamic University in Say and M. Abdou Malam Moussa, now the Ambassador of the Niger Republic in Kuwait, have also been of assistance.

Nearer to home I am grateful to Drs E. and S. Bernus, whose studies of the Islamic monuments of Aïr and Azawagh have contributed substantially to my assessment, likewise the critical and most helpful comments of Jean Louis Triaud, whose study of the *Khalwatiyya ṭarīqa* in Aïr, mentioned in this book, was the first comprehensive investigation to be published regarding the perennial heritage of Sīdī Maḥmūd al-Baghdādī in that region. Lastly, I have to thank three colleagues in London University, Dr Louis Brenner, Dr Humphrey J. Fisher, and Dr Murray Last, for help and advice and criticism of all kinds. The Editorial staff and the members of the Arts and Reference Division at Oxford University Press have been extremely helpful in seeing this book through to publication and I would particularly like to express my thanks to Penelope Johnstone for her advice on a number of matters connected with the translation of the Arabic text and its publication. The care that they have shown was greatly appreciated. Mohamed ben Madani, the editor of the *Maghreb Review*, was of help in obtaining copies of a text from the Bibliothèque Nationale in Algiers relating to the movement of Sīdī Maḥmūd. I hope that the help of all of the above is made plain at various points in the contents of this work.

H.T.N.

Newport, 1988

Just before this book went to press, both author and publisher were shocked and saddened to hear of the death of Dr Suzanne Bernus, whose work, along with that of her husband, is referred to throughout.

Contents

List of Plates

Arabic inscriptions on the graves, or meditation quarters, of mystics of the *Maḥmūdiyya*, or another Ṣūfī order, who were once resident within the ruined townlet of In Taduq in the Azawagh desert to the west and south of Agades, capital of Aïr. The inscriptions are either seventeenth or eighteenth century in date and show the Arabic lettering typical of this area. The formulaic phrases, together with others, indicate the 'illuminatory' character of the local Ṣūfism, also the initiation of women members separately into the order, which is unspecified, though it bears all the hallmarks of the *Maḥmūdiyya*, or the *Khalwatiyya*. Other graves in the vicinity appear to be of noteworthy members of the Ayt Awari Tuareg (including a former chief, Muḥammad Māṣil). The Ṣūfī movement and the *ineslemen* Arabic teachers and jurists are central to the way of life of many of the Kel Denneg Tuareg and the few Ḥassāniyya-speaking Kunta of this remote district (photograph kindly given to the author by Drs E. and S. Bernus). *Frontispiece*

Abbreviations

General

BIFAN	*Bulletin de l'Institut Fondamental* (formerly *Français*) *d'Afrique Noire*
BNP	Bibliothèque Nationale, Paris
BSOAS	*Bulletin of the School of Oriental and African Studies*, London
Ghubayd	[Ghubăyd ăgg-Ălăwjeli] *Histoire des Kel-Denneg, avant l'arrivée des Français*, publ. by K. Prasse (Copenhagen, 1975)
JAH	*Journal of African History*
Koran	The *Qur'ān*
Qudwa	*Qudwat al-muᶜtaqid fī siyar al-ajwād*
RBCAD	*Research Bulletin*, Centre of Arabic Documentation

References Cited Fully in the Bibliography

Corpus	Levtzion & Hopkins, *Corpus of Early Arabic Sources for West African History*
EI (1)	*Encyclopaedia of Islam*, 1st edn.
EI (2)	*Encyclopaedia of Islam*, 2nd edn.
GAL	Brockelmann, *Geschichte der Arabischen Litteratur*
GAL S	*Idem*, supplementary vol.
Lane	*Arabic-English Lexicon*, two vols., The Islamic Texts Society
Leo Africanus	*Description de l'Afrique*, trans. A. Epaulard
Rodd	Sir F. Rennell Rodd, *People of the Veil*
Sezgin	*Geschichte des Arabischen Schrifttums*, vol. i.
Shorter EI	*Shorter Encyclopaedia of Islam*
T	al-Tādilī: *Kitab al-Tashawwuf ilā rijāl al-taṣawwuf*, ed. by A. Faure
Arabic text:	The letter s (sād) indicates that this passage or variant is to be found in the text of *Ṣifat al-wird* by Mūsā Abatūl, though not in our text of the *Qudwa*.

Introduction

Some years ago, I was introduced to my Tuareg friend, Ghubăyd ăgg-Ălăwjeli (Ghubayd), who was then, and still is, an animator of Radio Niger (ORTN), in the Nigérien city of Agades, the capital of Aïr. He was at that time in the course of writing his history of the Kel Denneg Tuareg and during our correspondence he drew my attention to the conflicting legends and reports about Shaykh Sīdī Maḥmūd al-Baghdādī—Sidi Mekhmud Ălbăghdadi' amongst the Tuareg—who had come to the Aïr Massif 'from Baghdād' at an uncertain date in the sixteenth or seventeenth centuries.

According to Ghubayd, Sīdī Maḥmūd had converted men *à sa doctrine*, without a clear indication as to what that doctrine might have been, although, in the Tamasheq text which accompanies the history, Ghubayd renders 'doctrine' by the Arabic loan-word, *ṭarīqa* (*dăgh—etteriqăt—net*), thus indicating that what is clearly meant is a Ṣūfī 'Way', Sīdī Maḥmūd having been its founder or its missionary. This latter saint had been mentioned much earlier by noted travellers and explorers; amongst them Henry Barth in his *Travels and Discoveries in North and Central Africa* (1857), and Francis Rennell Rodd in his *People of the Veil* (1926).[1] Sīdī Maḥmūd was sometimes confused with the Algerian scholar Muḥammad b. ᶜAbd al-Karīm al-Maghīlī (died *c.*1503–6), who had passed through Aïr, possibly half a century before Sīdī Maḥmūd, and, even if he had died, as the Kunta maintain, as late as 1533–4, could have had no appreciable influence upon the curious life practised by the latter.

During a visit to Agades, Ghubayd took me to a house in an old quarter of the city where an Agades scholar allowed me to photograph a number of folios from the book entitled *Ṣifat al-wird* (The Description of the Prayer Litany), a *Khalwatiyya* Ṣūfī work whose author was called Mūsā Abatūl. In it there are a number of folios which describe Sīdī Maḥmūd and his followers. I paraphrased some of their sketchy content in my book, *The Tuaregs* (1975), pp. 63–7. It has not been possible since to see a complete copy of *Ṣifat al-wird*. Further parts of it, and much biographical detail about its author, have been presented in a recent, lengthy study by Jean-Louis Triaud entitled 'Hommes de religion et confréries islamiques dans une société en crise, l'Aïr aux XIXe et XXe siècles, Le Cas de la Khalwatiyya'.[2]

I visited Niger once more in late 1977 and I stopped on my route at the house of a leading Tuareg scholar and very good friend, Shaykh Muḥammad Ibrāhīm al-Aghlālī.

He then lived in the small village of Abalagh on the road between Tahoua, In Gall, and Agades. Amongst the folios of his, which he kindly allowed me to photograph, was a large and faded book, which he realized was of some importance although he could comment little on its content, so brief was my stay. Upon my return to London my films were printed by Paul Fox at the School of Oriental and African Studies, University of London. The book photographed proved to be the bulk of the contents of a work called *Qudwat al-muᶜtaqid fī siyar al-ajwād*, attributed to Shaykh Aḥmad al-Ṣādiq [b.] al-Shaykh Uwāyis al-Lamtūnī. The copy consists of some seventy to eighty folios. A number of the folios are not consecutive, and parts are in disorder and in a totally different hand. There is clearly some difference of date between the folios and, unfortunately, no date at all is given in the colophon which ends on a page of very tiny and untidy script, most of it illegible. There is a strong probability that the first three or four folios are eighteenth-, or early nineteenth-century in date. The bulk of the manuscript, however, would appear to be more recent. There is a risk therefore of a reworking and a rethinking of the content in some parts of the work. The ink is less faded, the hand is less artistic, and the Arabic grammar, at times, so crude and colloquial as to suggest that the copyist, or the writer, had a very imperfect knowledge indeed of Classical Arabic. Certain corrections made to the opening folios appear to be in this, or a similar, hand. Despite such faults, the content as a whole (save near its end) hangs together as a unified composition, however miscopied or marred.

Other parts of the text are written in the margins to these folios. Parts are untranslatable, and the task of decipherment is made worse by there being no clear indication as to the numbering of the pages. It is certain, though, that some passages of the later work, *Ṣifat al-wird*, have been quoted verbatim from the *Qudwa*, and that so too have shorter passages in Muḥammad Bello's historical work, *Infāq al-maysūr*.

The *Qudwa* is some sort of manual for novices or for the devout who were drawn to the *Maḥmūdiyya* during a period when it had undoubtedly declined. In sum, it is written in late medieval Arabic, in a non-Arabic-speaking region, and it is to be doubted that every part of it is solely the work of Shaykh Aḥmad al-Ṣādiq himself. My text, therefore, contains the biographical, historical, doctrinal, administrative, and catechizing parts of the *Qudwa*. Around it I have built 'chapters' which furnish the maximum amount of background material to enable the reader to understand the incomplete text. This includes a history, as far as it can be reconstructed, of early Ṣūfīsm in the Aïr Massif.

This most certainly had a considerable influence on the history of Islam in the southern Sahara, on Hausaland, on the Tuareg of Niger and Mali, and on Borno. From the study of the text a saintly figure of great courage and a deep spirituality emerges. He founded a brotherhood of men of differing backgrounds. This is not Ṣūfīsm in a cloistered library or in richly endowed *Zāwiyas*. It is Ṣūfīsm, even asceticism, amongst a small band of dervishes, in a harsh desert and mountainous environment, not unlike Arabia itself. Sīdī Maḥmūd softened the hearts and gained the devotion and reverence of these men, many of whom were like Tuareg nomads in their way of life, men who knew little of Arabic or Persian and who were living in a semi-pagan society. In comparison with the Middle East, the birthplace of Sīdī Maḥmūd, Agades and Aïr had, until then, been little influenced by Persian and Turkish Islamic civilization.

Much remains to be discovered, speculation, at times, is inevitable, but I believe that further research in Aïr amongst the Ṣūfī centres which are ruined and deserted will be very worthwhile.

Ṣūfīsm

Ṣūfīsm has been described by Carl W. Ernst as 'a vast spiritual enterprise, carried out in many lands that differ widely in culture and language, but are unified by the spiritual authority of the Qur'anic revelation and the example of the Prophet Muhammad'.[3] It is a living experience and a search for perfection.

The goals of Islamic mysticism (*taṣawwuf*) have been described by Ṣūfīs themselves in many different ways. Baba Rexheb—a distinguished *Bektāshī* mystic, writer, and spiritual leader—has remarked:[4]

> Islamic mysticism, *tasawwuf*, refers to the spiritual life of man. It is the ultimate reality for man who has freed himself from all materialistic needs and who through strict religious conduct has become the ruler of his own heart. Mysticism is that awareness which leads man to perfection; it endows a man with virtuous conduct and frees him from the pleasures of the world. Only then will man achieve the ultimate goal: total unification with his beloved, the almighty God.

He adds:

> The terms *sufi* and *sufism* mean different things to different people, yet the basic themes were the same:
>
> A sufi is that man who has purified his soul and whose heart has been filled with the purity of light. [Beshire Hafi]
>
> A sufi is that man who has chosen God and who is happy with him and whose worldly concerns are alien to him. [Bender Bin Al Huseyn]

> A sufi is that man who wears woollen cloth for the love of God and who has forsaken this world and has wholly embraced the way of the Prophet. [Abu Ali Rusbar]
> A sufi is that man who has cast away despair, who is free from temporal concerns and who with prayers and devotion has come close to God. To him gold and stone are the same. [Sali Tuster]
> Sufism is the awareness of spiritual endeavours and total rejection of any other matter. [Maaruf Qerhi]
> Sufism is the attainment of high moral virtue and the shunning of vice. [Abu Muhammad Jari]
> Sufism contains three major themes: rejection (*faqr*) of worldly possessions; reliance on God so as to hope only for God, to give all things for God alone, and to consider the needs of others before one's own; freedom from and total extinction of the needs of the flesh. [Ruveymi]
> Sufism is the denial of one's own selfish rights and total reliance on God. [Junaid Baghdadi][5]

He further adds:

The Persian scholar Jami in his book *Nefehat-ul Uns* [Inspiration to Intimacy] writes:

> Mystical knowledge is the complete knowledge which enters the heart of man [without the message of Gabriel to Muhammad] directly from the sea of divinity. This knowledge is of different kinds: of faith, of salvation, and of gifts. It is the knowledge of one's own inner self and the knowledge to learn the good from the bad. It includes the message, the word of God, his sight, revelation, and man's approach and unification with God.[6]

At one time, it was held that *taṣawwuf* was something grafted on to the stern monotheism of the Prophet's religion. The erotic language of the Persian and Turkish poets, the mathematical and pictorial mysteries of the *Ḥurūfīs*, and the savage and rhythmic and wound-inflicting *séances* of certain African and Asian Ṣūfī adepts were, each and all, sublime, barbaric, or bizarre. In short, 'pantheistic' Ṣūfīsm was a kind of parallel religion—parallel, that is, to Islam 'proper'. This view is still to be found in certain Soviet writers. It denotes to them the still-flourishing Ṣūfī circles in parts of the Caucasus and in Central Asia. As Annemarie Schimmel has pointed out,[7] Ṣūfīsm was once often dubbed, 'a foreign plant in the sandy soil of Islam'. The apparent connection with Gnostic, Hellenistic, and Neo-Platonic ideas that arguably attained their apogee in Ibn 'Arabī (died 1240) and elsewhere in the daring notion of the 'Ontology of Light' (*Ishrāq*)—'God is the Light of Lights (*Nūr al-Anwār*)'—which Ian Netton has so lucidly outlined afresh for us,[8] was highly appealing yet in no way appeared to offer us a guidance as to early origins and to spontaneous growth from within.

Massignon's great study of the life and death of Ḥallāj, who was executed in Baghdād in 922 and whose death was brought about for both religious and political reasons[9] underlined the fact that Ṣūfism grew and evolved due to the teachings, the example, the death, and the sanctification, even semi-deification, of saintly individuals. Annemarie Schimmel remarks:

> Ḥallāj's word *Anā'l-ḥaqq* 'I am the Truth', was interpreted as 'I am God' and seen as a stringent proof for his pantheistic outlook; his death at the hand of the government was taken as the model of the martyrdom of those who fight and want to die for an ideal, be it religious or socio-political. In fact, the suffering Ḥallāj has become a symbol not so much for those who seek God and long for union with him through death, but for those who have been imprisoned, killed or tortured by unjust governments; for the free spirits who suffer from narrow-minded ultra-orthodox leaders.

These remarks of hers preface the version in English of Tor Andrae's *In the Garden of Myrtles: Studies in Early Islamic Mysticism*, a valuable insight into the earliest phases of the Ṣūfī movement in Islam. It reveals those deep roots in the beliefs and teachings of the Prophet himself and in the life and the mentality of adjacent Arabia and its borderlands far better than any other study I have read.[10]

Ṣūfīs were representatives of orders (*ṭuruq*) and sub-orders (*ṭawā'if*) and the like. These began afresh to penetrate the peripheral Muslim world from the later Middle Ages onwards. They reflected in language, liturgy, and beliefs the traditional habits and ancient spiritual lore of the Central Asian Turks, the Khurāsānīs, the Egyptians, the Berbers, and the sub-Saharan world. These immensely important social, political, and military, or pacific, brotherhoods, have increasingly become the focus of attention of Western scholars. However, every 'Way' is made up of individuals. The *darwīsh*—the mendicant, the 'door-seeker', perhaps—whosoever he may be or whatsoever he may come to represent, is the bearer of a *silsila*, a chain of authority—golden and priceless—going back to the founder of his order and to Allāh himself, be he a *sharīf* or a shoe-maker or a scholar or a layabout or one who is possessed, or any one, or indeed almost all, of these things. He stores, cherishes, and, if need be, inculcates the esoteric essence of what he professes he has received from his teacher, be he a *shaykh*, an *ustādh*, or a *pīr*. His *murīd* or *tilmīdh*, his disciple, will memorize his word, imitate his example, preserve his garment, absorb his spittle, reflect his *baraka*. At his behest he may enter a seasonal retreat (as a *Kubrawī* or a *Khalwatī*). He will take part communally in a *dhikr* or *ḥaḍra*, a dance, or in an intense and intimate prayer with voice silenced or else raucous like a saw. He will be part of a company whom no man can number. He may well be a wanderer in the earth, a solitary bearer of a lantern of light or a flame of fire, discarding sandal after sandal, seeking shelter in cave or convent, housed in a palace or a prison. The *darwīsh* is the personalization, the physical embodiment of much of the essence of the Ṣūfī message, and he is looked upon, or depicted, as the popular spokesman of the inner vision of a community in the camp-fire happenings that are gripped, guided, and compèred by the story-teller.

Other men may take a backward step in their faith. They may fall and falter. The *darwīsh* will never look back. He will for ever remain restless and will ever seek distant horizons, since all these, in his beliefs, lead him to the presence of a divinity, that is beyond, beneath, and within. As Baba Rexheb remarks:[11]

> Once the spiritual approach occurs the distance traveled means nothing. If you are with me in spirit, you would be with me even if you were in Yemen. If you are not, even if you were beside me, you would be in Yemen.

This is how Hajji Bektash describes the road which leads man to God:

> I dreamed of God one night and asked him: 'Show me the right road that will bring me closer to you'. God replied: 'The moment you have rejected your own self, you have reached me'.

One day, a dervish approached his master, Hajji Bektash and asked permission to travel. The master asked him why he wanted to travel. The dervish replied that stagnant water begins to smell. Hajji Bektash quickly responded: 'The water of the sea remains stagnant and yet does not smell'. And then added:

> The birds cannot touch the sky. They fly, however, high enough to escape the snares.
>
> The dervish can do the same by leaving the material world. He can feel some peace in his heart. Whoever stays put in one place becomes a man; whoever travels meets men.

Within the great movement that is Ṣūfism it is, as we shall see, the *darwīsh* himself who is the person who combines two poles within himself: the sublime and the debased, the recluse and the rabble-rouser, the ascetic and the dissolute, the selfless servant and the importunate beggar. At times, one or other of these extremes is perceived in his behaviour and his utterances. Hence the love and the hatred, the adoration of him by some and the cry for his execution by others. One such *darwīsh*, who lived some two centuries before Sīdī Maḥmūd al-Baghdādī, the figure central to our study, typifies the bizarre figure of the *darwīsh* and the eclectic, even syncretic, religious doctrines that sustained his mission and that inspired the spiritual adventure that he offered to his disciples.

According to H. C. K. Köprülüzade Mehmed Fuad,[12] Barak Baba enjoyed great renown at the Ilkhānid Court at the end of the thirteenth century. He was a disciple of Sari Saltuk, himself a disciple of Ḥājjī Bektāsh Veli. Something is said about him, and his deeds, in Persian and Egyptian sources, and some of his words are even quoted. When Barak came to Damascus at the beginning of the fourteenth century, accompanied by a group of his disciples, the populace were astounded by the sight of their bizarre clothes. Popular songs were sung about them, and their extraordinary figures were even depicted in the shadow plays. Their beards were shaved, their moustaches long and uncut, and they wore caps made of felt. On these, two horns were fixed. Around their necks they wore necklaces of ox-bones dyed in henna. They carried crooked staves and little tinkling bells. Their extraordinary appearance was very ugly to behold and it frightened many. They had their own fanfare beaten out upon the drums and the other instruments that they had assembled. As they went their way, the sound of this music, joined to the percussive rhythm of the bells, the bones, and the staves produced a cacophonous din. Some Syrians said that Satan himself was afraid of it. Once, Barak was asked why he dressed in this way. 'I wished to be the laughing-stock of the poor', he said.

He possessed almost superhuman power. No tiger could face him, and in Damascus when a wild ostrich was set loose upon him he mounted its back and was seen to fly some distance upon it. Any money that was given to him he distributed then and there. His disciples were strictly disciplined, and a watch was kept upon their movements. If by chance one of them missed a prayer he was beaten forty times, and on that same day, after sundown, a *dhikr* was held by the assembly. Yet some maintained that they did not observe the fast of *Ramaḍān* and that they were known to commit all kinds of sinful practices.

Here was a paradox: the saint, the buffoon, the disciplinarian, the law-breaker. To those folk who made up the world beyond his small fraternity he was one or another or perhaps all of these things.

We shall see that Sīdī Maḥmūd from Baghdād was no stranger to this paradox within the *darwīsh* and the Ṣūfī. As centuries passed, his personality was seen to have changed. He became the divine man who is adored, an example for orthodoxy. Yet why did he die as a martyr? Much was forgotten, something extra was added. Such is the fate of the *darwīsh*. The remoter the region and the more credulous the faithful, so the *darwīsh* is transformed into a being that transcends the short span of his earthly life. He seems to tower above the lofty desert solitudes that encircle his humble grave that has become the place of pilgrimage of a countless multitude.

The Geography of Aïr: Mountains, Rain and Herbage

The Aïr Massif is a rocky complex of granite of rectangular shape, an uplifted outcrop of basement crystalline rocks. It occupies a central and southerly position in the Sahara. It is the most northerly part of the Niger Republic. Today, its capital is the important city of Agades. The whole Aïr region contains some 60,000 inhabitants, less than one person to the square kilometre. To the north of the Aïr Massif, in Algeria, lie the Ahaggar mountains, while to the north-east on the route to the Libyan Fezzan and to northern Chad are the towns of Kawar and the ancient salt workings at Bilma. Due west of Aïr is the region of Taggida n Tesemt, another region of salt, and once important for the smelting of copper. Called Takaddā in the medieval Arabic texts, it was once one of the Sahara's greatest cities.[13] Some one hundred and sixty km. to the north-west of Aïr is the mining centre of Arlit, something new to the district, though minerals, including tin, have been known to exist in Aïr for a considerable time. The uranium of Arlit is amongst the most important economic resources of the region, and, indeed, of the whole Niger Republic.

The central core of the Aïr Massif extends approximately four hundred and eighty km. from north to south and a maximum of about two hundred and forty km. from east to west. Its mountains are sharply etched and are marked out by their individual shapes. Their steep walls rise to considerable heights; up to six thousand feet in the Bagzan mountains. At the edges, Aïr vanishes into the surrounding deserts of Azawagh and Ténéré.

Within Aïr there is often a lush vegetation. In its northern parts acacias and perennial grasses grow in most of the valleys. Far richer than the vegetation which grows in the Ahaggar in Algeria, in places in Aïr it forms an impenetrable jungle of trees and brushwood. In the valleys, which can be raging torrents in August and September, there are *dūm* palms, date palms, and acacias. Plants of all kinds are abundant towards the southern foothills of Aïr and their valleys (*kōri*), where, to the north of Agades there are gardens and tiny fields of wheat and other cereals, and where onions, tomatoes, and other vegetables are grown in the village plots.

Among the first western travellers who have given us a detailed

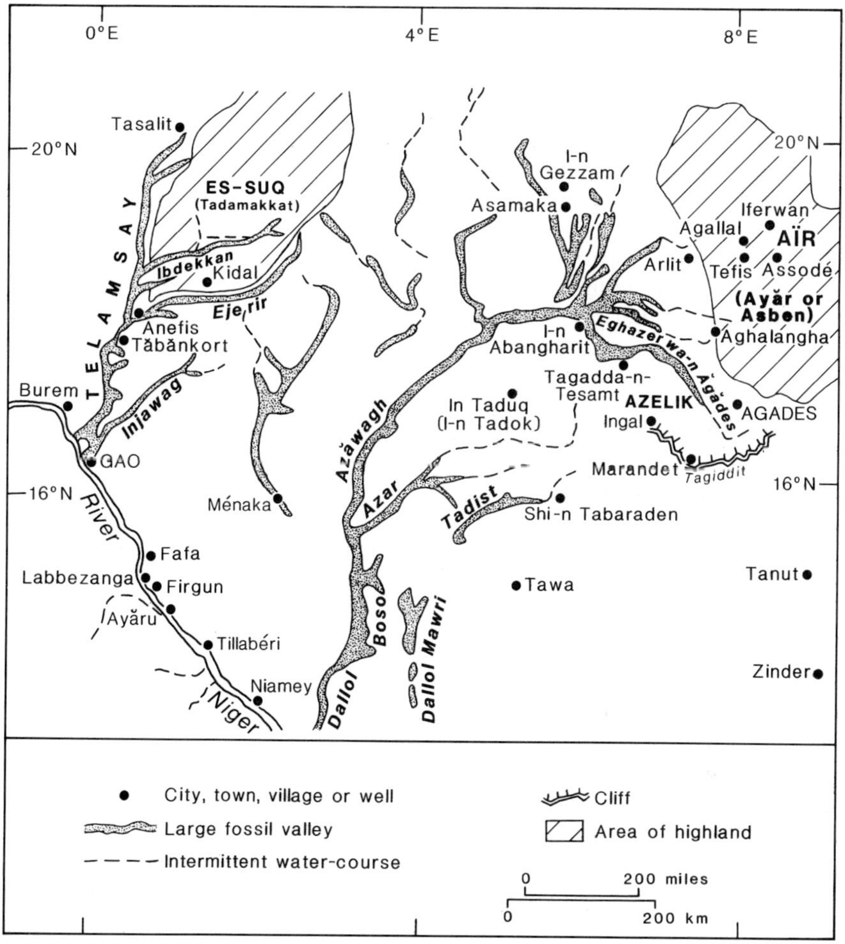

Azawagh and Aïr and the World of *Maḥmūdiyya* Ṣūfism

Note: Names on this map are spelt as those on the end-paper map in Ghubăyd ăgg-Ălăwjeli, *Histoire des Kel-Denneg, avant l'arrivée des Français* (Copenhagen, 1975).

description of the scenery of Aïr and the plan of the city of Agades, its walled quarters, its palace, and its mosques, was Henry Barth, who passed through it in the mid-nineteenth century. Francis Rennell Rodd, himself a great authority on Aïr, was quick to point out the debt which we owe to Barth:[14]

The first description of Aïr and its people in any detail was brought back to Europe by Barth after his memorable journey from the Mediterranean to the Sudan, on which he set out in 1849 with Richardson and Overweg, but from which he alone returned alive more than five years later. Prior to this journey there are certain references in Ibn Batutah and Leo Africanus, but they do not give us much information either of the country or of the people. From Ibn Batutah's description, the country he traversed is recognisable, but the information is meagre. The account of Leo Africanus written in the sixteenth century is little better. His principal contribution, in the English and original Italian versions, is a bad pun: 'Likewise Hair (Aïr), albeit a desert, yet so called for the goodness and temperature of the aire. . . .' It is an observation, in fact, of great truth, but hardly more useful than his other statement, which records that the 'soyle aboundeth with all kinds of herbes,' in apparent contradiction with the previous remark. He adds that 'a great store of manna' is found not far from Agades which the people 'gather in certaine little vessels, carrying it, when it is new, into the market of the town to be mingled with water as a refreshing drink'—an allusion probably to the 'pura' or 'ghussub' water made of millet meal, water and milk or cheese. He states that the country is inhabited by the 'Targa' people, and as he mentions Agades, it had evidently by then been founded, but beyond these facts his description is wholly inadequate. He unfortunately even forgets to mention that Aïr is mountainous.

Another traveller, who visited the Sahara, but not Aïr, in 1845, James Richardson, provides a most interesting description of Aïr and its people, although all the information which he quotes is derived from informants whom he met in the Libyan oases of Ghat. Richardson writes in his *Travels in the Great Desert of Sahara*:

The Touaricks of Aheer bear an excellent character as traders, and companions of travel, always assisting the stranger first at the well, before their own camels are watered. They seem, besides, mostly addicted to the peaceful pursuits of commerce, if we except their occasionally joining in the Razzias for slaves. A full third of the traffic of the South-eastern Sahara is in their hands, or under their control. I may add a few words upon their country and chief places, Aheer and Aghadez.

Aheer, or *Ahir*, which is often incorrectly spelt on the maps Aïr, is the name of a town and very populous district, including within its territory or jurisdiction the city of Aghadez. Aheer is also called Azben, and its district Azbenouwa, which appear to have been the more ancient names. The town of Aheer is also called *Asouty* on the maps Asouda,[15] the dentals /ṭ/ and /ḍ/

being convertible. These districts are bounded on the north by Ghat and its tribes; on the east by the Tibboo country and Bornou, on the west by the Negro, Touarick and Fullan countries of the north banks of the Niger; and on the south, by the Housa districts, vulgarly called by merchants, Soudan. Aheer is forty short days from Ghat, the Soudanese merchants who visit the Ghat mart always travelling much more *doucement* and in jog-trot style than the Moorish Arab merchants of the north. The line of the Aheer stations measures about thirteen days, from Tidik in the north to Toktouft in the south. In this portion of the route, and that previous to arriving at Tidik, there are twenty days of mountains. The Aheer route also abounds with springs and fine streams, which gush out from the base of rock-lands of great height, and some of which form considerable rivers for several months in the year, on whose banks corn and the senna-plant are cultivated. Aheer is the Saharan region of senna, where there are large wadys covered with its crops. The exportation, especially after a season of rain, is very great and profitable. Asouty is the principal town of the Aheer districts, and was formerly the capital of all the Kylouy Touaricks. No less than a thousand houses are now seen abandoned and in ruins. Here in former times all the Soudan trade was carried on and concentrated; its population is still considerable. The houses are nearly all constructed of hasheesh, or straw huts, and the city is without walls. Nevertheless, the people still honour it with the title of *Blad es-Sultan*, 'City,' or 'Country of the Sultan,' that is, where the Sultan occasionally resides, answering to our *Royal* city.

Aheer is the rendezvous of the salt-caravan of Bilma, in the Tibboo country, situate, almost in a straight line, about ten days east, the route to which is over barren stony ground.

Aghadez is the capital of the Aheer districts. This is the residence of the Sultan of the Touaricks of South-eastern Sahara. The present Sultan is called *Mazouwaja*,[16] who is represented as a friendly prince. But it was *En-Nour*, deputy Sultan of Aheer, to whom I wrote before leaving Ghat, begging his protection in the event of my return, to complete the tour to Soudan. Aghadez is now as large as Tripoli, or containing from eight to ten thousand inhabitants. In a past period it was four times as large. A great number of the people have emigrated to Soudan, where less labour is required to till the soil, and nature is more lavish in her productions. Aghadez is a walled city, but without any particular strength; the houses are but one storey high, built of mud and stone, and sun-dried bricks. Aghadez abounds in provisions of the most substantial kind, that is, sheep, oxen, and grain. The government is despotic, but the lesser chiefs have great power in their respective districts, like those of Ghat. The religion of the people is Mahometan; not a Pagan, Jew, or Christian, is found within these districts. Trade is carried on to a great extent, and Moorish merchants visit Aghadez, proceeding no further towards Soudan. The most interesting district near Aghadez is that of *Bagzem* (or *Magzem*, the labials /b/ and /m/ being convertible,) consisting of an exceedingly lofty mountain, requiring a full day's journey for its ascent. This mountain figures on the map under the ancient name of Usugala Mons, but for what reason God knows. The town is placed a good way towards its loftiest heights, the most of which heights are both cultivated and inhabited, and there is abundance of trees, grain, and fruits. Bagzem is three days' journey from Asouty.[17]

It is the rain which makes Aïr the fertile place it is. In good years, it benefits from the Sudanic summer rains. The southern part of Aïr, with up to 250 mm annual rainfall, benefits the most from the downpours which occur between July and September. Iferouane, in Northern Aïr, may experience up to 74 mm of rain, while Agades enjoys 179 mm. Compared with the Tuareg of the Ahaggar, the Aïr Tuareg are richer in camels and sheep than they are in goats. Some of them have herds of zebu. Human settlement is centred in the *kōri*, the valleys which have temporary water resources, like the *wādīs* of Arabia. Here the vegetation is concentrated, there is pasturage for herds, and beneath the surface there are subterranean sheets of water, which can be tapped, and the water raised to the surface, by buckets and well pulleys (*takarkarat*). These devices are not dissimilar to those known in the Middle East and in Libya. The water is channelled into rivulets and from these it is turned into the tiny allotments and fields. The villages, many of which are now deserted, are sited in side valleys or upon old terraces which are sheltered from the violence of the summer floods. Aïr enjoys a summer season and a winter season. Between these two seasons there are two others, *aḳăsa* and *gharat* in the Tuareg language. The former denotes 'green annual plants' and the latter 'dry annual plants'. The Aïr Tuareg use them as seasonal terms. Who has the right to this herbage and who has not, and whether the ruler of Aïr, the *Sulṭān* of Agades, is nominally, if not in practice, the master of the land, are problems which have faced the jurists of Aïr since the earliest days of the establishment of its Sultanate. It led to conflict, and occasioned the sending of letters to Cairo and elsewhere in order to obtain a ruling from the highest Islamic authorities.

One such letter from a scholar of the Agades region is to be found amongst the questions which were sent to the Egyptian polymath al-Suyūṭī (849–911/1445–1505), in Cairo. Agades was a remote city which occupied al-Suyūṭī's attention. However, this specific matter, which is included amongst the legal rulings collected in *al-Ḥāwi lil-fatāwī*, is not specifically about the city of Agades and its problems. Rather, it is about the mountainous Massif of Aïr, to the north, and the vegetation and the pasturage which grew there in abundance.[18]

In the land of Aïr is the town of Agades (*Agadaz*). It is a land of Islam and there are only Muslims within it. Every tribe which is amongst them has a terrain wherein it sojourns. In that terrain there is not found [that crop] whereby profit and gain may be made through tilling and ploughing and through sowing and by agriculture.[19] This is the prevalent situation. The bulk of the profitable food there is only the natural and lawful plant, be it tree or bush or shrub, such as the fruit of the *dūm* palm and of the lote, and there are others, the plant which shoots and sprouts without human husbandry. Like unto this are the grains and the berries which grow without tillage, nor toil, and which belong to the terrain. They acquire a worth and a value for him who comes to collect and to gather them.

The aforesaid land has been possessed by its aforesaid people. This is by the permission of the trustee of the land [or prince of the land?] who is the client (*mawlā*) of the Commander of the Faithful[20] and the said prince has divided it into fiefs for its aforesaid people who camp and sojourn there, for his interests and for those of the Muslims, in the assignment of it to them as feudal estates. It is lawful for him who is there to sell its herbage and anything from its trees? Can they prevent others from grazing and pasturing on it or from making use of it for themselves in any way?

The legal origin of the land and the terrain is quite unknown. It is not known whether it was conquered by force from pagans or whether it was conquered peacefully by the Muslims. Since time immemorial it has only been possessed by the hand of the guardian (*muqaddam*) of the country, who gives it as fiefs to whom he wills and they have proceeded in this way, first the forebear and then his successor. The bulk of their interests and their benefits are connected with that.

If you were to say, 'They have the right to sell its herbage and to deny it to others, then what is the purport of the *ḥadīth* of the Prophet wherein is mentioned the prohibition of the sale of surplus water in excess together with the sale of the herbage?[21] What is the purport of the *ḥadīth* of the Prophet wherein are mentioned four unprohibited things, amongst which both water and herbage were specifically mentioned.[22] Give us a legal ruling (*fatwā*) and we shall be rewarded servants. May Allāh, Almighty, guide you to the correct decision after bidding you farewell in peace.'

The answer—Praise be to Allāh and peace be upon His servants, whom He has chosen. The scholars have agreed that fresh herbage, if it be clipped from its plant and cut and acquired by taking and by transfer, then he who acquires it shall possess it and it is lawful for him to sell it. There is no need for him to give it away. As for that herbage which is to be found in the place where it grows and which has neither been clipped nor cut, if it be growing on 'dead' uncultivated land then the people who are there are all alike. It is like the case of water, lawful to all, and this is the purport of reported *ḥadīth* from the mouth of the Prophet, peace be upon him, regarding its prohibition. If it be growing on land which is owned, then it is the property of the owner of the land. There is no obligation upon him to give it away and he is allowed to sell it.

One other category remains [to be considered], namely, the fresh herbage which grows upon land which the Sulṭān has given to someone as an estate.

There is a point of detail to be noted here. If that land be 'dead' then its assignment as a fief is unlawful. Why this is so is because it is a *ḥimā*—a place of herbage or pasture, and of water, prohibited to the people so that they may not pasture their beasts upon it, nor approach it, nor venture upon it—and, therefore, prohibited in the *ḥadīth* of the Prophet, who said, the blessing and peace of Allāh be upon him, 'There is no *ḥimā* but it belongs to Allāh and to His Messenger.'[23] It is only lawful to assign a fief in land which is utterly devoid of any herbage or grass whatsoever. But if that land is not uncultivated 'dead' land and if it be of those lands which form part of the treasury of the state (*bayt al-māl*) which the Sulṭān currently bestows as estates and fiefs in the land of Egypt, then its division into fiefs is sound and correct. The feudal tenant is qualified to dispose of the fresh herbage in the land, to derive benefit from it and to sell it, because it is part of the treasury of the state. The Sulṭān has allowed this feudal tenant to exploit it, specifically, and so it would appear that the land of Agades is in this equivalent state of feudal benefice and in its usufruct. Allāh knows best.

This letter from an unnamed scholar of Agades and Aïr to al-Suyūṭī is, to date, the sole surviving Arabic document of the fifteenth century which was, without a doubt, sent from that region. Since the latter sent a letter, which was addressed jointly to Sulṭān Muḥammad Ṣaṭṭafan, the ruler of Aïr between 892 and 899 (1487 to 1493–4), and to Ibrāhīm, the ruler of Katsina, it would appear that this ruling on herbage and feudal estate in the Massif must date back to about this time, either during the reign of Muḥammad Ṣaṭṭafan himself, or, as seems possible, no mention being made of his name, during the reign of his predecessor or his immediate successor, though the latter seems unlikely.[24]

Aïr was by then a Muslim land, and the tribes who were 'people of the king', but whose names are not therein mentioned, were in the process of settling in parts of the Massif itself, much of which was pastureland. It should be noted that only The City of Agades is described as the seat of the 'Sulṭān of Aïr'. Nothing is said about Takaddā, nor Tadeliẓa, nor Assodé, and nothing is said about agricultural or religious settlement of any kind in the heart of the Massif. This latter, in the view of al-Suyūṭī, on the basis of the meagre information which had been given to him, was a feudal estate which formed part of the treasury of the state, administered by the Sulṭān on behalf of his investor, the Caliph. From the end of the fifteenth century this ruling, and no doubt others which are lost to us but which must have emanated from Cairo, if not from al-Suyūṭī himself, furnished a charter of land ownership in the Massif. It would be disputed; by the Songhai rulers, by the rulers of Borno, by the incoming Tuareg tribes whose allegiance was to others than to the rulers of Agades. As will be seen, it was not only these who had a claim to the land. The Ṣūfī brotherhoods also made claims to possess specific localities in Aïr.

Notes

1. The passages in Barth which relate to Aïr have been discussed and introduced in detail by Suzanne Bernus in her *Henri Barth chez les Touaregs de l'Aïr* (Études Nigériennes no. 28, Centre Nigérien de Recherche en Sciences Humaines; Niamey, 1972).
2. Published in *Cahiers d'Études africaines*, 91, xxiii 3 (1983), pp. 239–80.
3. Carl W. Ernst, *Words of Ecstasy in Sufism* (Albany, 1985), p. 1.
4. Baba Rexheb, *The Mysticism of Islam and Bektashism* (Naples, 1984), p. 23.
5. ibid. 40–1.
6. ibid. 43.
7. In Tor Andrae, *In the Garden of Myrtles: Studies in Early Islamic Mysticism* (Albany, 1987), p. viii.
8. Ian Richard Netton, *Allāh Transcendant* (London and New York, 1989), pp. 256–320.
9. Carl Ernst, *Words of Ecstasy*, pp. 63–73, and Tor Andrae, *In the Garden of Myrtles*, pp. 1–4.
10. See especially his p. 8.
11. *The Mysticism of Islam and Bektashism*, p. 135.
12. 'Influence du Chamanisme Turo-Mongol sur les ordres mystiques musulmans', *Mémoires de l'Institut de Turcologie de l'Université de Stamboul*, NS 1 (1929), pp. 5–19.
13. On the site of this major city, which has been located in the region of Azelik, see the recently published archaeological reports, more especially *Atlas RCP 322* (Programme Archéologique d'Urgence Région d'In Gall, République du Niger; Paris, Niamey, 1981), and also S. Bernus and P. L. Gouletquer, 'Du Cuivre au Sel, recherches ethno-archéologiques sur la région d'Azelik', *Journal des Africanistes*, 46 1–2 (1976), pp. 7–68. On Takaddā in the medieval Arabic sources, see N. Levtzion and J. F. P. Hopkins, *Corpus of Early Arabic Sources for West African History* (Fontes Historiae Africanae, Series Arabica IV; 1981).
14. Francis Rennell Rodd, *People of the Veil* (London, 1926), pp. 18–19.
15. Spelt Assodé (85 km. from Iferouane), it is considered by some to be of greater antiquity than Agades but to have declined at the beginning of the 17th cent. It is by no means impossible that the 'Takarkarī Sulṭān' mentioned by Ibn Baṭṭūṭah (see Levtzion and Hopkins, *Corpus*, p. 303, and 'Kāhir, belonging to the country of the Karkarī sultan') may relate to a ruler of the region of Assodé, particularly in view of the following remarks made by Erwin de Bary, *Le Dernier Rapport d'un Européen sur Ghat et les Touareg de l'Aïr* (1876–7), trans. and annotated by Henri Schirmer (Paris, 1898), p. 182: '*22 juil.*—Nous reprenons notre route en sens inverse. Nous marchons vers la montagne d'Asodi en laissant Aguéraguer à gauche. Mon guide me dit qu'Aguéraguer a été autrefois une grande ville, plus grande qu'Agadès, avant que les Kel-Guérès ne l'eussent détruite.'
16. Unidentified. The Agades Chronicles mention ᶜAbd al-Qādir as Sulṭān between 1251/1835 and 1270/1853.
17. James Richardson, *Travels in the Great Desert of Sahara*, vol. ii (London, 1848), pp. 141–5.
18. *al-Ḥāwī lil-fatāwī*, by the *Imām* Jalāl al-Dīn ᶜAbd al-Raḥmān b. Abī Bakr b. Muḥammad al-Suyūṭī, published by Idārat al-Ṭibāᶜah al-Munīriyyah (Cairo, 1352 AH), vol. i, 148–9.
19. A fact about Aïr stated earlier by the geographical writer, al-ᶜUmarī, died 749/1349, in his *Masālik al-abṣār fī mamālik al-amṣār*. He writes of the kingdoms of the 'Berber mountains': 'They live, as desert dwellers do, on meat and milk: grain is very scarce with them.' See Levtzion and Hopkins, *Corpus*, p. 274.
20. This statement would seem to confirm that the Sultanate of Aïr, and more specifically the Sulṭāns of Agades, probably prior to Muḥammad Ṣaṭṭafan, had been invested by a Caliph.

None of the Agades Chronicles, so called, is of help in regard to the inauguration of this investment. But see E. M. Sartain, *Jalal al-Din al-Suyuti* (Cambridge, 1975), vol. i. pp. 50–1, and vol. ii, pp. 158–9. Also see E.M. Sartain, 'Jalāl Ad-Dīn As-Suyūṭī's relations with the people of Takrur', *Journal of Semitic Studies*, 16/2 (1971), p. 195. What the local chronicles do suggest is that the house of Ṣaṭṭafan became a *de facto* dynasty to which the leading Tuareg groups in the Aïr Massif in the 15th cent. gave their allegiance, and that, following this, something like a *de jure* status was enjoyed by members of the house of Ṣaṭṭafan until the middle of the 17th cent.

See the full text of an Aïr document (undated), cited by Y. Urvoy, 'Chroniques d'Agadès', *Journal de la Société des Africanistes*, 4 (1934), pp. 145–7, specifically pp. 146 and 154–5. The following edition of the text is from the library of the Sulṭān of Agades. Part of it seems to date from the mid-17th cent. and makes reference to a correspondence with Cairo not dissimilar to the debate over rights to herbage and to land in the Massif. The author of it, al-Mukhtār b. al-Qādir al-Jīkatī, was apparently the son of ᶜAbd al-Qādir (al-Jīlānī) of Jīkat, who died in 1625 and who was the successor of Muḥammad b. Muḥammad Amezdennig of Teghzerin who was the leader of the Maḥmūdiyya in succession to Sīdī Maḥmūd al-Baghdādī himself. Hence this text must be contemporary with parts of the *Qudwa*. Note the favourable view it takes of the Agades Sultanate, as an institution, and of the tribes amongst the Tuareg which upheld it. Note also that there is no reference in it to Ṣūfism whatsoever.

'In the name of Allāh, the Compassionate and Merciful, blessings and peace in abundance be upon our lord Muḥammad and upon his [household] and his companions. I entrust my affair to Allāh, for verily He keeps a watch on the doings of His servants. My success is solely due to Allāh. Upon Him I depend and to Him I repent. This is the book of the origin of the Sultanate of Aïr and the book of the Sultanate of Bornu. As for the origin of the Sultanate of Aïr, there were four tribes, the Itesan, the Ijadanarnen [Ijădănranăn], the Izᶜaran [Izăghăran], and the Ifadalan [Ifădalăn]. They left the country of Aougila (Awjilā) [in Libya], and they banished the tribes of the negroes from the land of Aïr. They settled in Aïr for a long period without an appointed *Sulṭān*. Their circumstance was akin to that of the bedouin Arabs, because the latter in the age of yore were only ruled by their *shaykhs*. Such then was the circumstance of these four tribes. Only their *shaykhs* ruled them in the bygone age.

Then, after that time, the likes of them rose up and they began to consume and devour their families and their offspring and those who were weak and without a protector among them. That compelled them to seek for a *Sulṭān*. Then the five tribes—due to [the addition of] the Kel Sandal—sought out a *Sulṭān*. They found him in the country of the town of the [Kel] Ṣaṭṭafan. They carried him to the town of Tadeliẓa and they installed him there. After that they saw that it was unsuitable for him to reside in Tadeliẓa because the [presence of a] large number of animals which used to transport pearl millet to Aïr was trying and hurtful to them. So they moved him to Tin Shaman [in the north of the city of Agades] and they built a palace for him, he having no other companions other than those of the tribe of the four who had, individually and separately, built the seat of the Sultanate amongst the men of the tribe of Ilaswen [Ilasăwăn], the Balkorayen [Ibalkorăyăn], the Imaskikkin [Imaskikĭyăn], and the Inessufen [Inessūfa]. They were kingly lords, builders of residences facing the Friday Assembly mosque in the city of Agades.

Then, after that time, the sons of the *Sulṭāns* resided in these houses down to the day of writing [this document]. The five tribes were men of authority, with the [absolute] power to 'loose and to bind'. In that capacity no other tribe joins their number. When they are happy together before the *Sulṭān*, and are in accord with him, then all the world is at peace and the entire earth prospers. But when disharmony and discord occurs between the *Sulṭān* and those in authority with the power to 'loose and to bind', then the world is an empty wilderness. It is corrupt and evil and the whole country and the city endure severe trial, and [men] are anxious and needy. The cause of any dispute is due only to two patent matters which are obvious to them, but hidden from the minds of others who do not know the circumstances and who only know that which is apparent to them in their own time, but who have no knowledge of circumstances and deeds which happened in the past. Such, then, was the origin of the Sultanate of Aïr, as it happened in the past and right up to the present time. Whoever seeks to pervert it and to distort it, seeks to change the origin [of it all] and to distort it. He seeks for the impossible and he will grow weary having attained and profited nothing thereby, and he will repent of it when repentance will profit him nothing.

As for the five tribes, who carried [al Ḥājj] Alisaw [Ilaswen b. Taggagi, *c.* 833–53 (1430–49/50)], and who made him *Sulṭān* and who built a palace for him in their land, of their own volition and for their own satisfaction, their *Sulṭān* does not compel them, not force them, to act, for it was they who conquered the land of the negroes by force. On account of that they have become men who have the authority to 'loose and to bind'. They do not follow their *Sulṭān*, except out of favour and [to receive] benefit, and due to showing an honour, and due to the fact that he shows them deference and gives them an honour over and above all the [other] tribes. These others have no share in ruling and determining the destinies of the Sultanate of Aïr. He who amongst the other tribes seeks to be their equal or to bother them in their royal seat, acts so with injustice and he does them a wrong. He seeks for something which not one of the other tribes has attained before him.

As for the giving of horses to them [the ruling tribes], they have nothing imposed upon them by the *Sulṭān* in this respect. This is because the tax in horses imposed on the caravan traffic which comes to them from every direction [was fixed] at the time when they brought Alisaw [Ilaswen] and they set him upon their throne. Alisaw [Ilaswen] sent a man of note in a tribal group which journeyed to the land of Islam. He said [by the mouth of this mission] to the scholars of Islam, 'The company of the Tuareg who have seized the country of Aïr, by force, and who have conquered it, have made me to be chief over them. They have built a palace for me and made me *Sulṭān* over them.'

The situation [today] is that they take the poll tax in horses from the men of commerce who pass across their mountains and their deserts. I ask Allāh and I ask you, 'Is this tax lawful or is it unlawful?' They replied to him saying, 'The men who protect the route which runs between their mountains, and who have guarded it from robbers and marauders and from highwaymen, all the lot of them, you may take the horses and the raiment from the caravan trade and from the men of commerce and you may give it to the men who guard [the route] between Cairo and Timbuctoo, because it is the thoroughfare of the world. The raiment is transported from Cairo and the gold is transported from Timbuctoo. These men are those who are your arm of power and by them you conquer the terrain by force.'

This, then, [is the story] of the people of the Sultanate of Aïr, from the age of yore and up to the present time.'

21. This must refer to the *ḥadīth, lā yubāᶜ faḍl al-mā' li-yubāᶜ bihi 'l-kala'*, see the *Kitāb al-Musāqāh*, 38, in the *Muwaṭṭa'* of Mālik and also in *Kitāb al-Buyūᶜ* in al-Nasā'ī and in the *Musnad* of Aḥmad b. Ḥanbal, 2, 463, 3, 417.

22. Three things are mentioned by Ibn Māja and by Abū Dāwud: water, green herbage, and fire.

23. *lā ḥimā illā li-llāhi wa-li-rasūlihi* is recorded in the *Kitāb al-Jihād*, 146, in the *Ṣaḥīḥ* of al-Bukhārī. The ruling which is given in reply to the Aïr scholar follows ancient Arabian custom and tradition. According to A. F. L. Beeston, in a note in his *Epistle on Singing-Girls by Jāḥiẓ* (Warminster, 1980), p. 43, ' "Watered by the rains" alludes to ancient Near Eastern rules about land. Ground officially irrigated was the private property of the person who irrigated it; but ground not artificially irrigated, where the vegetation depends on natural rain (called *ba'l* land) was in principle free for all. Even here, however, a 'particular prohibition' limited the validity of the general rule, for ancient Arabian custom set aside certain areas as *ḥimā* ground, under the protection of local deities, where free grazing was not allowed; any animals straying within the boundaries of a *ḥimā* became the property of the deity. Islamic rules relating to the *ḥaram* areas around Mecca and Medina have certain analogies with these ancient rules.'

24. His successors reigned for a very short period. There was much confusion in the Sultanate, and it fell under the influence of the Askiyā, al-Ḥājj Muḥammad.

I

The Visit of Shaykh Aḥmad al-Yamanī to the City of Agades

Apart from the colophon of our manuscript of the *Qudwa*, the only other known document which has a reference to its author is *Nashr al-Mathānī*, composed by Muḥammad al-Ṭayyib al-Qādirī'.[1] This tells us that Abū'l-ᶜAbbās Sayyid Aḥmad b. Muḥammad al-Nūbī al-Khalīl Abī ᶜAbdallāh b. Sayyid Muḥammad b. Sayyid al-Walī al-Kabīr al-ᶜArif al-Shahīr Abī Filāḥa Idrīs al-Sharīf al-Ḥasanī al-Qādirī al-Yamanī al-Mālikī, who was born in 1040/1630, confirmed that amongst the scholars with whom he studied was Shaykh Abū'l-ᶜAbbās Aḥmad al-Ṣādiq b. al-Shaykh Abī Muḥammad Uways b. ᶜAbd al-Qādir al-Tārigī al-Lamtūnī, who was a Mālikī in his school of law and a Suhrawardī in his Ṣūfī 'Way',[2] and that this latter scholar was, at the time, a resident in the city of Agzad (Agades?). There seems little doubt that he and the author of the *Qudwa*, Ḥammād [or Aḥmad] al-Ṣādiq [b.?] al-Shaykh Uwāyis, the name as given in the colophon of the *Qudwa*, are the same person.[3]

In his initial study of the peripatetic scholars and holy men of Islam in Muslim Africa during the seventeenth and eighteenth centuries, John Lavers has demonstrated that Agades and Aïr were centrally situated on the routes which linked the Ṣūfī retreats of the Atlas, on the one hand, with those in the Upper Nile valley on the other. It is significant that Shaykh Aḥmad al-Yamanī himself hailed from this latter region.

Shaykh Aḥmad al-Yamanī (who, as John Lavers has discovered, was a Shādhilī Shaykh) was born in the village of M'allak which lay somewhere between Arbajī and Sinnār in the Sūdān, very possibly one or other of the two Maḥallas which were settlements of the scholarly ᶜArakiyyūn group.[4] After studies with his father he moved to Arbajī where he was initiated into the practices and the doctrines of Ṣūfīs. His principal guide was Shaykh Dafaᶜ Allāh b. Muḥammad al-ᶜArakiyyī al-Yamanī who taught many pupils in his *khalwa*. This Shaykh was a member of the *Qādiriyya* Ṣūfī order. He died in 1090/1679–80. Another of Shaykh Aḥmad's teachers was the Ṣūfī, Abū Najda Fāris al-Sanāsin, a resident of Arbajī. He was a Ḥanafī and he died about 1090/1679–80. To him many miracles and supernatural feats were attributed.[5] In 1075/1664, Shaykh Aḥmad left Arbajī in order to visit Borno, Aïr, and Morocco. The reasons for his journey appear to have been religious and scholastic. Borno was then at the height of its power, and the route between West Africa and the Sudan was much frequented by scholars, pilgrims, and merchants.

The goal of the first stage of his journey, which seems to have been planned in Arbajī, was the community of mystics which had been re-established at Belbelec, some eighty km. to the north of the Borno capital at Birni Gazargamu. Belbelec was also known as Kulumfardo or Kulumbardo. Its principal Shaykh was Shaykh ᶜAbdallāh al-Burnāwī. The latter is given his own biography in *Nashr al-Mathānī*.[6] His name was Abū Muḥammad ᶜAbdallāh b. al-Sayyid al-Imām Abū Muḥammad ᶜAbd al-Jalīl b. ᶜUmar al-Burnāwī al-Ḥimyarī. This South Arabian *nisba* would seem to indicate that he was either of Tubu or of Tuareg origin or may have laid claim to some relationship to the Kānemī royal house which boasted that Sayf b. Dhī Yazan was its forebear.

The *Nashr al-Mathānī* and other sources furnish details which suggest that this scholar, saint, and mystic in the second settlement at Kulumbardo could have been in regular contact with the brethren of the *Maḥmūdiyya* order, the order founded by Sīdī Maḥmūd, who were to the north in Aïr and in Agades at that time.[7]

ᶜAbdallāh al-Burnāwī was a mystic and an ascetic. He introduced strict rules amongst his community and he was himself, as we are informed, 'the *Quṭb* of his "Way" (*ṭarīqa*) and its *Imām*'.[8] *Quṭbāniyya* was the highest degree of sainthood, and it is clear from the reports about his community at Kulumbardo that his 'Way' was very much his own, despite the fact that in his youth he had studied in, or outside, Agades with Shaykh Aḥmad al-Ṣādiq b. al-Shaykh Uwāyis and in Arabjī, where he had studied under Shaykh Dafaᶜ Allāh. Despite his individual path, the facts indicated that a direct line of communication and contact, and a similarity of goal, characterized these Ṣūfī centres, however distant. ᶜAbdallāh was well versed in the practices of the *Qādiriyya* and extremely competent in regard to juridical consultations upon all four Sunnī rites. He was also a grammarian and was widely versed in all the Islamic sciences.

The community which he re-established was organized in a strict discipline. Great demands were made upon those who were initiated into it. Accounts of the life of his community are unanimous in regard to the vow of poverty which prevailed. According to Shaykh Sirāj al-Dīn b. ᶜAbd al-Ḥayy al-Ḥalabī, in his work entitled *Rayḥān al-qulūb fī-mā lil-Shaykh ᶜAbdallāh al-Burnāwī min asrār al-ghuyūb*, the Shaykh received a complaint from one of his companions that he only possessed two *mudds* of millet, whereupon the Shaykh replied that he had even less and that all the gifts which were bestowed upon him were set on one side and were forgotten. 'He went with his companions to a desert place and he ordered them to sit apart, the one from the other, and he withdrew on his own until the hour of the *ẓuhr* prayer. Then he returned, united his companions together and they returned together to their village. This was his daily ritual.'[9] His only attire was a single shirt which reached to his knees and which had narrow sleeves.

His novice, Shaykh al-Yamanī, said that he only saw him once in a bad humour. Someone had said to him 'May Allāh destroy the Tuareg', they being a large Arab tribe which severed routes and waylaid travellers. The countenance of the Shaykh changed and he said to the man, 'Leave my presence'. Then his disciples intervened in favour of the offender and the Shaykh pardoned him.[10]

In addition to the Shaykh's initiation of a large number of novices into his Ṣūfī 'Way', he was also instrumental in the conversion of a number of non-Muslims. Not infrequently he received young girls as gifts considered as a form of alms-giving. Rather than reject these girls he married them. Later, after they had borne him offspring, he gave them in marriage to the *fuqarā'* of his community and also to Tuareg and Tubu 'robbers and bandits'. Thus his own offspring became the adopted sons and daughters of the robbers, and he himself was able to modify their conduct to a lesser or greater degree.[11]

Relations with Mai ᶜAlī of Borno, who had approved the renewed foundation of Kulumbardo, were good. However, circles at court viewed the activities of the community with disfavour. A certain *Qāḍī* Abū Bakr, in a manner which, as will be seen, recalls the behaviour of the counsellors to the *Sulṭān* of Agades in regard to Shaykh Sīdī Maḥmūd, warned the Mai that the Shaykh represented a threat to his throne. The motives behind his action were those of a personal jealousy at the success of the Shaykh who had drawn away a large number of his following by his personality and charisma. His attempt failed.[12]

Another report of Shaykh Aḥmad al-Yamanī is furnished by Shaykh Abū'-l-ᶜAbbās al-Wallālī in his *Mabāḥith al-anwār fī akhbār baᶜḍ al-akhyār*:[13]

In his country the Shaykh engaged in no commerce and conserved nothing. All the *fuqarā'* who lived with him were totally consecrated to Allāh and had no worldly preoccupations. They feared none. It was their habit that when they had finished the morning litany (*wird*) they separated. They scattered, each to his own place, in the bush which surrounded the town, be it hot or cold. There they adored Allāh, and they paid no heed to raiment, nor food, until the noon hour (zawāl). Then they left the bush like wild beasts and they filled the mosque to join with the Shaykh in the prayer. Their invocations shook the earth. Thus they spent the rest of the day and all the night until morning and then they separated.[14]

However, the fate which was to befall the second Kulumbardo community was to be as violent as that which destroyed the first, and in a manner which recalls what is known to have taken place amongst the community of Shaykh Sīdī Maḥmūd in Aïr.

The Shaykh died a martyr at the age of 63 on Monday, 16 *Rabīᶜ al-Thānī*/18 May 10988/1678. Despite droughts, the community had thrived, but this had attracted the attention and the envy of the Immikitan Tuareg of Alakos and Kutus who attacked the town of Kulumbardo. A massacre took place, and it was only after several days that the body of the Shaykh was discovered by his son, ᶜAmr, who had fought beside his father but had been sent away by the latter to look after the womenfolk. The Tuareg responsible for the massacre were themselves subjected to slaughter by a 'Sudanese usurper'—a punishment which was meted out to them as divine retribution, according to the writers. In all likelihood they have in mind the reverses which the Tuareg of Aïr suffered at the hands of ᶜAlī b. al-Ḥājj ᶜUmar b. Idrīs, who launched an invasion of the Sulṭānate of Agades during this period, or else the rifts and revolts which took place amongst the Tuareg groups themselves.[15]

Notwithstanding the slaughter, the second Kulumbardo community dispersed into parts of Niger and Nigeria, though ᶜAmr b. ᶜAbdallāh al-Burnāwī returned eventually to Borno region, where, at Gueskero (now in Niger), another town was built with royal backing. The brother of ᶜAmr, Muṣṭafā, succeeded him and organized what amounted to a theocratic state, guarding the frontiers of Borno from Tuareg incursions.

Aḥmad al-Ṣādiq [b.] al-Shaykh Uwāyis al-Lamtūnī[16]

After an extended stay amidst the community of Shaykh ᶜAbdallāh in Borno, Shaykh Aḥmad al-Yamanī was advised by the latter to journey to Morocco. His route took him through the region of Agades where he was to sojourn for some time at the *zāwiya* or *khalwa* of Shaykh [Abū'l-ᶜAbbās] Aḥmad al-Ṣādiq [b.] al-Shaykh Uwāyis/Uways b. ᶜAbd al-Qādir al-Tārigī.[17] This *zāwiya* of his, which was apparently founded by his father, Uwāyis, was of a wide renown in African Islam. Muḥammad b. al-Ṭayyib al-Qādirī adds at this juncture:

Amongst his pupils is to be found the Shaykh and *Faqīh al-ᶜĀrif bi-llāh* Abu'l-ᶜAbbās al-Yamanī. The latter had a great respect for this person whose biography we pen. He gave him his highest praise and made known his good actions and declared his merits. The uncle of my father heard him say that his 'Way', that is the *ṭarīqa* of this person of the biography, was the *Suhrawardiyya ṭarīqa*. I have seen it written down in his own hand.

Our lord and grandfather, ᶜAbd al-Salām al-Qādirī, remarked in the text of his *Nuzhat al-fikrī* that 'a virtuous man, amongst those who were worthy of faith and whose statements are trustworthy had crossed the land of the Tuareg in order to reach the Sudan. While he was there he met the sons of Shaykh al-Ṣādiq. They said to him, "In the furthest Maghrib there is an illustrious family which belongs to us, namely that of Shaykh Abū Bakr al-Dilā'ī. This man is of very good faith and he is truthful in what he says. One can count upon what he says and there is no doubt that he spoke truthfully." The intention behind the words of the sons of al-Ṣādiq would appear to be that "this family is our own, in the sense that the men of [the *zāwiya*[18]] of Dilā' are cousins to them in relationship, or that both families have a common origin. One can also understand the meaning to be that their tie is only that of Islamic science: in short these two families are houses of science and sanctity. It is equally possible that this tie stems from the fact that both families belong to the Lamtūna. All the Tuareg are Lamtūna in fact. This is not to be doubted. The historians have said as much and they all concur on this point. The Lamtūna are numerous, strong and courageous." '[19]

The sojourn of Shaykh Aḥmad al-Yamanī in Agades, or nearby, first took place in 1078–9/1670. Some ten years later, in 1089–90/1680, accompanied by Abū Bakr b. Muḥammad al-Khaḍir b. al-Shaykh Sīdī Abī Bakr b. Muḥammad al-Dilā'ī, he left Fez with the expressed intention of once more visiting Shaykh ᶜAbdallāh al-Burnāwī in Kulumbardo. However, when he and his companions reached Agades they learnt of the martyrdom of Shaykh al-Burnāwī at the hands of the Tuareg and, at the same time, of the recent decease of Shaykh Aḥmad al-Ṣādiq [b.] al-Shaykh Uwāyis al-Lamtūnī. The occasion inspired a eulogy by Shaykh Aḥmad al-Yamanī, his former pupil, as well as by Shaykh Abū Bakr al-Dilā'ī. Shaykh Aḥmad al-Yamanī returned from Aïr to Morocco. He reached Fez and died there in 1113/1712.

From the above documentation the following appear to be the only sure facts which we have regarding the author of the *Qudwa*:

(*a*) He was a Tuareg and a Lamtūnī[20] and he was a resident for the last years of his life in, or near, Agades itself (spelt Agzad in the Arabic text) and not in the heart of the Aïr Massif.

Pl. 1. The Colophon of the *Qudwa*, giving the full name of the author

(*b*) He was a member of the *Suhrawardiyya ṭarīqa*. No specific mention of the *Maḥmūdiyya ṭarīqa* is made here.

(*c*) Shaykh Aḥmad al-Ṣādiq died between 1670 and 1680, though in all likelihood nearer the latter date. Either much of the *Qudwa* text was composed between these two dates,[21] or it may have been composed before. If the latter, then Shaykh Aḥmad al-Yamanī may have read it and taken some of its content with him to Morocco.

However, an important piece of corroborative evidence has come to light recently, due to the archaeological survey carried out by the mission led by Edmond and Suzanne Bernus to Shin Wasagharan in the Niger Republic. This site lies to the south of Agades, to the east of the well of Abalama. The site contains ruins of a mosque and other buildings and a cemetery which contains a large number of epitaphs and gravestones with Arabic inscriptions of varied dates. According to the Tuareg poet, M. Hawad, who accompanied the mission, this site is one of the places of pilgrimage of Aïr and is of religious importance. Few of the Kel Ferwan, who live locally, go near it, and they hold the locality in awe and reverence. One inscription, heavily weathered and of doubtful date, is sufficiently readable to make it likely that it is the last resting-place of Shaykh Aḥmad al-Ṣādiq. The inscription is to a Shaykh called Aḥmad al-Ṣādiq b. al-Shaykh Ways. It is numbered Gravestone 13.8. *Shin Wasagharan*. Part of the inscription reads:

In the name of Allāh, the Compassionate and Merciful. Blessing of Allāh be upon our lord, Muḥammad, upon his family and upon his Companions. I testify that there is no god but Allāh and I testify that Muḥammad is His Messenger. This is the tomb of Shaykh Aḥmad/Aḥmād al-Ṣadiq [*sic*] b. al-Shaykh Ways (Uwāyis), who died in the year ninety . . . [unclear: 1090?], in the month of Allāh, Shaᶜbān(?), on a Tuesday(?) . . .

Problems of decipherment apart, the deceased is surely none other than the author of the *Qudwa*.

Notes

1. *Archives Marocaines*, vol. xxiv (Paris, 1917), pp. 308–9. The trans. was made by Graulle Maillard and Michaux Bellaire.

Muḥammad b. al-Ṭayyib b. ᶜAbd al-Salām al-Qādirī al-Ḥasanī was one of the most important historians of the Maghrib during the 17th and 18th cents. He was born in 1124/1712 and died in 1187/1773. His most important work was *Nashr al-mathānī bi-ahl al-qarn al-ḥādī ᶜashara wa-l-thānī* (The Diffusion of Praises of the People of the Eleventh and Twelfth Centuries). In regard to this work and to other matters relating to this author, see

Norman Cigar, *Muhammad al-Qadiri's Nashr al-Mathani: The Chronicles* (Fontes Historiae Africanae, Series Arabica VI; London, 1981), pp. xi–xv.

2. The Ṣūfī 'Way' founded by Abū'l-Najīb ᶜAbd al-Qāhir b. ᶜAbdallāh al-Suhrawardī (died 563/1168) and by his nephew and pupil Abū Ḥafṣ. It is the oldest of the universal Ṣūfī 'Ways'. The name of the founder also appears in the 'chains' of initiation in other 'Ways', including the *Mawlawiyya* and the *Shādhiliyya* orders. The latter was one of the earliest to be established in the Sahara.
3. This name appears at the conclusion of the text of the *Qudwa* which would appear to have been dictated by the Shaykh himself. It is almost certain that the great bulk of the copy is much later than the 17th cent., and some allowance has to be made for errors by copyists.
4. For the background to this Ṣūfī activity in the Sudan, see R. S. O'Fahey and J. L. Spaulding, *Kingdoms of the Sudan* (London, 1974).
5. *Archives Marocaines*, pp. 309–10.
6. Ibid. 251–60.
7. Communication between Borno and Morocco would at that time have taken the traveller through Agades in either direction.
8. The rather curious statement appears in the French trans. of *Nashr al-Mathānī*, p. 259, 'Cette Tarîqa est peu répandue: nous n'avons jamais entendu parler d'une Tarîqa analogue, à aucune époque ni dans aucun pays; ce que nous en avons vu dans notre Maghrib, par le Chaikh Aboûl-ᶜAbbâs al-Yamanî, que Dieu l'agrée, nous suffit.'
9. Ibid. 253.
10. Ibid. 253. No explanation is given for the outburst, whether it was due to the desire of the Shaykh to change the way of 'robbers', including the Tuareg, by peaceful conversion, as seems likely, or whether it be due to friendship with Tuareg Ṣūfīs in Aïr, or whether it be due to the Shaykh himself being related to the Koyam (Kel Yetti) Tuareg, which is also another possible reason.
11. See n. 10. On the term *fuqarā'* see n. 14.
12. *Nashr al-Mathānī*, pp. 253–4.
13. Cited ibid. 258–9.
14. The term of *fuqarā'* (singular *faqīr*), 'poor man', applied to a Ṣūfī novice or to a man of a brotherhood without a special office is, as will be seen, used throughout in the *Qudwa*, and the term was much used in the *Maḥmūdiyya*. However, P. M. Holt draws attention to a special use of the word in the Sudan, where *fuqarā'* is a dialect plural form of *fakī* (*faqīh*), meaning a Ṣūfī, as well as a secular 'teacher'. The colloquial term for a Qur'ānic school is *khalwa*, as well as indicating a Ṣūfī retreat; see *Studies in the History of the Near East* (London, 1973), p. 122. With such variation of meaning some regard must be paid to local usage where such terms occur.
15. *Nashr al-mathānī*, p. 256.
16. Ibid. 308–9.
17. Uways is spelt Uwāyis in the colophon of the *Qudwa*. This name appears in one or two of the known lineages of the Kel Es-Sūq scholars and mystics of Aïr during the age of Shaykh Sīdī Maḥmūd (see my *Tuaregs*, Warminster (1975), p. 44), e.g. Shaykh Uways Wa-n-Barwa. The name of the copyist of the 17th- or 18-cent. dated copy of the ode of Muḥammad b. Tighna of Tadeliza—composed as a satirical attack on the *jihādist* Ḥadāḥadā and the *Qāḍī* Ḥamidtu and their excesses around 1650—is given as Ilyās b. al-Sharīf Ibrāhīm b. al-Shaykh Uwāyis al-Jakti̱ (of Jīkat). It is very possible that al-Sharīf Ibrāhīm was related to Shaykh Aḥmad al-Ṣādiq, even a brother of his. Chronologically it is reasonable. See my *Tuaregs*, pp. 125, 133, and 220.
18. In regard to some aspects of life at Dilā' at this time, see Magali Morsy, *Les Ahansala: Examen du rôle historique d'une famille maraboutique de l'Atlas marocain* (Paris, 1972).
19. Other Lamtūna of Takaddā and Agades region are discussed on p. 16. *Nashr al-mathānī*, p. 309.
20. See passages from *Salwat al-anfās* by Muḥammad b. Jaᶜfar al-Kattānī, vol. ii, p. 335, and the colophon of the *Qudwa* (Abalagh copy) on Plate 1. No mention is made of any *nisba* in the *Qudwa*.
21. It appears to have been dictated. Stylistically it is not one of a piece and suggests that its author was very old when he dictated it.

2

The Daghūghiyyūn *Sharīfs* and Scholars of the Family of al-Ḥājj Settle in the Central Sahara

The scholars and mystics who made their homes in the Mali Adrār and in the Aïr Massif, and who established cells and hermitages there, were of diverse Saharan origin. Many of them came from Arab and Berber tribes which had been settled in those districts for many centuries. They included the Massūfa Ṣanhāja, who were reputedly ancestors of the Inessūfa Eshsherifen. These latter are centred today around the town of In Gall in Niger, around Azelik (Takaddā), and also in Agades itself. They formed the ruling class in the medieval copper and salt complex of Takaddā. They were also citizens of the 'town of scholars', Anū Ṣamman, the ruins of which appear to lie to the west of Agades.

Many of the Massūfa scholars were jurists rather than mystics. The Egyptian writer, al-Sakhāwī (died 1497), mentions two of them from this district: Ibn Sugan *al-faqīh*, and his son, Abū Yaḥyā b. Yaḥyā b. Muḥammad b. ᶜAlī al-Massūfī al-Nākanatī (from Wa-n-Gānet?) who died in the Takaddā desert (*bādiyat Takaddā*) on 19 Dhū'l-Ḥijjah 948/19 March 1543. This date would have made him a near-contemporary of Shaykh Sīdī Maḥmūd al-Baghdādī who would have been living in the adjacent Aïr Massif at that time.[1]

The Massūfa of the Moroccan Draa and the Central Sahara were devotees of Ṣūfism as far back as the twelfth century. The Moroccan writer al-Tādilī mentions one Saharan Ṣūfī in his hagiographical work, *Kitāb al-Tashawwuf ilā rijāl al-taṣawwuf*.[2] He was called Abū Isḥāq Bārān b. Yaḥyā al-Massūfī:

> He was one of the companions of Abū ᶜAbdallāh al-Daqqāq. He died in Sijilmāsa in 570/1174–5. I was told by Abū ᶜAbdallāh Muḥammad b. Abī'l-Qāsim, who said, 'I was told by Abū Bakr b. ᶜAlī, and by others, that Abū Isḥāq said to one of the Ṣūfī *mashāyikh* in Marrakech, "How can I join those who follow the Ṣūfī path?" He said to him, "By removing this mouth muffler (*lithām*) and on the condition that you go to the market and that you return to us wearing a rag to cover your head." He was one of the chief men [of the Massūfa]. He left them and was absent for some time. Then he

Pls. 2–3. A passage referring to the Ṣūfī movements in the region of Aïr during the sixteenth century (Jalāl al-Dīn Sīdī Mawlāy Muḥammad al-Hādī al-Sūqī, *Naṣīḥat al-umma fī'-isti*ᶜ*mal al-rukhṣa*)

Plate 3

entered where they were once more, and behold, he had removed the mouth muffler from his face and upon his head he wore a rag. The Shaykh said to him: "You have joined those of the Ṣūfī path, and your pompous pride has taken leave of you." He left for Sijilmāsa and he directed himself towards Allāh, by his devotion and worship, until he died and departed to dwell in His presence, mighty and glorious He is.'

An important centre for Moroccan Ṣūfīs was the district of Dukkāla, the region lying between Azemmur and Safi. This had been so since the time of the Almoravids. It was from this region, and from Sijilmāsa, that the Eshsherifen mystics of the Kel Es-Sūq, in both the Adrār of Mali and in Aïr, claim that their ancestors wandered at an early date. This is particularly true of the Kel Es-Sūq Daghūghiyyūn of the Mali Adrār. They sometimes claim to be Lamtūna, and therefore 'Almoravids', possibly because of the close links between them and the Āl Amghār Ṣanhāja family which was prominent in the region of Dukkāla. The Ṣūfīs of this family drew upon many of the ideas and the teachings of the Ṣūfīs who dwelt in the Moroccan Sūs. The Daghūghiyyūn claim a line of descent through ʿAlī b. Yaḥyā b. Ibrāhīm al-Daghūghī, to Isḥāq b. Mawlāy Idrīs, a descendent of ʿAlī b. Abī Ṭālib, the son-in-law of the Prophet. An important scholar of the Kel Es-Sūq of Mali, Sīdī Mawlāy Muḥammad al-Hādī, wrote:

This Idrīs was the brother of Muḥammad b. ʿAbdallāh b. al-Ḥasan b. ʿAlī b. Abī Ṭālib. He was the first of the household of the Prophet to come to the Maghrib. All the *shurafā'* of the Maghrib are of his lineage, save for the *shurafā'* of Sijilmāsa.[3]

The statement is confirmed, independently, by a noted Sūsī scholar, Muḥammad al-Mukhtār al-Sūsī:

Al-Daghūghiyyūn: a family of the Daghūghiyyūn Bū Jān, the grandsons of Abū Ibrāhīm b. Ibrāhīm al-Daghūghī who was famous in the sixth [twelfth] century, as is shown by the book *al-Tashawwuf*. Much scholarship was handed down amongst them, together with sound literary learning from that century, even though the bulk of the biographical reports of the men of this family are unknown to us, save for the summary statements about them by the men of the eleventh [seventeenth] century.[4]

A representative example of reports about the early Daghūghiyyūn is to be found in al-Tādilī's book, under Scholar number 224:[5]

Abū Muḥammad Tīlijjī b. Mūsā al-Daghūghī: One of the great men of the *mashāyikh* of the country of the Banū Daghūgh of Dukkāla. He died there in the year 605 [1208]. He lived to be one hundred and twenty years old. He was a preacher in the *Ribāṭ* of Shākir [a companion of ʿUqba b. Nāfiʿ] at a time when only a few individuals mounted the pulpit there. I heard Dāwūd

b. ᶜAbd al-Khāliq say, 'I and a group of the Ṣūfī novices (*murīdūn*) were with Abū Muḥammad Tīlijjī. We spoke about continuous fasting (*wiṣāl*) and about the length of time which a man should practise it. One of them disapproved of a man doing so for a long period. Abū Muḥammad said, "I knew a servant [of Allāh] who continued to fast for a whole year." So we kept quiet, one dared not ask the question, who is this man? I used to say, if I meet him I'll ask him about him. Whenever I visited him I forgot to ask him and when I departed then I remembered. I continued thus until he died, may Allāh have mercy upon him, and I had not asked him.'

Dāwūd said, 'I was told by Abū Muḥammad who said, "In the days of trial and hardship I was hotly pursued and were I to have been found I would have been killed. One summer day I fled to a tent and I sat there while my riding beast stood at the door of the tent. Lo, horsemen had followed my tracks and they came to the tent. They looked towards it but none of them saw me nor did they see my beast. I heard them say, 'What is wrong with this tent, why have its people departed?' " '

I was told by Muḥammad b. Jaldāsun[6] who said, 'I was told by Muḥammad b. Tīlijjī that his mother told him, saying, "In the night I beheld a person visit Abū Muḥammad. He woke him up from his sleep and he gave him a copper vessel and he performed his ablutions out of it." She continued, "I saw an animal which resembled a white camel which had come to him. He mounted it and it ascended with him to the roof of the house and it journeyed forth with him as I watched it." When she had said this she was struck dumb and uttered no further word. She stayed for a little while and then she died.'

The Ṣūfīs of the Mali Adrār are, in part, heirs to the Moroccan Daghūghiyyūn. Sīdī Mawlāy Muḥammad al-Hādī expands a little, citing what further evidence he had about the earliest Ṣūfīs in the Mali Adrār:

As for those who claim Sharifian status in our land [the Eshsherifen of the Mali Adrār], their claims are facts which are certain and can be proved correct. They can be cited from the words of our past scholars who lived in the tenth [sixteenth] century and afterwards. Such men [Eshsherifen] were Aḥmad al-Burjī (?), Muḥammad b. ᶜAlī and Muḥammad b. Ibrāhīm b. Imkaḥūl and those of whom they have proved the status of *Sharīf* according to the reported tradition of this ancestor, namely Āyya. Among them also there was that one whose name was Muḥammad al-Mukhtār. We have seen, in what they have quoted, that they are in accord in regard to the Sharīfian status of the latter. His lineage is soundly based, because he was the paternal cousin of the *Quṭb*, Abū'l-Ḥasan al-Shādhilī'.[7] His name was Muḥammad al-Mukhtār b. Ibrāhīm b. ᶜAbd al-Raḥmān b. ᶜAbd al-Jabbār. His name appears thus in the work entitled *Laṭā'if al-minan*.

I have also been informed, by one whom I do not suspect, that Shaykh Sīdī'l-Mukhtār al-Kuntī said to him, the unsuspected one, that, 'Whoever [amongst the Kel Es-Sūq] proves to me that his lineage goes back to [Agg]

Āyya,[8] then I can prove that he is a *Sharīf*.' This is because known lineages have been mixed due to resemblances between names [which are much alike], and also due to the great number of those who claim to the status of *Sharīf* amongst those who are not entitled to it or whose claim is unproven.

I have put forward the name of this forebear [Muḥammad al-Mukhtār], because, in date, he is either from amongst those men who lived in the seventh [thirteenth] century, or else from those of the eighth [fourteenth]. As regards the ninth [fifteenth] century, I cannot believe this to be so. Allāh knows best, but al-Shādhilī was amongst those who lived in the seventh century. I have also found in one of the ancient texts that the Shaykh and *Quṭb*, Muḥammad b. Yūsuf, and Shaykh Aḥmad b. Abī Ruways, were both amongst the *mashāyikh* of the Ṣūfīs. It appears thus to me. They were men who took the *wird* of Abū Ruways.[9] The latter teacher was the possessor of a profound mystical perception (*ᶜārif*), and the same was also reported on the authority of his pupil, al-Ḥājj [Muḥammad b. Muḥammad] Abū'l-Hudā al-Sūqī. The latter was the author of two sets of questions; one was sent to al-Suyūṭī, and the other was sent to al-Maghīlī.[10] As for the other Shaykh, that is, Muḥammad b. Yūsuf, his name is well known.

I maintain that these men [cited above] were from the tenth century, though they had some knowledge of the ninth, taking into account the judgement which was given by Muḥammad b. Yūsuf. It was prompted by a conflict in respect to two matters of his. One was the Sunni ᶜAlī, the infidel, who died at the end of the ninth century (1493),[11] and the second was with Muḥammad b. ᶜAlī on account of a matter which was told to me by my Shaykh, Muḥammad Ḥanna, may Allāh have mercy upon him.[12]

These traditions of the Kel Es-Sūq stress the important influence of the Sharīfian Daghūghiyyūn, claimants to descent from the *Ahl al-Bayt*, amongst the Ṣūfīs of the Central Sahara in the late medieval period. At the same time, one or two names of the mystics associated with the Algerian saint, Abū Ruways, who appear also in the text of the *Qudwa*, are brought to the fore. Amongst these, al-Ḥājj Abū'l-Hudā al-Sūqī is the most important. Not only was he amongst the chief followers of Sīdī Maḥmūd, but two extracts from his writings appear as quotations in the very heart of the text of the *Qudwa*.

Scholars of the Ḥājjiyyūn

The group of scholars, known collectively as the family of al-Ḥājj, with noteworthy judges and men of letters amongst them, played an important part in the history of Timbuktu, more especially during the so-called 'Tuareg period'. Allied in culture, origin, and calling, also by marriage, to the Tuareg family of And-Agg Muḥammad al-Kabīr, to the allegedly Massūfa families of Muḥammad Aqīt and

Aqītūn, and to the Inessūfa of Takaddā, this family was singled out for harsh treatment by Sunnī ᶜAlī. Humiliated and stripped of possessions and power, its members fled for safety to Walāta, possibly to Tīshīt and to Wādān, all in Mauritania, and to the borders of Aïr, more especially to Takaddā and to Anū Ṣamman, which was at no great distance from Agades and which had rapidly developed at that time. Elias Saad in his book, *Social History of Timbuktu*,[13] remarks:

The school associated with the al-Ḥājj family had exercised a great though ill-documented influence before the rise of Sunni 'Ali. The Songhai monarch persecuted and killed some of the scholars from this family, including a number among them who lived, as we are told, at the Alfa Gungu. However, the family seems to have maintained wide Sahelian connections, much like the Kunta of the eighteenth and nineteenth centuries. Al-Qāḍi al-Ḥājj, and his brother Ibrāhīm, are associated at once with Walāta and Banku, besides Timbuktu. Their sons and relatives fled Sunni 'Ali both to Walāta and Tagedda, while Ibrāhīm b. 'Umar, reputed to be a *walī*, became a judge at Jenge during the reign of Askia Muḥammad. Today there exists an *ijāza* in the possession of al-Shaikh 'Īsa wuld Muḥammad Mawlūd, of the Keltina al-Ḥājj, which traces a long chain of transmission backwards to al-Amīn b. Abu Bakr b. al-Qāḍi al-Ḥājj. The latter studied under al-Suyūṭi and, although he may have been the first to study under the illustrious Egyptian, he is not mentioned in the Timbuktu chronicles any more than his son Aḥmad and his nephew Muḥammad Ṣāliḥ. It may be that the activities of these scholars during the Songhai period were distributed over a wide area and left little impact on Timbuktu. Indeed, excepting the possibility that Al-Amīn b. Aḥmad and 'Abd al-Raḥmān al-Mujtahid were products of their school, their impact on Timbuktu was not revived until after the Moroccan conquest when Muḥammad b. Aḥmad b. al-Qāḍi 'Abd al-Raḥman became Judge. He taught some influential scholars and thereby kept alive the *sanad* going back to his great-uncle, Muḥammad al-Amīn. It is possible that his family later migrated from Timbuktu, much as happened to the And-Agh-Muḥammads. Alternatively, both families may have continued to contribute to the transmission of learning among the limited circles of their immediate relatives.

Anū Ṣamman was a centre for these Massūfa scholars. Amongst these, it was al-ᶜĀqib b. ᶜAbdallāh al-Anuṣammanī who died some time after 955/1548–9, whose name appears as a solitary individual in later sources.[14] Regarding his literary and scholarly legacy, J. O. Hunwick and R. S. O'Fahey remark:

He originated from Anū Ṣamman near Tegidda-n-Tagait on the plains to the west of Agades. His only known teacher is al-Maghīlī, whom he met when the latter visited the Tegidda area in the early 1490s. He performed the pilgrimage to Mecca, evidently some time before 1505, since he met al-Suyūṭī in Egypt and the latter died in that year. A. Bābā records that he disputed with [al-Makhlūf] al-Balbālī over points of *fiqh* (*masā'il*).

After him, one scholar who resided in Anū Ṣamman, but who was of the family of al-Ḥājj, has received most notice. This was al-Najīb b. Muḥammad Shams al-Dīn, who died after 1004/1595–6. He had noted pupils. According to Hunwick and O'Fahey:

> Originating from Anū Ṣamman, he studied under Aḥmad (or Isḥāq) Suḥūliyya (of whom nothing is currently known) and was still alive, though very old, in 1004/1595. Among his pupils was Sh. al-Bakrī, an influential teacher of the next generation.

Commenting upon his pupil, Shaykh al-Bakrī, they add:

> This scholar is presumably to be identified with al-Najīb b. Muḥammad Shams al-Dīn al-Takandāwī al-Anṣamānī, whose biography Bello gives, and who, in turn, is to be identified with the man whom Aḥmad Bābā calls al-Najīb b. Muḥammad al-Kiddāwī al-An.ṣ.m.nī. These two *nisbas* relate the man first to the Tegidda (Tegidda-n-Tagait) region to the west of Aïr and then to the village of Anū Ṣamman within it. The reading 'al-Takandāwī' in both texts of IM is an obvious scribal error for 'al-Takiddāwī'. According to Aḥmad Bābā, this al-Najīb was still living at the time he wrote in 1004/1596, but he was an old man.
>
> If this information is correct, it would argue strongly for Sh. al-Bakrī having been born no later than *c.* 1575 and having studied under al-Najīb when the latter was already aged. After studying in Yandoto, Sh. al-Bakrī is said to have travelled to 'his land' (*li-bilādihi*), or, according to the variant reading to 'the land' (*al-bilād*), where he met and studied with Sh. al-Najīb. After completing his studies with him he again returned to 'his land' where, after a teaching career, he eventually died. Sh. al-Bakrī's homeland was apparently Borno, but he most probably studied with Sh. al-Najīb in the latter's homeland which was Anū Ṣamman in Tegidda-n-Tagait.

It seems most probable that chronology requires that it is this Shaykh al-Najīb who is nicknamed *al-sayf* (the sword) in the text of the *Qudwa*. He is referred to as 'Muḥammad *al-faqīh*, or, al-Najīb Muḥammad b. [Muḥammad] *al-faqīh* known as "the sword" (*al-sayf*)', and according to the *Qudwa* it was he who counselled in vain the Sulṭān of Agades, Ahmad b. Tilẓay (Taluẓa), to give Sīdī Maḥmūd al-Baghdādī his full backing. This scholar, al-Najīb, is very highly regarded in Agades, and numerous stories are told about his miracles.[15] However, it is this scholar's other compositions which are better known to us, since a copy of at least one of his works is now accessible, and the thoroughness and breadth of his erudition—especially his lexicographical competence, spurred on by his love for and deep study of the ᶜ*Ishrīniyyāt*, in praise of the Prophet, by the

Berber scholar, ᶜAbd al-Raḥmān b. Yakhlaftan al-Fāzāzī (died 627/1230)—is most readily apparent from the manuscripts.[16] Although the exact familial relationship of Muḥammad al-Najīb is still not clear, Hunwick and O'Fahey enter his works separately as unquestionably his.

It is not clear if he is the same person as MUḤAMMAD al-NAJĪB b. MUḤAMMAD Shams al-Dīn b. MUḤAMMAD al-NAJĪB b. MUḤAMMAD b. ᶜABD AL-ṢAMAD al-Anṣamānī (*sic*). Two works attributed to him are known:

1. *Sharḥ ᶜIshrīniyyāt al-Fāzāzī*
   MSS: Kaduna (NA), 1 copy.
2. *al-Ṭarīqa al-muthlā ilā 'l-wasīlat al-ᶜuẓmā*
   MSS: Paris (BN), 5372 (inc.)

The second of these works is barely distinguishable from the first. It gives rise to the belief that they are one and the same composition, or else that little more than a page or two exists of a work called *al-Ṭarīqa al-muthlā*. There is no colophon to the incomplete Paris (Kel al-Sūq) manuscript. Nevertheless, the Exordium indicates that its author is Muḥammad al-Najīb b. Muḥammad Shams al-Dīn b. Muḥammad al-Najīb b. Muḥammad b. ᶜAbd al-Ṣamad al-Anuṣammānī (Anuṣammanī). He resided in Anū Ṣamman and he was possibly an al-Ḥājjī (from Timbuktu or Wādān) by descent. After praise to the Almighty and to His Prophet, in eloquent Arabic style, although with nothing particularly Ṣūfī in its phrasing, the author discloses his passion for the *ᶜIshrīniyyāt*; for al-Fāzāzi's original and for the poem composed on it (*al-takhmīs*) by the Shaykh and *faqīh* Abū Bakr Muḥammad b. Mahīb. Muḥammad al-Najīb then explains how much time was spent helping his pupils, and others, to resolve thorny passages where Qur'ānic verses and Prophetic *ḥadīths* were quoted or expounded. Most of these matters related to the meanings of obscure expressions or else to the inflection of Arabic words in a grammatical context. These questions suggested a clear division into two of the material within his dictionary, or work of lexicography, which had been slowly forming in his mind after much prayer and intercession and contact with other scholars whose reference works in manuscripts were few or non-existent and who depended upon borrowing from colleagues. One scholar, al-Ḥājj Muḥammad al-Amīn b. ᶜUthmān, is mentioned by name. The final format, *Uns al-muḥibbīn fī sharḥ manāqib al-mursalīn*, is somewhat loose in its style yet bears witness to an impressive command of Arabic syntax surpassing that found in the *Qudwa*, which was written at a later and in a decadent time.[17]

Notes

1. See al-Sakhāwī's *al-Ḍaw' al-lāmiᶜ*, pub. Cairo in 1354/1936, vol. x, p. 147. Al-Nākanatī suggests a *nisba* relating to Djanet in the region of the Algerian Tassili, or is a misreading for Tākaddāwī.

   Takaddā, by the age of Sīdī Maḥmūd, had lost its status, as a town of commerce and culture, to adjacent Agades. We have no knowledge as to who preceded these scholars in that district. Ibn Baṭṭūṭa (died 770/1368) records that the *Qāḍī* of the town, Abū Ibrāhīm Isḥāq al-Janātī, was a Berber. There is a distinct possibility that his *nisba* bears a relationship to these scholars.

   It is perhaps worthy of note that nowhere does Ibn Baṭṭūṭa record that the scholars and their colleagues had any Ṣūfī affiliation whatsoever. Ian Netton in his article, 'Myth, Miracle and Magic in the *Riḥla* of Ibn Baṭṭūṭa', *Journal of Semitic Studies*, 29/1 (1984), pp. 131–40, has drawn attention to the strong Ṣūfī interests of the Moroccan traveller, to the extent that he joined the *Rifāᶜiyya ṭarīqa* in Jerusalem and the *Suhrawardiyya* in Isfahan. The initiation he received is described in some detail and also the *silsila* of the *ṭarīqa*. H. A. R. Gibb in his *Travels of Ibn Battuta, AD 1325–1354* (Cambridge, 1962), pp. 297–8, translates the passage as follows:

   'He invested me with it accordingly on the fourteenth of Latter Jumādā in the year 727 in his convent afore-mentioned, as he had been invested with it by his father Shams al-Dīn and his father had been invested with it by his father Tāj al-Dīn Mahmūd, and Mahmūd by his father Shihāb al-Dīn 'Alī al-Rajā, and 'Alī by the Imām Shihāb al-Dīn Abu Ḥafṣ 'Omar b. Muḥammad b. 'Abdallāh al-Suhrawardī, and 'Omar had been invested by the great shaikh Ḍiyā al-Dīn Abu'l-Najīb al-Suhrawardī, and Abu'l-Najīb by his paternal uncle, the Imām Waḥīd al-Dīn 'Omar, and 'Omar by his father Muḥammad b. 'Abdallāh, known as 'Amawaih, and Muḥammad by the shaikh Akhū Faraj al-Zinjāni, and Akhū Faraj by the shaikh Aḥmad al-Dīnawarī, and Aḥmad by the Imām | Mamshād al-Dīnawarī, and Mamshād from the shaikh, the seer of the truth, 'Alī b. Sahl al-Ṣūfī, and 'Alī from Abu'l-Qāsim al-Junaid, and al-Junaid from Sarī al-Saqaṭī, and Sarī al-Saqaṭī from Dā'ūd al-Ṭā'ī, and Dā'ūd from al-Ḥasan b. Abi'l-Ḥasan al-Baṣrī, and al-Ḥasan b. Abi'l-Ḥasan al-Baṣrī from the Commander of the Faithful, 'Alī b. Abī Ṭālib.

   Ibn Juzayy comments: In this manner did the shaikh Abū 'Abdallāh [Ibn Baṭṭūṭa] cite this chain of authorities. But it is a matter of common knowledge that Sarī al-Saqaṭī was the disciple of Ma'rūf al-Karkhī, and Ma'ruf was the disciple of Dā'ūd al-Ṭā'ī; likewise that between Dā'ūd al-Ṭā'ī and al-Ḥasan there was Ḥabīb al-'Ajamī. In regard to Akhū Faraj al-Zinjānī, it is known only that he was the disciple of Abu'l'Abbās al-Nihāwandī, and that al-Nihāwandī was the disciple of Abū 'Abdallāh ibn Khafīf, that Ibn Khafīf was the disciple of Abū Muḥammad Ruwaim, and Ruwaim the disciple of Abu'l-Qāsim al-Junaid. As for Muḥammad b. 'Abdallāh 'Amawaih, he it was who was the disciple of the shaikh Aḥmad al-Dīnawarī 'the Black', without any intervening person; but God knows best. The person who became the disciple of Akhū Faraj al-Zinjānī was 'Abdallāh b. Muḥammad b. 'Abdallāh, the father of Abu'l-Najīb.'

   The *silsila* of Shaykh Sīdī Maḥmūd differs from this (see chapter 8) and seems in keeping with the *Khalwatiyya*. Though the dedication of Ibn Baṭṭūṭa to Ṣūfism was not wholehearted, it does seem possible that he would have referred to it during his visit to Takaddā had it been established there.
2. See al-Tādilī, *Tashawwuf*, pp. 241–2.
3. See my *Berbers in Arabic Literature* (London, 1982), p. 229.
4. Muḥammad al-Mukhtār al-Sūsī, *Sūs al-ᶜālima* (Fedala, Morocco, 1380/1960), p. 129. The contemporary Ṣūfism that is still to be found amongst the Daghūghiyyūn, who are in Morocco, has been little studied. However, Vincent Crapanzano, in his chapter entitled 'The Ḥamadsha', in Nikki R. Keddie (ed.), *Scholars, Saints and Sufis* (Berkeley, Calif., 1972), p. 327 ff., has drawn our attention to the influences in Ṣūfī ritual of an extreme kind which emanate from regions to the south of the Sahara. In the early 18th cent. Sīdī Aḥmad al-Daghūghī allegedly paid a visit to the Sūdān, where he was sent by his master, Sīdī ᶜAlī, 'to bring back the *hal*, or ecstasy'. He did so by 'stealing' from the king of the Sūdān a flute, a drum, and the *ᶜifrīta* or *jinniyya*, ᶜĀ'isha Qandisha.

5. al-Tādilī, *Tashawwuf*, pp. 414–15.
6. There is a full biography of this scholar, ibid., 210.
7. Abū'l-Ḥasan ᶜAlī b. ᶜAbdallāh al-Shādhilī, the founder of the *Shādhiliyya ṭarīqa*, died in 1258.
8. See p. 13 and my *Tuaregs* (Warminster, 1975), p. 144.
9. Neither the *Minan al-kubrā*, by ᶜAbd al-Wahhāb al-Shaᶜrānī, nor the *Kitāb Laṭā'if al-minan*, by Aḥmad b. Muḥammad b. ᶜAṭā-Allāh al-Iskandarī, mention this person, Muḥammad al-Mukhtār. As for the *wird* of Abū Ruways there is nothing to indicate what *ṭarīqa* this was, or who Abū Ruways was, or where Abū'l-Hudā studied and by whom he was initiated. Since this nickname is not uncommon amongst Ṣūfīs, no further information can be gathered from Saharan and Sahelian sources.
10. Little is known about the Ṣūfī activities of al-Maghīlī (died 1503–4 or 1505/6), and the reader is referred to the article by ᶜAbd al-ᶜAzīz ᶜAbdallāh Batrān, 'A Contribution to the Biography of Shaykh Muḥammad b. ᶜAbd al-Karīm b. Muḥammad (ᶜUmar—Aᶜmar) al-Maghīlī al-Tilimsānī', in the *Journal of African History*, 14/3 (1973), pp. 381–94.

    Respected Tuareg scholars like to identify Abū'l-Hudā Muḥammad b. Muḥammad with Muḥammad b. Muḥammad al-Lamtūnī, the unknown enquiring scholar, writing from Agades or Aïr, or from the Mali Adrār, who appears in al-Suyūṭī's *Ḥāwī li'l-fatāwī*; see *The Tuaregs*, pp. 43, 45–7, and 67, and John Hunwick's 'Notes on a Late Fifteenth Century Document concerning al-Takrūr', in C. H. Allen and R. W. Johnson (eds.), *African Perspectives* (Cambridge, 1970). Their case cannot be proved, and in many ways it seems unlikely. There are also problems of date. All this makes their case a weak one. Shaykh Aḥmad Abū Ruways may have been a Qādirī Shaykh, but the questions asked from Aïr region are almost exclusively concerned with *fiqh*. As for al-Maghīlī, we know that he stayed in Aïr and Takaddā but it seems curious that Abū'l-Hudā had to correspond with him rather than to visit him in person.
11. Latest thinking on this much-maligned and misunderstood Songhai ruler is to be read in Elias N. Saad, *Social History of Timbuktu* (Cambridge, 1983), pp. 41–5.
12. Cited from Document No. 94 in the Arabic archives housed in Niamey, Institut de Recherche Scientifique, formerly Boubou Hama collection, written about 1867/8 by Jalāl al-Dīn Sīdī Mawlāy Muḥammad b. al-Hādī al-Sūqī, who lived in Gao district and in the Mali Adrār.
13. Elias N. Saad, *Social History of Timbuktu*, pp. 63–4. Regarding Wādān and the Ḥājj families, see Rainer Oswald, *Die Handelstadte Der Westsahara* (Marburger Studien zur Afrika und Asienkunde, Serie A: Afrika, Band 39; Berlin 1986), which corrects and updates some of the information furnished by Mauritanian scholars in my 'Ṣanhājah scholars of Timbuctoo', *BSOAS*, 30/3 (1967), pp. 638 ff.
14. *Arabic Literature in Africa*, No. 1, ed. J. O. Hunwick and R. S. O'Fahey (Program of African Studies; Evanston, Ill., 1985), pp. 26, 27–8, 76–9.
15. See Adamou, *Agadèz et sa Région* (Etudes Nigériennes No. 4; Niamey, 1979), pp. 64–6, where he includes the following remarks about al-Najīb Muḥammad 'al-sayf':

    'Ngib al Quidaly Tigdawi, de son vrai nom Mohammed Ibn Mohammed, est très connu pour son livre Nagibi ou commentaire sur El Acharnia. Mais sa grande réputation lui vient surtout de son héroïsme. On disait qu'après la fin de la construction de la grande mosquée par Zakaryā, des diables menaçaient chaque vendredi le muezzin qui du haut du minaret appelait les fidèles à la prière. Ngib décida alors de monter lui-même un vendredi sur le minaret pour dire l'appel à la prière. Lorsqu'il descendit, son sabre était trempé de sang. Depuis ce jour on l'appela Al-Mogharib-bi-Sefi (le connaisseur de sabre) ou encore Mohammad Maï Takobi (Mohammed possesseur du sabre). Les diables cependant ne désarmèrent pas car, apres avoir émigre et transporté le cavadre de leur patriarche assassiné par Ngib, ils ensorcelèrent la place destinée à l'Imam. Ce maléfice découvert, on fit encore appel à Ngib qui organisa des prières collectives, des sacrifices, pour libérer le lieu saint de ces mauvais esprits. Il conseilla également de changer la place destinée ă l'*imām*.'

    It seems possible that two scholars called Muḥammad al-Najīb b. Shams al-Dīn were confused, in fact, into one person. However, one person is suggested by verse 92 of Muḥammad b. Tighna's poem (composed in the mid-17th cent.) directed against Ḥadāhadā (see my *Tuaregs*, p. 133):

'And the view of *the* scholar of Anū Ṣamman, [the *faqīh* al-] Najīb, who was distinguished and a man of noble standing. The ruin of his town is not to be wondered at.'

Al Quidaly may well indicate some connection with the Igdalen maraboutic group of In Gall region. No mention is made of the other works attributed to this scholar. The importance of the *ᶜIshrīniyyāt* for the Shehu ᶜUthmān dan Fodio, and for mystics of the region, is the subject of a remark by Mervyn Hiskett in his *Sword of Truth*, (Oxford, 1973), p. 37.

'The next major branch of study he was concerned with was the biography of the Prophet Muhammad, the story of his life and mission; the revelation of the Koran to him; the wars he fought against the unbelievers and how he finally overthrew paganism and established Islam in Mecca, the town of his birth. This story is to be found both in Arabic prose sources and in Arabic verse, in the form of poetic panegyrics addressed to the Prophet. Well-known works of this genre the Shehu is known to have studied are *al-'Ishriniyyat* (The Twenties) of the thirteenth-century Moroccan poet, al-Fazzazi and the *Burda* (The Cloak) of the Berber poet al-Busiri. Both tell the Prophet's story in an allusive rather than allegorical style, making constant references to the *mu'jizat*, the 'evidentiary miracles' through which God singled out Muhammad as 'The Chosen One'. Although cast in a formal style, they are often very beautiful and full of reverence and deep longing to express worship. There is no doubt this type of poetry, much loved by Muslim mystics, had a profound effect on the young Shedu and helped him to compose his own poetry in praise of the Prophet.'

16. See *GAL*, *S* i. pp. 482–3.
17. The Paris manuscript 5372 in the Bibliothèque Nationale is subtitled 'Volume de 189 Feuillets, les feuillets 1, 95, 139 sont mutilés, 14 Novembre 1896'. Much of the text is now unreadable, particularly at the end, which is incomplete, and the concluding pages are lost. The Arabic script is typical of the Kel Es-Sūq and is in a Maghribī hand with some 29 lines to each page. Fo. 101 contains a poem in profuse praise of the Prophet.

3

Shaykh Sīdī Maḥmūd al-Baghdādī and his Arrival in Aïr in the Sixteenth Century

The Prophecy of Ḥadīth

The opening folios of the *Qudwa* present special problems over legibility, readability, and the possibility of any very satisfactory translation. The handwriting is different from that which appears in the rest of the text. The opening folios appear to be older. Many passages have faded completely, or have been covered over by a later writer or by a copyist. Part of it is now unquestionably untranslatable. Are we closer in this part to the original copy of Aḥmad al-Ṣādiq b. Uwāyis? The style is certainly more formal, literal, and classical; furthermore it is followed by a general portrait of Shaykh Sīdī Maḥmūd. This, as will be seen, is also to be found in Muḥammad Bello's *Infāq al-maysūr*, where this passage is quoted from the *Qudwa* almost verbatim. It is followed by the biographies of his first disciples. This whole section of the *Qudwa* therefore must date from the eighteenth century at the very latest, whatever the date may be of other passages towards the end of the Abalagh text.

The bulk of the discussion in these early folios is concerned with the signs of the *Mahdī* who will appear at the end of time. The author is anxious to make clear his view regarding the precise role played by Sīdī Maḥmūd in the divine plan, there having been some misunderstanding over this amongst his followers, and an open hostility on the part of the Sulṭān of Agades and his religious advisors. In the second passage here, the author indicates that the appearance of the holy man of Aïr was foretold in prophecy and in the *ḥadīth* of the Prophet, but that any claim to his role as the eschatological *Mahdī* was baseless. As passages further on within the text of the *Qudwa* reinforce this point—for example, the appeal of Shaykh Abū'l-Hudā to the Sulṭān—its appearance at the opening to the whole composition reveals that this was a matter of importance nearly a century after the death of Shaykh Sīdī Maḥmūd. None the less, the status of the Shaykh is never clearly defined. The matter is left unclarified. We have no information about the identity of Shaykh Abū ʿUbayda b. al-*faqīh* Muḥammad b. al-*faqīh* al-Ḥasan, who is quoted here.

The beliefs about the events which are to take place at the end of time, which are expressed in the *Qudwa*, appear to be derived from the following sources:

(*a*) The cosmology of the days which are to precede the Last Judgement and the region of the world where the *Mahdī* will make his appearance. Ideas such as these are derived from early *ḥadīths* about the support of the people of the Maghrib for a man who is descended from the Prophet's daughter, Fāṭima, who will march to Mecca and who will be master of Justice and Equity at the end of the age.[1]

Such ideas were considerably expanded and developed by later writers. Prominent amongst them was al-Qurtubī (died 671/1272) in his *al-Tadhkira fī aḥwāl al-mawta wa-umūr al-ākhira*.[2] The following passage illustrates several sources for statements that are to be found in the early part of the *Qudwa*:

The Chapter regarding the *Mahdī*, his description, his name, his gift, his stay, and his going forth with Jesus to assist him to fight the Anti-Christ. . . . Regarding the sign of his departure, the twice taking of the allegiance and how he will fight the Sufyānī and will slay him.

The *ḥadīth* of Umm Salama and Abū Hurayra has already been mentioned, namely, that the *Mahdī* will take the oath of allegiance betwixt al-Rukn and al-Maqām. This makes it clear that the oath of allegiance will not occur hitherto. The situation is otherwise, since, it is reported, from the *ḥadīth* of Ibn Masᶜūd and others of the Companions, that he will come forth at the end of time from the Furthest Maghrib. Victory will precede him for forty miles. His banners will be white and yellow and within them signs will be written with the name of Allāh Almighty. No banner of his will be defeated. The unfurling aloft of these banners and their being sent forth will be at the sea shore *at a place called Māssa* in the direction wherein the sun sets.

In the Maghrib there shall be a tumult, and fear and hunger will prevail there, and high price. Feuding will be widespread, and some of mankind will devour others. At that time a man of the Furthest Maghrib of the family of Fāṭima, the daughter of the Messenger of Allāh will go forth. He is the *Mahdī* who will arise at the end of time and he will be the first of the conditions of the hour.[3]

(*b*) The belief that a charismatic religious leader would appear from a Saharan region, or build a castle or a religious centre within it, was a widely held view in North Africa during this period. This Saharan region is often identified with the Sāqiya al-Ḥamrā' in the Western Sahara from whence certain 'maraboutic' groups in Southern Tunisia, the Awlād Muḥammad in the Fezzan, the Kunta of Mauritania, and Azawād, allegedly emigrated to other North African regions.[4]

R. G. Jenkins in his article on 'The Evolution of Religious Brotherhoods in North and Northwest Africa 1523–1900' writes:

In the light of the available evidence, it appears that from the fifteenth century, the diffusion of the Qādiriyya and Shādhiliyya, together with the increasing role of *sharīfs*, and mounting fixation on the person of the *walī*, progressed far more rapidly than it had done in the previous two hundred years. The Maghribian tradition which held that *walīs* came from the Muslim West at this time, particularly from the Sāqiyat al-Ḥamrā', should not be lightly dismissed. Nor should Delafosse's belief that these *walīs* dispersed to the south, as well as to the north. This dispersion of *walīs* and diffusion of Ṣufism, was closely connected with political events. The Shādhiliyya and Qādiriyya did not only increase their influence; they competed with each other. The important result of this religious and political activity was the emergence of the *ṭuruq*.

He adds:

There are two basic elements in the diffusion of Ṣūfi *ṭuruq*, as distinct from the diffusion of Ṣufism before 1523. Firstly, the increase in the number of affiliates of a particular brotherhood was partially due to its appeal. Here, sociological and religious factors are significant. For the lay brothers, it appears that affiliation was undertaken upon a corporate rather than an individual basis. This was the case with the Kunta and Idaw Alī, two of the Zawāyā groups in the western Sahara. And Evans-Pritchard suggests that a parallel may also be drawn with the Sanusiyya. Closely linked with ethnic affiliation was the prominent role acquired by *sharīfs*. Attention has been drawn previously to the conditions in which a local following developed around the person of the *walī*, whereby his descendants became a type of aristocratic caste, within the ethnic group, which often took its name from the *walī*. The widespread diffusion of this phenomenon can also be seen, in some measure, as a reflection of ethnic particularism—each ethnic group requiring its own *walī*.[5]

(*c*) Though the precise status of Sīdī Maḥmūd is not defined, the author of the *Qudwa* would appear to have regarded him as a *mujaddid*, the renewer of the faith, one who was to prepare the way for the *Mahdī* who one day was to follow him. J. Hunwick has shown that during the age of Sīdī Maḥmūd it was possible for there to be more than one *mujaddid* at any one time, and for more than one district and discipline, even though the districts in question were linked in some way. Even so, the lack of mention of the very existence of Sīdī Maḥmūd by other leading scholars in his lifetime is decidedly strange:

The view that more than one regenerator was necessary in a given age in order that the benefit of *tajdīd* might teach the whole *umma* was taken up in West Africa by the well-known Timbuktu jurist Aḥmad Bābā (d. 1627), who apparently went so far as to assert that each locality might have its own local *mujaddid*. He wrote an *urjūza* 'on those sent at the head of each hundred [years]' and for the tenth century named the regenerator as 'our imam Muḥammad'. Al-Maqqarī, who quotes this line in his *Rawḍat al-Ās*, a bibliographical compendium of scholars from whom he had received *ijāzas*, explained Aḥmad Bābā's view that God assigns a regenerator to each locality and that he was claiming that his shaykh (evidently Muḥammad Baghayogho, the Dyula teacher, d. 1002/1593) was the regenerator for Timbuktu.[6]

This view was inherited by the Shehu ʿUthmān b. Fūdī, as has been shown by Mervyn Hiskett in his studies. The Shehu saw himself as the last of the renewers: 'Fifthly, we praise God because he has rendered us fit in the time of the renewing of His religion, by the choice He has made of us.'[7]

B. G. Martin has mentioned how these expectations were more specifically centred around Sīdī Maḥmūd, or else were specifically inspired by his example:

In Hausaland, the *hijra* year 1200/1785–6 became the focus of peculiarly intense expectations. 'Twelve centuries,' it was said, and 'twelve caliphs' had come and gone, but the mahdi had not yet shown himself. In the minds of the people, the concept of a savior was intertwined with their hopes for a 'renovator' (*mujaddid*). This was no new trend; it had been fermenting in the region for centuries. The era close to the millenium of the *hijra* (1000 H./1591–2) had probably witnessed the episode of Shaykh Mahmud al-Baghdadi. Al-Baghdadi 'showed proofs of spiritual power . . . his companions preached that he was the Expected *Mahdi* . . . a great battle took place, between him and the learned men of the land in which he was killed and his following broken up.' Even before the sixteenth century, prophecies had been current about the coming of a 'renewer'. Muhammad Bello preserves the following prophecy, allegedly spoken by a Fulani lady, Umm Hani bint Muhammad al-'Abdusi (d. 1455): 'There will appear in this Sudanic land one of God's saints who will renew religion, revive orthodoxy, and create a religious community. The fortunate will follow him and spread his fame in distant places . . . One of his signs will be that he will not tend cattle as the Fulani custom is. Whoever lives until that time should follow him.'[8]

(*d*) We may note also the story of the death of al-Ḥallāj, who is referred to in the *Qudwa*, who was executed in Baghdād on 6 March 922; also, perhaps, the story of the death of al-Suhrawardī al-Maqtūl, executed by the order of Saladin's son, al-Malik al-Ẓāhir, in Aleppo in 1191. Such models have obviously inspired certain details in the story of the martyrdom of Sīdī Maḥmūd. His biography, which in the *Qudwa* is so slight as to be little more than a shadowy sketch, is largely modelled upon the idealized lives of earlier Ṣūfī martyrs.

(*e*) The likening of the brotherhood of Sīdī Maḥmūd to those who had boarded an 'ark of salvation', together with references to the esoteric and to the exoteric and literal division of his teachings, is a feature of the inculcation of Ṣūfī ideas within the *Qudwa*. In a paragraph at the beginning of his text, the author points out, after his opening doxology, that the 'Way' (*ṭarīqa*) has been effaced (*indarasat*) due to the decease of those who guarded and preserved it and those who were serious in maintaining and perfecting it. Hence, everything which is to be told to a people within it, whether by instruction or by sign, calls for a clear statement of interpretation. Apparently, the *Qudwa* was written down at a time when numbers were few and the whole *Maḥmūdiyya* fraternity at the point of disappearing. It is a nostalgic work, addressed to a few of the pious, rather than serving as a textbook for an active and flourishing Ṣūfī *ṭarīqa*. Yet, as will be seen, there were developments of a hopeful nature a while after the work's composition.[9]

The concept of the 'ark', together with the importance of Noah, hearkens back to the *Rasā'il* of the Brethren of Purity, who lived in tenth- or eleventh-century Baṣra. See the following passage from Ian Netton's study of their teachings:

> Noah is one of the prophet-warners who appear in that favourite Qur'ānic *Sūra* of the Ikhwān's, *Sūra* 7, and he also ranks beside Abraham, Moses, Jesus, and Muhammad as one of 'the Messengers possessed of constancy'. He and his people are saved by God in the ark but Noah's son is drowned after trying in vain to save himself on a mountain. The *Rasā'il* refer to the great flood several times by the Qur'ānic name *al-ṭūfān* and the word is also metaphorically: the brother who reads the *Rasā'il* is asked whether he would like 'to embark and ride with us in the ship of salvation (*safīnat al-najāt*) which our father Noah built, peace be upon him, so as to be saved from the flood of nature (*ṭūfān al-ṭabīᶜa*) before "heaven shall bring a manifest smoke (*bi-dukhān mubīn*)" '. This is a singularly striking and evocative metaphor, providing a good indication of just how rich in overtone, yet compact in style, some of the writing of the Ikhwān can be, often uniting themes and phrases from other parts of the *Rasā'il*: when speaking of Noah the Ikhwān use the word 'ship' (*safīna*) and, indeed, the same metaphor elsewhere, while in another place a Noachic-type flood of water (*ṭūfān min al-mā'*) is envisaged beside a flood of fire (*ṭūfān min al-nār*) like that which the Ikhwān see promised for the end of time in the Qur'ānic words 'when heaven shall bring a manifest smoke'.[10]

This specific image of the Ark is one of the few instances in the *Qudwa* where ᶜAlīd influences may perhaps be detected. An example from the *Bektāshiyya ṭarīqa* is furnished in the *Hutbetül Beyan* (the Sermon of Explanation—the alleged response of ᶜAlī to Muᶜāwiya

Pls. 4–10. The opening folios of the *Qudwa*: the eschatological significance of Sīdī Maḥmūd and the prophecies allegedly made about them

Plate 5

Plate 6

Plate 7

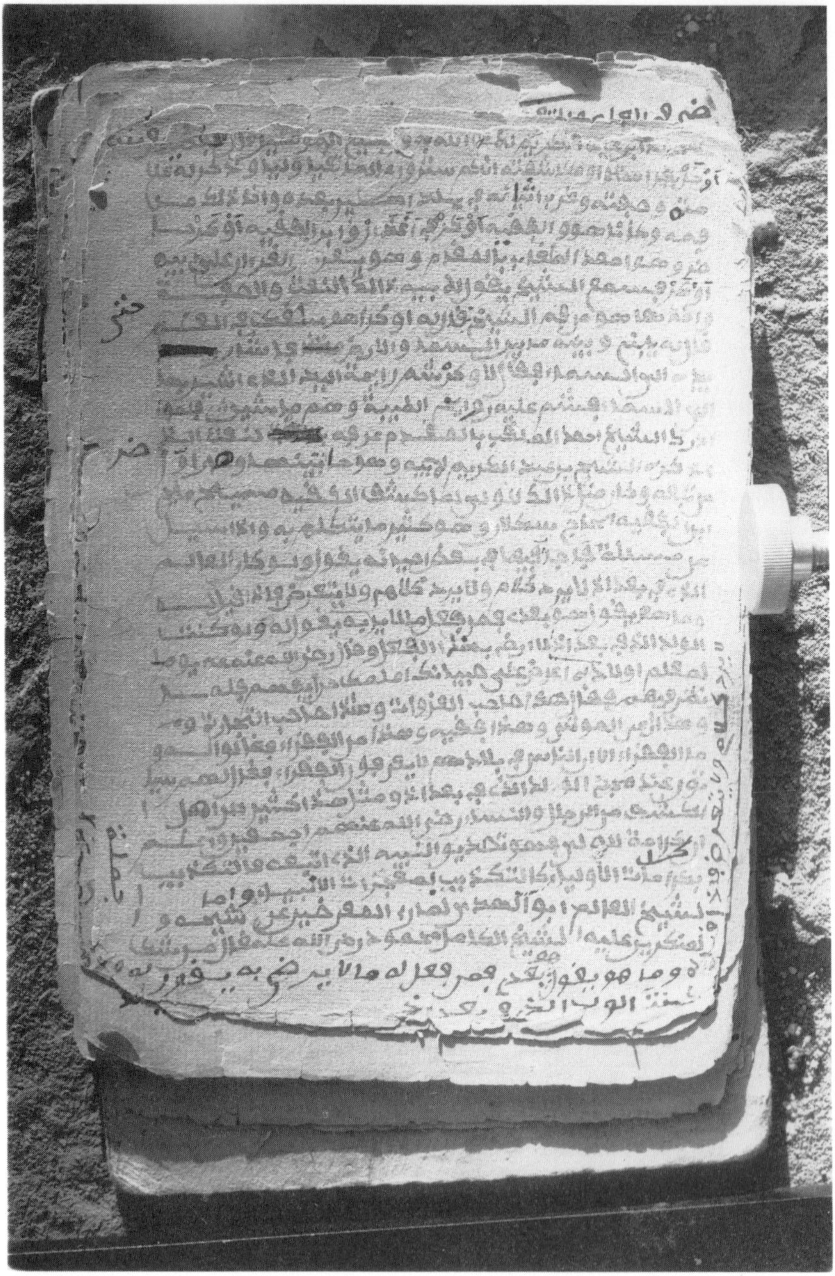

Plate 8

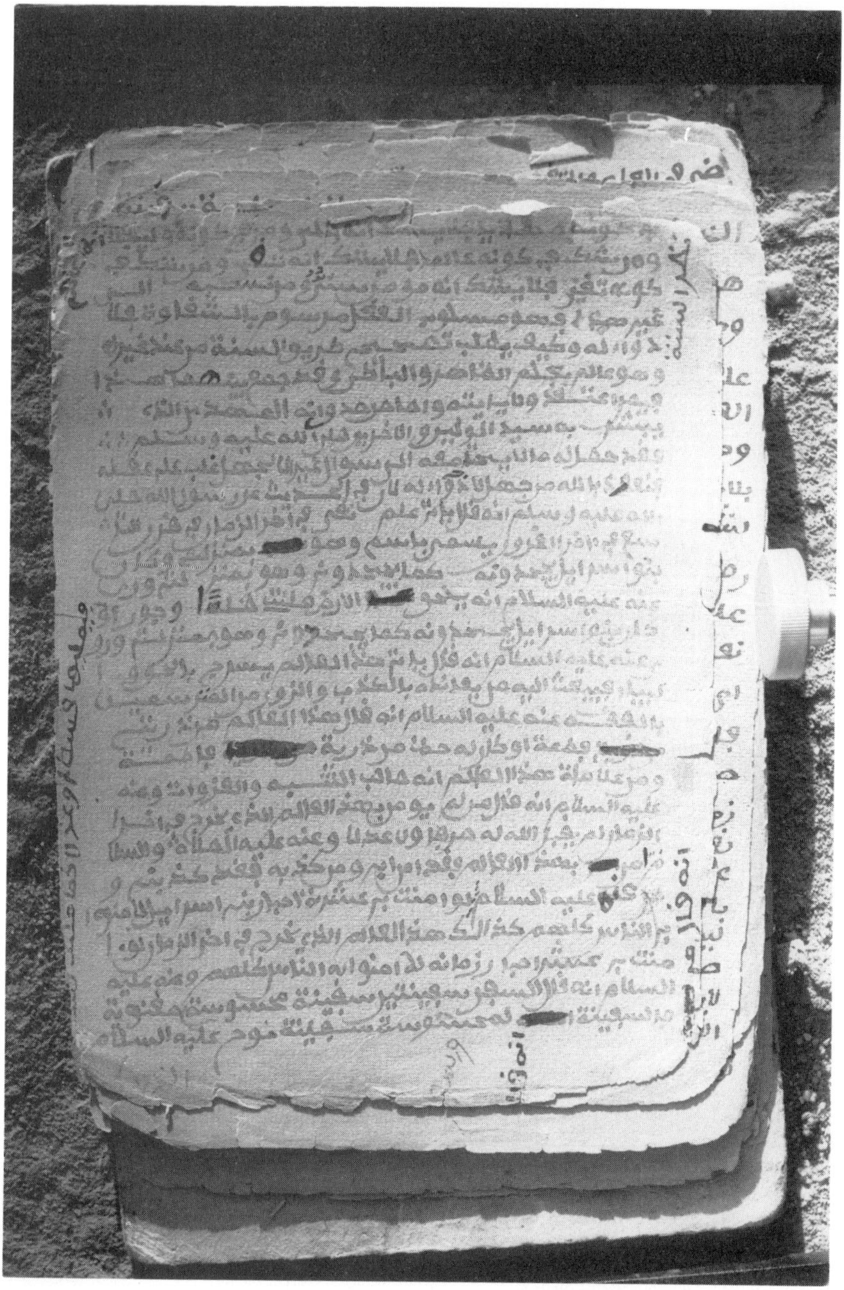

Plate 9

Plate 10

over the dispute between them regarding their respective rights to the Caliphate). To ᶜAlī are ascribed the following words:

'I am the first Noah and I am the Ark of Noah.' *Anā nūhuni l-awwalu wa anā safīnatu nūhin.* As the Prophet of God said: 'The Ark of Noah is a parable, *misal*, of the love of the People of My House.' As salvation came to Noah by the Ark, so it comes to humanity by Ali.[11]

Translation: the Doxology and its Message in the Opening Folios of the *Qudwa*

In these folios the role of Sīdī Maḥmūd in history is explained, together with his mystical and eschatological significance in God's unfolding plan for His community.

Passage 1

In the name of Allāh, the Compassionate, the Merciful, Blessings be upon our Lord, Muḥammad. Praise be to Allāh who guides whom He wills by His light, He who bestows success and happiness upon him through his obedience to Him. It is He who facilitates [affairs] for him and who makes close a relationship to Himself. He it is who endows him with His love and the love of the Messenger of His, Muḥammad b. ᶜAbdallāh, and with the love of his Companions, and with the love of the other Prophets and those sent forth by Him, and with the love of His saints and of the pious and devout from amongst His servants and all the other Muslims.

Passage 2

Verily, he—peace be upon him—said: 'This learned man is one of the offspring of Fāṭima; amongst the signs of this learned man are that he will be a master of an informed knowledge, and of an alert attention, and of military expeditions.' He [the Prophet] is quoted as having said that: 'He who does not believe in this learned man who will go forth at the end of time, Allāh will not accept his repentance nor his ransom.' It is reported that he also said, the blessing and peace of Allāh be upon him: 'He who believes in this learned man, believes likewise in me and he who disbelieves in him does not believe in me either.' It is also reported that he said, peace be upon him: 'Were ten learned men of the Children of Israel to believe in him then all mankind would do so. So likewise is this learned man who will go forth at the end of time. Were ten learned men amongst the people of the Book of his time to believe in him, then all mankind would do likewise.'

It is also reported that he said, peace be upon him: 'The ships [which are arks] are two ships, a ship which is perceived through the senses and a ship which is an ideal [of spirituality]. The ship which is an object of sense is the ark of Noah, peace be upon him, which was at the beginning of time, while the ship which is related to the mind and to the spirit is the ship of this learned man who will go forth at the end of time. He who boards it and sails in it will be safe, but he who does not board it, nor sail in it, will drown.' It is also reported that he said, peace be upon him: 'Amongst his signs will be that he will build the castle betwixt the Maghrib and the Sūdān, and he will suspend feuding and the people will follow him after five years into the tenth century of the *hijra*.

Amongst his signs is that he will come from the Saharan country, while he, in his origin, will come from the Maghrib. He will conquer the entire Maghrib.' We have quoted thus from the hand of the Shaykh and scholar, Abū ʿUbayda b. *al-faqīh* Muḥammad b. al-*faqīh* al-Ḥasan, may Allāh be pleased with them. Also, in *ḥadīth*, the Messenger of Allāh, His blessing be upon him, said, 'Woe to my community (*umma*)! They will go up to this man and they will slay him. How excellent a martyr he is! Would that I were together with him in his time so that I could help and succour him against those who do wrong to him and who unjustly treat him.' A man said to him, 'From what tribe does he hail?' He said to him, 'From the offspring of Fāṭima.' He was alarmed . . . [he asked] 'from the offspring of Fāṭima?' 'Yes,' he said.

If you reflect on this learned man, who was mentioned by the Messenger of Allāh, His blessing and peace be upon him, [observe that] he extolled him and he bore witness to him. He wished that, were he to be living in his time, he could come to his assistance against those who wronged him. His time of coming he declared. He foresaw his century amidst the others and the time when the people would follow him, saying, as he did, 'five years into the tenth century of the *hijra*'. He described him by saying that some of the people who were appointed to the offices of jurisprudence and theology (*fiqh*) would rise up against him, rejecting him and killing him wrongfully. [If you reflect], then, you would know for sure that he is not that Fāṭimid man of learning who will meet with Jesus in the city of the Messenger, the blessing and peace of Allāh be upon him, it being also said [the meeting will take place] in Jerusalem, because, according to *ḥadīth*, it is said that the *Mahdī* will only be rejected by the Anti-Christ (*Dajjāl*) and his legions who are out to substitute unbelief for

Islam. As for the Muslims, one amongst them has only to behold him and he will follow him. Praise be to Allāh for his meeting with him [then].

Notes

1. See the article on the *Mahdi* in the *EI* and the bibliography which appears in it.
2. See pp. 168–72 of my book, *The Arab Conquest of the Western Sahara* (London, 1986), where the North African context of these prophecies is discussed.
3. al-Qurṭubī, *al-Tadhkira fī aḥwāl al-mawtā wa umūr al-ākhira*, ed. by Aḥmad Ḥijāzī al-Saqqā (Cairo, n.d.), pp. 723 and 734–5.
4. See, e.g. G. W. Murray, *Sons of Ishmael* (London, 1935), pp. 275 and 280, and esp. F. de la Chapelle, 'Esquisse d'une histoire du Sahara occidental', *Hespéris*, 11 (1930), pp. 72 ff.
5. John Ralph Willis, *Studies in West African Islamic History*, vol. i, (London, 1979), pp. 46–8.
6. John O. Hunwick, *Sharīʿa in Songhay: The Replies of al-Maghīlī to the Questions of Askia al-Hājj Muḥammad* (Oxford, 1985), p. 117.
7. Mervyn Hiskett, *The Sword of Truth* (Oxford, 1973), pp. 121–5.
8. B. G. Martin, *Muslim Brotherhoods in Nineteenth Century Africa* (Cambridge, 1976), pp. 25–6.
9. See pp. 124 ff.
10. Ian Richard Netton, *Muslim Neoplatonists* (London, 1982), p. 84.
11. J. Kingsley Birge, *The Bektashi Order of Dervishes*, (London, 1937), p. 143.

4

The Followers of Sīdī Maḥmūd and their Disciples

Translation

The passages in the folios of the Qudwa *that refer to the prophecies of al-Maghīlī, and others, regarding Sīdī Maḥmūd, and some details regarding those scholars who were his disciples and where in Aïr they are laid to rest.*

1. When he entered the land of Aïr [covered in light and guidance], the people [hastened] to him in order to acquire something of his light and of his guidance [intended] for those whom he saw were in need of it and who were [likewise] in need of something which would save them from error, so bringing them [back again] to the path of the Truth, from the darkness into the light, from ignorance to knowledge, from heedlessness to a lively awareness, from a preoccupation with things ungodly to a preoccupation with the ways of Allāh, and from wilful fancy to piety. Allāh show His mercy unto them and pardon them.

He bore witness to it by his promotion, from amongst pious men, of a [godly] band—may Allāh be pleased with them—men amongst whom were included the scholar, *faqīh* and exemplary Shaykh, Abū'l-Hudā al-Sūqī,[1] may Allāh be pleased with him, also the *faqīh* Muḥammad b. *al-faqīh* Muḥammad b. *al-faqīh* ᶜAbd al-Raḥmān b. Tnkrsh Allāh (ṣ, Nkrsh),[2] the mercy of Allāh Almighty be upon him, and Muḥammad *al-faqīh*, the saint, Ibn *al-faqīh*, he who is related to al-Qundus [ṣ, al-Qundusī],[3] because his tomb is located in that place, and who is known as 'the sword' (*al-sayf*). [Together with him he chose], also Muḥammad b. Muḥammad , who was nicknamed Mazdānnak [*sic*] b. *al-faqīh* ᶜAlī, the saint, known as Akhīd(?)[4] [and Muḥammad b. Muḥammad b. *al-faqīh*, *al Walī*, known as Inirgaray and Muḥammad the pious *faqīh*, the father of the orphans and widows, who is known as Akhīd]. His tomb is visible and located at Tinqas(?)[5] and it is visited after the mosque, may Allāh pardon him. [He chose] also, the *faqīh*, Muḥammad b. ᶜAbd al-Raḥmān.[6] May Allāh pardon him and enlighten his sepulchre, also the *faqīh*, Shaykh

Pls. 11–15. Folios in the *Qudwa* that specifically refer to the role the specific scholars played in the acceptance and dissemination of the *Maḥmūdiyya* during the lifetime of Sīdī Maḥmūd

Plate 12

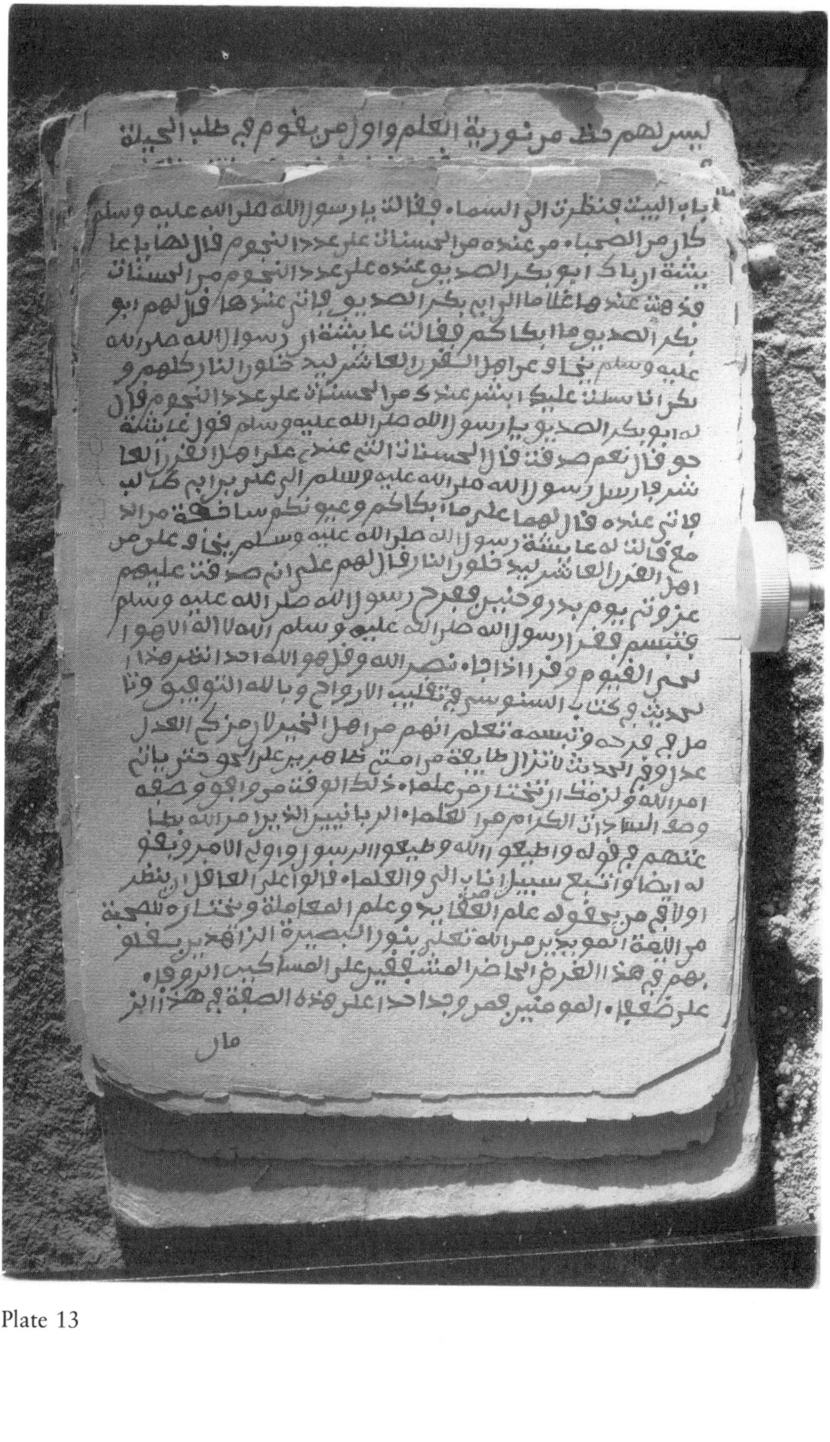

Plate 13

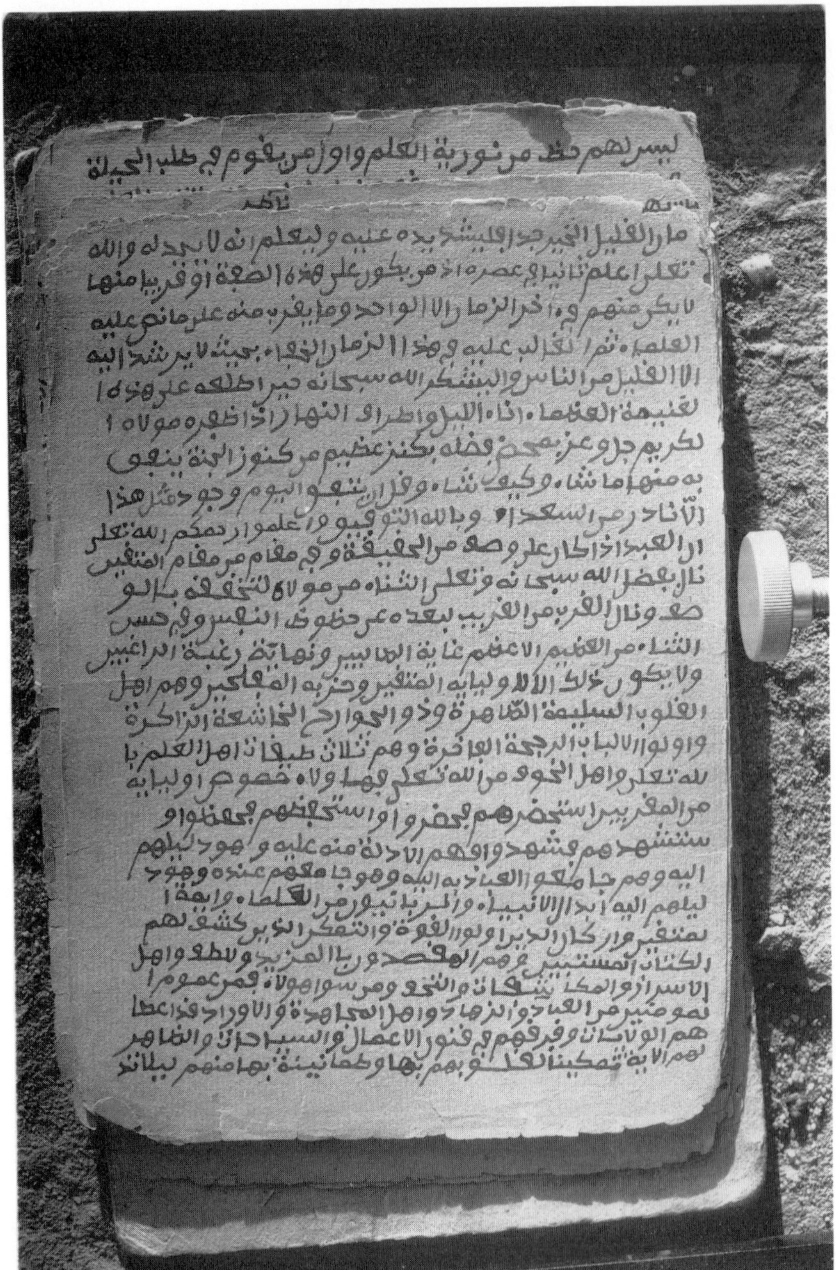

Plate 14

Plate 15

Aḥmad b. *al-faqīh* Awgar al-Fullāni, known as *al-muqaddam.*[7] His tomb is to be seen and is visited at Tmzk/Nzkrn(?).[8] Allāh pardon them. [He chose] also, the Sūqī Shaykh, Muḥammad b. Yūsuf, known in the Adrār-n-Īfōghās, [ṣ, Tadamakkat] and Shaykh Abū'l-Ḥasan b. *al-faqīh* and Shaykh Abū'l-Hudā and others amongst the men of true guidance and piety.

When the advent [of Sīdī Maḥmūd] was imminent, mutual rejoicing at the good news heralded it, as had been the case with saints and men of learning before, for example with his [spiritual] father, ᶜAbd al-Qādir al-Jīlānī (Jīlī),[9] and with [Aḥmad b. ᶜAlī] al-Rifāᶜī,[10] and with Abū Ḥāmid al-Ghazāli[11] and with Ibrāhīm al-Dasūqī[12] and with other saints and scholars. When the birth of ᶜAbd al-Qādir al-Jīlānī drew nigh, the men of vision and mystic revelation and insight began to announce the good tidings about him. Some of them made prognostications about him during his youth and they said, 'this boy will enjoy the highest rank [and notoriety]'. Such is their wont in regard to many scholars and saints because the light of sanctity is never extinguished.

Such was the case of the Shaykh, the noble scholar, the *Sharīf*, the lordly Maḥmūd, may Allāh be pleased with him. When the time of his entry into the land of Aïr was at hand, some of the saints announced the glad tidings before he came. Amongst them was the Shaykh, the perfect scholar, Muḥammad b. ᶜAbd al-Karīm al-Maghīlī, Allāh show kindness to him and to all true believers. . . .[13]

· 2. The *faqīh*, Awgar, said, on account of the religious insight which he possessed and due to his vision, 'Verily you will set eyes upon a pure and a saintly scholar.' He made mention of his signs and his characteristic quality and the imminence of his coming into the land of Aïr, following him [that is, al-Maghīlī]. He heard this from the latter, who was in Agades with the *faqīh*, Awgar. The son of the *faqīh*, Awgar, Aḥmad nicknamed *al-muqaddam*, was present whilst he was displaying the expounding of the Qur'ān to Awgar, his father. He heard the Shaykh [al-Maghīlī] say to his father that it was his [Sīdī Maḥmūd's] description and quality of his true portrait in person. He learnt it from the mouth of Shaykh al-Maghīlī. Then Agwar said to him, 'Will he attain the level of learning which you have attained?' He, [al-Maghīlī], said, 'The difference between him and me is as the celestial [object] to the terrestrial.' He pointed his hand towards the sky and he said to Agwar, 'Smell the odour of the hand which I am pointing to the sky.' He smelt sweet odours while the two men were walking on their way.

When Shaykh Aḥmad, who was nicknamed *al-muqaddam*, met Shaykh [Sīdī Maḥmūd], he recognized him through the description given by ᶜAbd al-Karīm [al-Maghīlī] to his father, when he had been present in their company. He became the first of those who followed after him. A meeting similar to this was the encounter of the saint and clairvoyant, the *faqīh*, Malīḥ b. *al-faqīh* al-Ḥājj Saklan. After he had been speaking about him, and when he was asked about some matter, he replied at times by saying, 'The scholar who is in Baghdād, were he to be here, he would not refute what I am saying and he would not take exception to it.' When he was asked about what he had to say about someone who had committed an act which he disapproved of, he answered, 'Were I the boy who is in Baghdād I would not tolerate such behaviour.' One day he said—may Allāh be pleased with him—to the teacher of his children, 'Make it known to your boys that I shall be informing you about who such a person will be from amongst their number.' When he beheld them before him he said, 'This one will be in charge of raiding expeditions, this one will control the trade and the commerce, this one will be the shepherd and the herder, this one will be a *faqīh*, and this one will be among the *fuqarā'*.'

They said to him, 'What is meant by the *fuqarā'*?'. The people of their country [up to that time] had no knowledge of the [term] *fuqarā'*. He said to them, 'They will come when the youth who is in Baghdād comes.' An occurrence such as this is common amongst those who possess extra-sensory perception, both men and women, may Allāh be pleased with them all.

Know that every miracle which is performed by a saint confirms the truth of the prophet whom he follows. To disbelieve in the miracles of the saints is like disbelief in those loftier miracles performed by the prophets.

As for the scholarly Shaykh, Abū'l-Hudā, when he saw those who had turned aside from his Shaykh, and had disapproved of him, the perfect Shaykh Maḥmūd, may Allāh be pleased with him, he said, 'Whosoever doubts that he is a *mahdī*, then undoubtedly he is a saint, and whosoever doubts his sainthood then undoubtedly he is a scholar, and whosoever doubts that he is a scholar then undoubtedly he is pious, and whosoever doubts his piety then undoubtedly he is an orthodox believer. Whosoever attributes something else to him other than this is bereft of his reason and is marked by wretchedness. No physic will cure him. How can the rectification of the path of the *Sunna* be sought from anyone else other than from him? He is a scholar, he knows the truths, outwardly made manifest and inwardly sensed and comprehended, and he has combined the two. I believe in his sanctity. As for those who believe that he is *the Mahdī*, who is commended by the Lord of the first and of the last, the blessing and peace of Allāh be upon him (Muḥammad the Messenger), then he has experienced something about which it is not his business to ask another, unless it be due to ignorance which is bereft of a remedy, because in *ḥadīth* it is reported that the Messenger of Allāh, His blessing and peace be upon him, said "Learning of a saint will come about at the end of the age in the ninth century [of the *hijra*], in the last of the centuries. He will bear his name and he will be in his rank and in his status. The Children of Israel used to deny him. In the same way they [in that age] will deny him, he being of the Prophet's rank and status." It is also reported from the Messenger, the blessing and peace of Allāh be upon him, that he said that this scholar will come adorned with the Truth and the Clear Statement, and those who oppose him with falsehood will send [evil mischief] to him through those who are the readers and the doctors of jurisprudence. It is also reported from the Messenger of Allāh, peace be upon him, that he said that "this scholar will be a descendant of mine". O Allāh, do not deny us his *baraka*.' *Here ends the statement of Abū'l-Hudā.*

As for the *faqīh*, Muḥammad b. *al-faqīh* ᶜAbd al-Raḥmān b. Tnkrsh-Allāh, may Allāh be pleased with him, he wrote a book, and in it he urged the *fuqarā'* to follow just as they were commanded by their Shaykh Maḥmūd; in regard to [the ritual] of purification, the *dhikr*, the statutory prayer, and the knowledge of Allāh, of His attributes and of the belief in His *baraka*. He said to them after a long discourse, 'I must declare it. The deeds which you do must be done sincerely towards Allāh Almighty and only done for His sake. I caution you against three things; the wiles of Iblīs,[14] that is to say, entering into a dispute with him who has not entered into the "Way" [of Sīdī Maḥmūd], secondly, that you will pay no heed to anyone who has not joined the order, and thirdly, beware lest Iblīs arouses your aversion to taking [religious] knowledge from men who know the canonic law and its branches. If you accept my statement to you then cleave to what you have been commanded by your Shaykh.' *I have abridged what he said.*

As for the *faqīh* and saint, al-Najīb Muḥammad b. [Muḥammad] *al-faqīh*, known as 'the sword' (*al-sayf*),[15] he said to [the Sulṭān of Agades], Aḥmad b. Tilzay: 'Your Shaykh Maḥmūd is not the *Mahdī*. Be clear in your mind in regard to what I am telling you, because Allāh, mighty and glorious He is, has His eye on His servants. Allāh is sufficient as an advocate.' He also said to him, 'It is your duty to exalt the scholars and the *fuqarā'*. Whosoever exalts the scholars, exalts the Messenger of Allāh, His blessing and peace be upon him, and whosoever exalts the *fuqarā'*, exalts Allāh Almighty, mighty and glorious He is.' He also said to the Sulṭān, 'Allāh, Allāh, I warn and I beseech, for the sake of the angels who pray for blessings for your Shaykh, O Allāh, [Sire] join with those who join with him and cast off those who spurn him, give shelter to those who shelter him.' *Here end the words which he uttered in response concerning him and the words which he pressed upon him [the Sulṭān]. In Allāh success is to be found.*[16]

As for the scholar, Shaykh Muḥammad b. Muḥammad b. al-Walī, known as Inzugrayn,[17] his affair with Shaykh [Maḥmūd] is made plain to all. He was amongst the closest of his beloved associates and amongst those who shared his secret and his authority to go forth to the *murīdīn*, may Allāh be pleased with him. As for Muḥammad *al-faqīh* b. Muḥammad b. Ibrāhīm,[18] when he was asked about Shaykh Maḥmūd, he said, 'He is a pious scholar and a saint. The rejection which he endured and the death which he suffered are evidence of a dearth of happiness [amongst some] over what [acts] he did, since a clear and true guidance that was made manifest came to them [from him] and they rose up in order to extinguish it at a time when it was meet and right for them to show [him] honour and esteem, to offer [him] a welcome and to give thanks to Allāh Almighty, who favoured them with this gift of His,' *to the end of what he said.* May Allāh Almighty have mercy upon him. His tomb is to be seen at Tefist,[19] and it is visited on pilgrimage.

It is a fact that the scholars who witnessed to Sīdī Maḥmūd's pre-eminence, and to his superior virtue, were those men who were distinguished in learning. Some amongst them were those who were the companions of Shaykh Muḥammad b. al-Karīm al-Maghīlī, men who took their learning and their religious discipline from him. Others amongst them were those who had met him and who [also] had met Shaykh Abū Ruways.[20] Others had met both these men and had also met the *Imām* al-Suyūṭī in Egypt and had derived benefit from him. Some had met Shaykh Aḥmad al-Zarrūq[21] and had profited from him. Others had met Allāh's saint, ᶜUthmān al-Mawhūb b. Afalāwas.[22] These men, and other scholars like them, were men of learning and the lords of the people of the ninth [fifteenth] century of the *hijra*, men like Shaykh Abū'l-Hudā b. Muḥammad.

He (ᶜUthmān al-Mawhūb b. Afalāwas) said, 'I was in receipt of correspondence from my Lord, the Shaykh, the (*ᶜārif*) possessor of mystic knowledge, the clairvoyant, the one who is exalted by Allāh over all, in praise of him [the Prophet], who cannot be thanked enough for his bliss and his favour, the blessing and peace of Allāh be upon him, the seal of the prophets. By Allāh, the Unique Lord, I have not prayed for fifty-six years except it be in the company of men who are devoted to Allāh, Muslims *and true believers*, men pious and upright, *who bow the knee in prayer and who kneel in adoration.* They know Allāh's Truth and His Reality, they who are the attainers, who reach, with purity of vision, the light of the Lord of the Worlds. Whosoever should doubt this to be so, then the secret of it is best known to Allāh, the Almighty. Its manifestation is apparent without my voice needed to proclaim it. These are the words of the runaway slave who is in need of requesting and of seeking the mercy of his Lord who created him without any need for Him to do so, of ᶜUthmān b. (al)-Mawhūb b. Muḥammad [Afalāwas]; blessing and peace and pardon and forgiveness and safe keeping be upon all who say, "There is no God but Allāh, and Muḥammad is the messenger of Allāh, His blessing and His peace be upon him." So be it, at the first and at the last, between the East and the West. Amen, Amen, peace be upon you and the mercy of Allāh and His blessing.'

He corrected [*this statement*] *by his own hand, may Allāh have mercy upon him.*[23]

At the beginning of the tenth [sixteenth] century of the *hijra*, Shaykh [Sīdī Maḥmūd] appeared. He knew, and met, those who bore witness to him, and who confessed to him that he knew far more than they did and that his piety, his godliness and his asceticism surpassed their own. Yet, despite this, they were the lords of their age until they passed away in the tenth century, may Allāh be pleased with them all and with us, on account of their *baraka* and the *baraka* of those like them, the people of the tenth century. The Messenger of Allāh had fears on account of them and he cautioned regarding them. It is our hope that Allāh, through him, will show His favour to them in view of what is said in prophetic *ḥadīth* concerning his weeping, the blessing and peace of Allāh be upon him. He did so one day and ᶜĀ'isha said to him, 'Why do you weep, O Messenger of Allāh, His blessing and peace be upon him?' He said to her, 'O ᶜĀ'isha, I fear for the people of the tenth century, lest they enter the fire of Hell, all of them.' So she wept with him.

She went to the door of the house and she looked upward to heaven and she said, 'O Messenger of Allāh, His [God's] blessing and peace be upon him, is there, amongst the Companions, one who has virtues which are as numerous as the stars?' He said to her, 'O ᶜĀ'isha, let Abū Bakr al-Ṣiddīq fill you with hope, for his virtues are as numerous as the stars.'

She sent one of her slave boys to Abū Bakr al-Ṣiddīq and he came to her house. He said to those who were there, 'Why are you weeping?' ᶜĀ'isha said, 'Verily, the Messenger of Allāh, His blessing and peace be upon him, is fearful for the people of the tenth century, lest all of them should enter into the fire of Hell, but I asked about you. Rejoice, for yours are good qualities and virtues, as numerous as the stars.' Abū Bakr al-Ṣiddīq said to him, 'O Messenger of Allāh, His blessing and peace be upon him, is what ᶜĀ'isha says indeed true?' 'Yes,' he answered, 'she spoke truly.' Then Abū Bakr said, 'Those good qualities which I possess will be as a charity bestowed upon the people of the tenth century.'

The messenger of Allāh, His blessing and peace be upon him, sent for ᶜAlī b. Abī Ṭālib and he came to his house. ᶜAlī said to them both, 'Why do you weep? Why are your eyes inflamed and why do they flow with tears?' ᶜĀ'isha said to him, 'The Messenger of Allāh, His blessing and peace be upon him, is afraid for the people of the tenth century lest they enter into the fire of Hell.' ᶜAlī said to them, 'I bestow as a charity upon them my raid which I carried out on the day of Badr and Ḥunayn.'[24]

The Messenger of Allāh, His blessing and peace be upon him, rejoiced and smiled and the Messenger of Allāh, His blessing and peace upon him, said aloud, 'There is no God but Allāh, the living and the self-existing,' and he recited, 'When the assistance of Allāh comes, then say, "He is the One True God." '[25] *See this* ḥadīth *in the book of al-Sanūsī, in his Taghlīb al-Arwāḥ.*[26] *Success is with Allāh.*

Ponder upon his joy, and upon the way that he smiled on account of his knowledge that they were men of good qualities, for [it is said that] he who bestows an increase to the balance is just. It is also said in *ḥadīth*, 'A party of my *Umma* will continue to have a knowledge of the Truth until the command is given by Allāh. It is incumbent upon you to choose from the lordly scholars those whom Allāh has commanded you to obey, according to His Word, "Obey Allāh, and obey the Messenger and those who are in authority," and also, in accordance with his word, "follow the path of those who are my deputies".'[27]

The scholars have said, 'It is the duty of the man of good sense and of reason first of all to observe closely him whose fields of knowledge are the science of the faith, knowledge of its creeds and of its dogmas, and who has a knowledge of conduct towards others. He should choose him for his companionship from amongst those *Imāms* who are endowed by Allāh Almighty with the light of vision, men who are in heart ascetics amidst the age's goal and its ambition, men who care for the poor and for the needy and who show pity for the weak amongst the true believers. If one finds such a person who possesses these qualities in this age, which is so bereft of goodness, then let him tightly clasp him with his hand and let him know that he will not find—Allāh Almighty knows best—another like him in his age, since he who possesses these qualities, or approximates to them, at the end of time, will be unique amongst men. This accords with that which the scholars have recorded in their writings. The bulk of wisdom in this age is concealed, so that the one who guides towards it is rarely to be found amongst mankind. Thank Allāh, glory be to Him, when He has given a man knowledge of this supreme gain.'

3. Shaykh Maḥmūd did not take leave of his companions until some of them had become Shaykhs, may Allāh be pleased with them all. He gave them authority to go forth [as leaders] to the novices and to the neophytes (*murīdīn*) and to take the oath from those who came to them, be they novices or be they not. He gave his authority to the rest to quote and cite those transmitted teachings which were handed down to his close companions.

Amongst the latter was Shaykh Muḥammad b. Muḥammad who was known by his agnomen which had been given to him by the scholarly *Imām*, al-Suyūṭī, that is to say, Abū'l-Hudā,[28] may Allāh be pleased with him. He used to remark, 'I said to my lord, Shaykh Maḥmūd, "Give me your counsel and your advice".' He answered, 'I counsel you to fear Allāh, for verily if you live in the fear of the Lord, He will show you marvels and wonders in your person. If you fear Him, truly, then ever afterwards there will be a divine blessing (*baraka*) bestowed.' I said to him, 'What is it to fear Allāh, explain it to me?' He said, 'If you follow the canonic law to the letter and if a black slave were to beat you, then you would know that it is Allāh Almighty, Him no less, who is beating you.' Shaykh Abū'l-Hudā used to give Shaykh Maḥmūd preference over his own *mashāyikh*, for example, Muḥammad b. ᶜAbd al-Karīm [al-Maghīlī], ᶜAbd al-Raḥmān al-Suyūṭī, ᶜUthmān b. Afalāwas, Shaykh Aḥmad al-Zarrūq and Shaykh Abū Ruways. He [Abū'l-Hudā or Abu Ruways?] said, when he met him [Sīdī Maḥmūd], after having met them [the *mashāyikh*], and having taken the Ṣūfī 'Way' from them, 'I discount and renounce everything which I said to you [all] before my meeting with Shaykh Maḥmūd. Come to me today and I shall speak to you afresh, because, on account of this light, I have been told of secrets unknown to me before.' He said, 'Those who look for a *mahdī*, then let them wait for him. There is no other *mahdī*, only him.' After that he was his devoted follower and admirer until he died in Sanbaba.[29] His tomb may be seen and it is visited. He died in the year 940 [1534], or on about that date. Success is in the hands of Allāh.

Shaykh Abū'l-Hudā was the teacher and the master of *fuqahā*'. Amongst his closest companions was the Shaykh of perfection, Muḥammad al-Amīn,[30] may Allāh be pleased with him. Later, the latter journeyed to the Orient and was met by [eminent] Shaykhs, and the pupils of some of them, until permission was granted to him and he was told to return after some years. He, may Allāh be pleased with him, used to say, 'My Shaykh [in the Orient] said, "What man said to you, 'Forsake the path of your Shaykh [Maḥmūd] which you have learnt through your Shaykh, Abū'l-Hudā'? Have nought to do with that man." '

When he [Shaykh Abū'l-Hudā or Shaykh Muḥammad al-Amīn?] reached Aïr, and he called men to Allāh, to obey Him, mighty and glorious He is, he [Shaykh Abū'l-Hudā or Shaykh Muḥammad al-Amīn?] called aloud for His creation to be given guidance, that mosques should be built for the love of Muslims, for religious help to be given to them, help in their mundane affairs, for kindness and tenderness towards them, mercy for them and for charity to all whom he met. His remarkable deeds and miracles are many in their number. He acted thus until he died, may Allāh be pleased with him, on a Monday night in the year 982 [1575], at [In] Taduq,[31] aged 63,[32] having built the mosque of the saint, al-Mawhūb ʿUthmān b. Afalāwas, may Allāh be pleased with him. This was after the locality had fallen into ruin. He was buried in front of the mosque.[33] His tomb may be seen and it is visited at the present time. May Allāh cause his *baraka* to return to us, also the *baraka* of others like him. Amen. Success belongs to Allāh.

Amongst them [the companions] was the scholar Shaykh and saint, Muḥammad b. Muḥammad, who was nicknamed Amezdennig, the son of the saint known as Inzakrīn.[34] He was the companion of Shaykh Maḥmūd. The latter ordered him to guide the disciples and the novices. He was a scholar and pious saint, the pillar of Islam and the *Imām* of the chosen elect and of the masses. In his doctrine and belief he was a follower in his [Shaykh Maḥmūd's] belief in the gnostic emanatory and illuminatory principle of the divinity. His way was the way of Muḥammad and in his inner nature he was divinely inspired and his guidance true. May Allāh be pleased with him.[35]

He was amongst the group of *mashāyikh* who had a vision of al-Khaḍir[36] and Elias,[37] peace be upon both of them. Shaykh Aḥmad b. *al-faqīh*, may Allāh be pleased with them both, one of his companions, said, 'I came to my Shaykh and he told me that the prophet of Allāh, Elias, peace be upon him, visited him. He showed him the mat which he had spread out before him. He sat upon it and both of them engaged in a conversation for some while.' Then Shaykh [Muḥammad b. Muḥammad] told Shaykh [Aḥmad], 'He moved his body due to the longing which he felt to meet my Prophet Muḥammad, the blessing and peace of Allāh be upon him, until I lauded him before him, then, in his body he felt [the presence of] the

Prophet, the blessing and peace of Allāh be upon him. He activates the communion between two of the brethren when one of them praises [him], though not the other, [that is], praise of the Messenger of Allāh. His blessing and peace be upon our Prophet.'

He told me, when he was addressing his Qur'ān reciters, 'Call them publicly and observe our [rule of] entrusting them with a secret, to be followed by another secret. Use your tongue to counsel them wisely and empty your heart in their discourse. Confide your secret to those who bear witness to it. All that I have entrusted to you in their affairs is to convey the message of the truth. The one who is the originator of affairs and who is the master of them is I myself.' He used to say, 'It is your duty to remember Allāh Almighty in the *dhikr*. You must control your feelings and emotions and control your breath. It is the nearest and the shortest path to [the presence of] Allāh Almighty.' He used to say, 'Whosoever from amongst the novices sits with me for a period of forty days beneath this tree will have his need fulfilled by me if Allāh Almighty wills it.' He used to say, 'A man knows the place where his tomb will be. He builds the mosque facing it and he adores Allāh in that place until he dies and he enters his grave.' He himself is an example [of this] because [once] he was in Assodé (Asuṭay) and he journeyed to Teghzerin (Taᶜdhrin) and he notified his descendants that his tomb was to be sited there. He built the mosque and dug the well.[38] Then he died, may Allāh be pleased with him. His tomb is near his mosque. It may be seen and it is visited [as a holy place]. Many were the miracles which he performed. Success is in the hands of Allāh.

It was from him[39] that the *fuqarā'* learnt the 'Way' (*ṭarīqa*) and he took their oath and their vows in this wise. The novice (*murīd*) carried out the ritual purification. He sat before him and he rested his knee against the knee of the Shaykh or close to him. The latter took the hand of the novice and called on Allāh's protection. Then he would recite the *basmala*[40] and the Qur'ānic passage, 'Verily those who swear allegiance (*bayᶜa*) to you . . . ', to the end of the verse.[41] Then would follow, 'O those who have believed, repent to Allāh . . .' to the end of the verse.[42] Then he would thrice repeat, 'Ask pardon of Allāh. I have believed in Allāh, His angels, His books, and His Messengers, and the last day, and in the Divine predestination, for good and for evil. I am content with Allāh as Lord, and in Islam as a religion, and in Muḥammad as Messenger and Prophet and in [Abū Bakr] al-Ṣiddīq and [ᶜUmar] al-Fārūq and in [ᶜUthmān] the lord of the two lights, and in ᶜAlī, the guide of the *Imāms*, al-Murtaḍā, the pleasure of Allāh Almighty be upon them all.' The novice would follow him in all this.

Then the Shaykh would command him to be silent so that he would say to him, three times, 'There is no God but Allāh,' placing his hand upon the [novice's] head, avoiding the right side of it and keeping to the left. Then the novice would repeat what he said. If anyone else was present he would do likewise. Then he would recite the *fātiḥa* [the opening Qur'ānic *sūra*] and he would tell the novice to perform two bendings of the torso (*rakᶜatayn*), the first with the *fātiḥa* and 'Say, O unbelievers . . .',[43] and the second with the *fātiḥa* and 'Say He is Allāh, the Solitary . . .',[44] and with a prayer for himself and for his guardian. As for the women-folk, their initiation was from behind the veil of a hem of a garment as was the custom with the Messenger of Allāh, His peace and blessings be upon him.

4. Amongst his [Muḥammad b. Muḥammad's?] close companions were two Shaykhs, amongst his brethren, both of them famous. One of them was a son of Shaykh Abū Yaḥyā[45] and the other was a son of Shaykh Muḥammad b. al-Ḥājj because the woman who nursed these boys gave them one breast to suck in the home of their Shaykh Sīdī Maḥmūd.[46] The two sons were, firstly, Shaykh Sīdī ᶜAbd al-Qādir. He was the son of Shaykh Abū Yaḥyā. The latter was one of the close associates of Shaykh Ibn Amezdennig.[47] He entrusted him to call men to Allāh.

The second son was Hārūn. He was the son of Shaykh Muḥammad b. al-Ḥājj [Aḥmad], may Allāh be pleased with them all. He [Shaykh Muḥammad b. Muḥammad] entrusted Shaykh Sīdī [ᶜAbd al-Qādir] to give his licence to teach (*ijāza*) and he entrusted him with the initiation of novices amongst those who came to him seeking it. Shaykh Sīdī [ᶜAbd al-Qādir] entrusted that in turn to his [?] companion, Shaykh Hārūn, so that many were initiated by them both.

The first of the two [Shaykh Abū Yaḥyā?] died on Monday night when he was aged seventy-five years and he was buried at the place where his retreat (*khalwa*) was located behind the mosque. This was in the year 1004 [1597]. It was in *Rabīᶜ* II, may Allāh be pleased with him. He (ᶜAbd al-Qādir?) succeeded him amongst his sons and companions until he too died, may Allāh be pleased with him, thirty years after, in the year 1033 [1625], in the month of *Rajab*, on the eighteenth of that month.[48] The date corresponds to the date of the death of Abū Bakr al-Ṣiddīq, may Allāh be pleased with him. He was buried opposite [the mosque or his retreat?] in the village of Jīkat.[49] May Allāh be pleased with them all.

When the time drew nigh that Shaykh Sīdī ᶜAbd al-Qādir b. al-Shaykh Abū Yaḥyā was to dwell in the place [in Jīkat] where he was to build, the saint, Muḥammad b. Badr, may Allāh be pleased with him, was informed of it. He said to the people of that village, 'The

Shaykh [Sīdī ᶜAbd al-Qādir] will come with the *fuqarā'* and they will build in this locality.' He named it *Rabwat al-yamīn*.[50] 'In the eyes of Allāh they are of mighty esteem. All those with whom they will become acquainted will have priority in their eyes and they will enjoy their honour and their esteem, because they are a mercy which is bestowed upon you.' An episode similar to this is also recounted. When the Shaykh [Abū Yaḥyā], his father, died, may Allāh have mercy upon him, the people said, 'Who will be his successor amongst his descendants and companions?' The Shaykh, Sīdī Mūsā al-Sūdānī, said, 'He will only be succeeded by Sīdī ᶜAbd al-Qādir, by Allāh the Blessed,' and he repeated what he said. Likewise, the scholar, Shaykh Muḥammad b. al-Ḥājj,[51] may Allāh be pleased with him, said when he saw him, 'Glory to Allāh who lays hold on a man from amongst the men who have the divine secret. He places them amongst men and he walks amongst them.

Now that was prior to the people following him. Such, then, is the joyful announcement, made public, of some of the men who enjoy the company of a divine secret. When he became old, he emigrated [to join with] the *fuqarā'*, in the pursuit of the "Way", and he became a companion amongst the companions of Shaykh Maḥmūd, this he did to a great extent and he drew benefit from them. He did so even from the women companions of Shaykh Maḥmūd. He was one of those who had the vision of the men who had the divine secret and he met with the prophet of Allāh, Elias, and with others beside him, the blessing and the peace of Allāh be upon our Prophet and upon him. On this night all the men of the divine secret come, such and such being their number.' He used to say when he perceived something, 'One of them has perceived . . .', this was because he had no love of attributing anything [directly] to himself. Were it not for the fact that he would have objected to its appearing, we would make mention [here] of some of his virtuous acts and his miracles, may Allāh be pleased with him.

Amongst them [the companions of Sīdī Maḥmūd] was the brother Shaykh of them both, Aḥmad al-Galālī b. *al-faqīh*.[52] He, may Allāh be pleased with him, used to meet Elias, the prophet of Allāh, and Jesus, the son of Mary, and others besides these two amongst the people who were inspired by the divine secret. Many were his pious works and miracles, may Allāh be pleased with him. He died in the month of *Jumādā* I, on Tuesday night, the tenth, in the year 1018 [1610] or about that date. He was buried at Agallal.[53] His tomb is visible and it is visited [as a holy place], may Allāh be pleased with him, may He bring him contentment, and bestow it upon all Muslims, both men and women.

Shaykh Ibn Najjār al-Badrānī[54] used to say, 'As he caused good works to abound, so obstacles and opposition mounted against him. Beware lest anyone band against you to falsify and to invalidate the assembly for the *dhikr*, or prayer for the Messenger of Allāh, His blessing and peace be upon him, so that your preoccupations be with them [that band]. Rather, devote your prayer and adoration to your Lord. Verily in His hand is the power to set free and to bind.'

Notes

1. By repute one of the greatest saints amongst the Kel Es-Sūq who lived during the late 15th and early 16th cent. Two passages which are attributed to him may be read on pp. 43, 100. All that is known about him from the Tuareg traditions of Aïr is that he was a novice of Shaykh Abū Ruways, he performed the pilgrimage to Mecca, and he addressed two sets of questions to al-Suyūṭī and al-Maghīlī. It is a tradition in Aïr that he died at In Taduq in 1500, but so far no trace of a grave that may be identified as his has been discovered, despite reports of an Arabic inscription bearing his name. It is also said that he wrote a commentary on the Qur'ān.
2. His name is spelt either Tkrsh Allāh or Nkrsh Allāh or Tnkrsh Allāh. If the latter is correct, the name may indicate the Tamajeq *tanakra*, namely 'resurrection'.
3. Unidentified. In Arabic this word denotes 'the beaver'. Does he relate in some way to another scholar, nicknamed 'the sword'? See n. 15.
4. The reading of Akhīd is uncertain. *Ṣifat al-wird* is very different at this point. It reads: 'Muḥammad b. Muḥammad, the *faqīh* and saint known as Inirgaray and Muḥammad the pious *faqīh*, "the father of the orphans and widows who is known as Akhīd".' On this saint (also called Amezdennig), see pp. 156, 157.
5. Tinqas. Perhaps this name should read Tefis. *Ṣifat al-wird* appears to read Tinfas. About the mosque at the latter locality, see Rodd, pp. 256, 258, and 418, and F. Nicolas, 'Contribution à l'étude des Tuareg de l'Aïr', in *Contribution, à l'étude de l'Aïr* (Paris, 1950), p. 487 (n. 40).
6. Unidentified.
7. About Awgar al-Fullānī and his family, see pp. 131, 132. The *muqaddam* or 'overseer' in a Ṣūfī *ṭarīqa* is responsible for the smooth administration of his *zāwiya*, to propagate the *ṭarīqa* and to win new members for it. A *murīd* or novice is initiated after the *muqaddam* has read out the rules and regulations governing the *ṭarīqa*. The *muqaddam* is expected to further a friendly atmosphere of co-operation amongst the *murīdūn*. On occasions he may have to offer his house as a *zāwiya* or else assume responsibility for its construction. His duties include the bestowing of the *wird*.
8. According to Aboubacar Adamou, *Agadez et sa région*, p. 64, the tomb of Muḥammad *al-faqīh* is at Inzagarne to the west of In Gall and that of Aḥmad *al-Muqaddam* at Ammalag, to the east of Agades. Probably the reading Nzkrn relates to Inzagarne, and the obscure 'His tomb' perhaps to the tomb of the *faqīh*, Muḥammad. *Ṣifat al-wird* has Ammalag and it appears to be correct.
9. The first real Ṣūfī order founded by ᶜAbd al-Qādir al-Jīlānī/Jīlī (1077–1166).
10. Aḥmad b. ᶜAlī Abū'l-ᶜAbbās, the founder of the *Rifāᶜiyya ṭarīqa*, (1106/1118–1183).
11. Abū Ḥāmid Muḥammad b. Muḥammad al-Ṭūsī al-Shāfiᶜī (1058–1111), Islam's greatest theologian.
12. Ibrāhīm b. Abī'l-Majd ᶜAbd al-ᶜAzīz, saint and thaumaturge (1235–1278), see *EI* under *Dasūḳī or Dusūḳī.*
13. There is no evidence in any of al-Maghīlī's writings, or in those of his contemporaries, suggesting that his interest in Ṣūfism embraced the sort of discipline and doctrine which Shaykh Sīdī Maḥmūd represented. Kunta accounts tell of al-Maghīlī being an initiate of

the *Qādiriyya ṭarīqa* but the alleged proofs and claims for this in the texts are highly suspect, even spurious: see J. Hunwick, *Sharīʿa in Songhay* (Fontes Historiae Africanae, Series Arabica V; Oxford, 1985), pp. 42–6. The *Qudwa* here seems to integrate al-Maghīlī into its list of founders of the *Maḥmūdiyya*, together with al-Suyūṭī, in a manner not dissimilar to the Kunta stories. On the subject of the confusion between al-Maghīlī and Sīdī Maḥmūd at the site in Aïr known as *Maqām* Shaykh b. ʿAbd al-Karīm, see Hunwick, ibid., p. 40, n. 1, and Rodd, pp. 291–3. In the latter a total confusion between the two men is made apparent.

14. Regarding *Ṣūfī* ideas about the Wily Iblīs, see Peter J. Awn, *Satan's Tragedy and Redemption: Iblis in Sufi Psychology* (Leiden, 1983), pp. 57–90. According to Boubou Hama, cited in *Programme Vallée de l'Azawagh, Nov.–Dec. 1984*, (ORSTOM–CNRS, 1985), Annexe to Ch. 11, p. 32, the *faqīh* ʿAbd al-Raḥmān b. Tnkrsh Allāh (spelt Takarcha) was of the Kunta and is also buried at In Taduq. Since a number of the Arabic-speaking nomads who now inhabit the region of In Taduq are related to the Moors of Mauritania and to the Kunta, it is possible that a claim of relationship to this Tuareg saint is relatively recent in date. It may well be that there is a misreading of the *nisba*, al-Nākanatī, in al-Sakhāwī (see ch. 2), as al-Kuntī.

15. He is probably to be identified with Muḥammad al-Najīb b. Muḥammad Shams al-Dīn b. Muḥammad al-Najīb b. Muḥammad b. ʿAbd al-Ṣamad al-Anuṣammanī of Takaddā, the author of the commentary on the *ʿIshrīniyyāt* of al-Fāzāzī and *al-Ṭarīqa al-muthlā ilā'l-wasīla al-ʿuẓmā*. It seems probable that he is the same scholar as al-Najīb b. Muḥammad Shams al-Dīn al-Takiddāwī al-Anuṣammanī who died after 1004–1595/6, the teacher of Shaykh al-Bakrī; see ch. 2 where this problem of identification is fully discussed.

16. No source is given for these alleged statements. Al-Najīb's work *al-Ṭarīqa al-muthlā* is referred to by the Tadeliẓa scholar, Muḥammad b. Tighna, in his ode against Ḥadāhadā, see *The Tuaregs* (Warminster, 1975), pp. 125 and 133. The Sulṭān Aḥmad b. Tilẓay was deposed either in 964/1556 or 961/1554.

17. See n. 8. Is this the same scholar, and the name of Inzugrayn or Inzakrīn the same as Inzagarne?

18. The founder of the mosque at Tefis (spelt in some Arabic texts as Tifis), to the south-east of Agallal, by repute the 'mother of mosques' in the Massif and the most ancient. He appears to have been one of the Eshsherifan from the Adrār-n-Ifōghās. The Kel Tefis regard him as their ancestor. According to legend he came from the west on an elephant which then brought his family to Tefis and then the beams for the building of its mosque.

19. According to F. Nicolas, 'Étude sur l'Islam, les confréries et les centres maraboutiques chez les Toureg du Sud', in *Contribution á l'étude de l'Aïr* (Paris, 1950), p. 487, the tomb is still visible in a vast cemetery. Sacred dust from the area of the tomb is collected by pilgrims. See also Rodd, pp. 256–8.

20. See p. 14.

21. Aḥmad b. Aḥmad b. Muḥammad al-Burnusī al-Fāsī, 1442–93, see Brockelmann, *GAL*, ii, 253, *S* ii, 360–2.

22. ʿUthmān al-Mawhūb b. Afalāwas (variant Afalāwus), Ṣūfī divine and lineal ancestor of the Iberkorāyān Tuareg of Azawagh, and founder of the *temenukela* of the Ayt/Ait Awari, in particular, is an important figure in the early history of the *Maḥmūdiyya*. In a note in the manuscript of an unpublished history, Boubou Hama remarks: 'Maître Aflâouss ben Jabir-ben Ahmed-ben Mohamed ben Aibyad el Ouajhi-ben Malam Abou Abd-allahi-ben Alhousseine-ben Ali-ben Abi Talib (que Dieu soit saisfait d'eux). Cette généalogie correspond exactement à celle citée dans une vieux commentaire du Coran intitulé: "Johavahir el-issâne" écrit par Maître Abderrahmane Essa-Alibi, originaire d'Alger, décédé en 1467 de l'ère chrétienne.' Boubou Hama supplies no source whatsoever for his note, though elsewhere he attributes information to the Agades *marabout*, Hamane ben Ahmed Bougounou, see p. 165, n. 7.

It should be noted that this 'Arab' lineage, as distinct from a 'Berber' line, corresponds to that given by Ghubayd, pp. 26 and 34, with only minor variants.

An examination of the *Kitāb al-Jawāhir al-ḥisān fī tafsīr al-Qur'ān*, by ʿAbd al-Raḥmān al-Thaʿālibī, 2 vols. (Algiers, 1905) has failed to reveal this genealogy. This is hardly surprising as Afalāwas or Afalāwus (his name *afalawas*, in Tamasheq, means 'joyful', 'contented') was a Tuareg Ṣūfī divine of Azawagh and Aïr. There is no reason whatsoever why he should have ever met or come into contact with the Shādhilī scholar, ᶜAbd al-Raḥmān b. Muḥammad b. Makhlūf al-Thaᶜālibī al-Jazā'irī, 1384/5–1470/1, to whom a number of highly suspect links in Ṣūfī *silsilas* are attributed (see J. Hunwick, *Sharīᶜa in Songhay*, pp. 31, 44, 46).

The ᶜAlīd lineage of Afalāwas contains a number of ancestors who appear frequently in other lineages of holy families. Jābir, a descendent of ᶜAlī b. Abī Ṭālib, for example, occurs in the Sūdān in somewhat similar circumstances (see P. M. Holt, *BSOAS*, 30 (1967), 142–57). The names given by Ghubayd are: Jābir, Aḥmad, Jaᶜfar, Bayāḍ al-Wajh, ᶜĀlim (?), al-Faḍl, Yūsuf, ᶜAbdallāh, al-Ḥasan, ᶜAlī, al-Ḥusain and Abū Ṭālib. These do not form a consistent lineage. The names are selected and arranged from a literary source. Bayāḍ al-Wajh relates to *Sūra* 48, *Fatḥ*, of the Qur'ān, where the followers of Muḥammad are portrayed as bowing down, adoring, craving grace from Allāh and His goodwill, 'their marks are in their faces from the effects of adoration'. ᶜUthmān al-Mawhūb specifically alludes to this Qur'ānic reference in passage [A] in the text of the *Qudwa*.

In the commentary of al-Thaᶜālibī (part 4, pp. 182–5) this mark on their faces, due to an excess of adoration, is described as a 'whiteness, a golden glow and a brightness'. It is apparent that the name Bayāḍ al-Wajh relates to this concept and Qur'ānic context. However, if one examines this whole passage in al-Thaᶜālibī, it seems that other names in the lineage of Afalāwas (underlined here) are likewise derived from a literary source and are lifted bodily from it. They have been arranged in a suitable manner leading back to ᶜAlī b. Abī Ṭālib.

A lineal descent from ᶜAlī b. Abī Tālib is what one expects. As A. J. Arberry remarks in his *Muslim Saints and Mystics* (London, 1966), p. 3: 'A strong tradition connects the growth of this movement with the Prophet through his cousin and son-in-law Ali b. Abi Taleb, the fourth caliph whose abdication led to the greatest schism in the history of the faith, the separation between Sunni and Shi'a. According to this version, the Prophet invested Ali with a cloak or *kherqa* on initiating him into the esoteric mysteries, imparting to him therewith the heavenly wisdom which transcends all formal learning. In his turn Ali invested his own initiates, and through them the *selselas* or chains of affiliation passed on the inner lore of mystical truth to succeeding generations.'

If the *Qudwa* is correct, ᶜUthmān b. Afalāwas, the father of Aḥmad (Ăkhmăd), chief of the Aït Awari, though himself of the Iberkorăyăn, became an active participant in the Takaddā and Aïr Ṣūfī movement of the late 15th and early 16th cent. and he became a follower of Sīdī Maḥmūd. His work was continued by his disciple, Abū'l-Hudā (died 1534 or 1575). The *Qudwa* states that the mosque of ᶜUthmān b. Afalāwas fell into disrepair during the lifetime of Abū'l-Hudā. It was either the latter or his pupil, Muḥammad al-Amīn, who restored it. The mosque was severely treated at a later date, and in particular during the reign of Ḥadāḥadā (Khădakhăda), and his successor, Muḥammad Wă-ysmudăn, the son of Abū Yaḥyā, predecessor of Ḥadāḥadā, between 1650 and 1700, when the *Qudwa* was first compiled, but which makes no reference at all to these alleged events. In Taduq is of such importance in the history of the *Maḥmūdiyya* that it ranks with Agades, Jīkat, Abatūl, and Aghalangha as a principal centre for Ṣūfī teaching and practice in the Aïr region.

It has been, and still appears to be, on a pilgrimage route, especially for Ṣūfīs going from West to East or on their way back from the pilgrimage. Like certain sites in the Massif itself, it is a necropolis-cum-mosque, or mosques, a classical example in its way—like al-Bahnasā in Middle Egypt, the resting-place of countless Companions of the Prophet and *shuhadā'*, martyrs of early *jihād*—of an Islamic *Jabbāna*. To cite Lane's *Lexicon*, Jabbāna or *Jabbān* denotes a 'common place of prayer in a desert tract'. At the same time the word indicates a burial-ground 'because the place of prayer is generally in the burial-ground' (see Lane, vol. i, p. 377). As will be observed in our text, Sīdī Maḥmūd himself paid great attention to these burial grounds. He regularly visited them, prayed in them, and encouraged his followers to make this their practice whenever they journeyed within or without the Aïr Massif.

23. If authentic, this is among the earliest passages of Arabic text from Aïr.
24. A wholly spurious *ḥadīth* which is to be dated hardly earlier than the 17th cent.

25. Passages from the Qur'ān, *Sūra 2, al-Baqara*, verse 255, and *Sūra* 60, *al-Naṣr*, verses 1 ff, respectively.
26. I have been unable to trace any work by al-Sanūsī with this title.
27. See the Qur'ān, *Sūra 4, al-Nisā'*, verse 59.
28. No independent evidence exists to support this dubious statement. See n. 32.
29. A locality, so far unidentified, in Aïr, the Adrār-n-Īfōghās or elsewhere in the Central Sahara or Sūdān. It is possible that the name is a misspelt form of In Taduq.
30. Muḥammad al-Amīn is an important scholar of Aïr, although almost nothing is known about him.
31. See n. 22.
32. This date of 1575 is specific. There is no indication in the text of the *Qudwa* where the author obtained it. Is it oral tradition, or from a text, or read on a gravestone at In Taduq? The passage raises other problems of chronology. The syntax of the whole passage is highly ambiguous. The expression 'the Shaykh' might refer either to Abū'l-Hudā or to his disciple, Muḥammad al-Amīn. Read as an entity the whole extended passage suggests that the former, and greater, scholar is meant. Furthermore, most of the oral traditions of Azawagh and Aïr concur that Abū'l-Hudā was indeed buried at In Taduq within the precincts of the mosque of ʿUthmān b. Afalāwas, which he had restored. This is specifically stated in the *Ṣifat al-wird*.

    However, if Abū'l-Hudā died in 1575, at the age of 63, he could not possibly have met al-Suyūṭī (died 1505) or al-Maghīlī, nor could he possibly have corresponded with either of them. Both men would have died before he was born. If, on the other hand, Muḥammad al-Amīn was also buried at In Taduq, though this also cannot be proved, then this date may refer to his decease and not to the decease of Abū'l-Hudā, who might well have died earlier. The date given here therefore casts grave doubts on early contacts between the Aïr *Ṣūfīs* and al-Suyūṭī. It eliminates any possibility that the scholar Muḥammad b. Muḥammad al-Lamtūnī, see p. 19, n. 10, can possibly have been this Abū'l-Hudā. Such is the view held by certain scholars of Niger and Mali. Any possible contact between al-Maghīlī and Abū'l-Hudā would likewise have to be discounted. The person referred to in the earlier passage, buried at Sanbaba (see the second paragraph of Section 3), may be Abū'l-Hudā, and not Abū Ruways. If this were the case, then Abū'l-Hudā would have died about 1534. His meeting, as a young man, with al-Suyūṭī would thus have been possible. However, this means that Abū'l-Hudā lies buried at Sanbaba and not at In Taduq, that Muḥammad al-Amīn lies buried at In Taduq and not at Ṭawāz. Abū Ruways would have to be excluded from the list of scholars whose tombs were visited in this section of the *Qudwa*. The texts of the *Qudwa* and *Ṣifat al-wird* cannot be squared at all at this point.
33. To date no tomb with inscription has been discovered.
34. Amezdennig means 'the easterly', see pp. 156, 157. On the name Inzakrīn, see n. 17.
35. His key role in the *silsila* of initiation into the *Maḥmudiyya ṭarīqa* is explained on pp. 156, 157.
36. On the role played by al-Khaḍir in *Ṣufī* thought see the article by A. J. Wensinck in the *Shorter EI, al-Khaḍir* and Khʷādja Khiḍr.
37. See the article *Ilyās* by A. J. Wensinck in the *Shorter EI*.
38. Nicolas has an extended note about Muḥammad b. Muḥammad, nicknamed Amezdennig, in his 'Étude sur l'Islam', p. 488 (no. 45). He spells Teghzerin as Tyîr'ezrin. Its founder, Ames-Dennég (*l'oriental*) is obviously Amezdennig, who is also named H'âmed-Elennég of the Itesen. Described as the adopted son of Sīdī Maḥmūd al-Baghdādī, who is said to have spent three years at Teghzerin [on the western edge of the Massif], Muḥammad b. Muḥammad Amezdennig then went to Tagzut and founded a small mosque. He returned to Teghzerin where he founded its much larger mosque, dug its well and was buried there. All this accords with the *Qudwa*. According to Nicolas, the Shaykh had a son called Muḥammad, known as Ekadéy-Môlen, who later enlarged this mosque. Ekadéy-Môlen is the name of the mosque of Tyimélen founded, it is said, by Sīdī Maḥmūd himself. See Nicolas, n. 42.
39. This initiation ceremony may be compared with those of the *Qādiriyya* and the *Bektāshiyya*, recorded by J. P. Brown in his *Dervishes or Oriental Spiritualism* (London, 1868), pp. 97–105 and 166–74. A more recent account of a *Bektāshī* initiation ceremony is described by Helmer Ringgren in 'The initiation ceremony of the Bektashis', in

Initiation, ed. by C. J. Bleeker, *Studies in the History of Religions*, Supps. to *Numen*, 10, Initiation (Leiden, 1965), pp. 202–8.

40. The invocation 'In the Name of Allāh, the Compassionate, the Merciful.'
41. *Sūra 48, al-Fatḥ*, verse 10.
42. *Sūra 66, al-Taḥrīm*, verse 8.
43. *Sūra 109, al-Kāfirīn*,, verse 1.
44. *Sūra 112, al-Ikhlāṣ*, verse 1.
45. See Nicolas, 'Étude sur l'Islam', p. 486 (26, Jékat) and p. 489 (54, Tyések'). The relationship of these scholars one to another is shown in Fig. 1.

FIG. 1

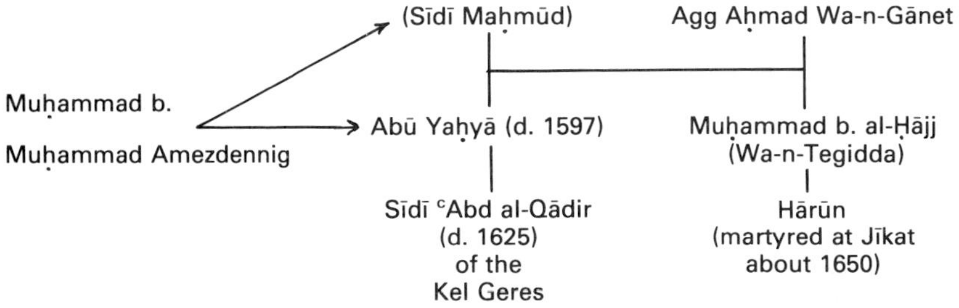

46. The text does not make it clear whether the wet-nurse was a wife of Sīdī Maḥmūd, as is reported in some Aïr traditions.
47. Muḥammad Amezdennig.
48. This date confirms a composition of the *Qudwa* at a date no earlier than the 17th cent. The probable date of the composition of the bulk of the text is fully discussed elsewhere, see n. 49 below and Introduction.
49. On Jīkat or Jākat, with variant spellings, see *The Tuaregs*, pp. 42, 51, 65, 94, 118, 121–2, 126, 133, and 220, where the manuscript indicates Jakṭī as a *nisba*. Nicolas, 'Étude sur l'Islam', p. 486, mentions traces of a large settlement, an extensive cemetery and a ruined mosque, and there are a number of funereal inscriptions. Jīkat is one of the most important of the Islamic sites in Aïr and several scholars of Agades appear to have come from it, although the *Qudwa* suggests that it was settled in the 16th cent. as a centre for Ṣūfīs. Nicolas says that the Shaykh Hārūn, son of Muḥammad b. al-Ḥājj, was killed by the Iberkorăyăn, and other Aïr accounts tell of the destruction of the settlement by Ḥadāḥadā. The *Qudwa* does not confirm the historicity of these reports. No mention is made at all of the martyrdom, or even the death, of Hārūn which must have occurred about 1650. The omission suggests perhaps that the original texts at this point could have been written prior to 1650.
50. *Rabwat al-yamīn*, meaning 'Dune of the right hand', or 'of the oath'.
51. This curious wording, with its family references, suggests that there is some biographical data here supplied by a scholar familiar with Jīkat and its holy men. This has found its way into the substance of the *Qudwa*. This data also (see no. 49 above) would appear to refer to life in Jīkat prior to its alleged sack by Ḥadāḥadā during the latter half of the 17th cent.
52. Aḥmad of Agallal. According to Nicolas, 'Etude sur l'Islam', p. 484, (No. 7, Agalal), the great mosque there was founded by Shaykh Aḥmad al-Rabbāni agg/b. Muḥammad Wa-n-Tefis about 1480. It is not clear what relationship this scholar, who died in 1610, had with its founder of the same name.
53. Some Kel Agallal claim descent from an alleged son of Sīdī Maḥmūd, Mūsā agg/b. Sīdī Maḥmūd Wa-n-Takriza, according to Nicolas, 'l'Étude sur l'Islam', p. 484. However, on p. 487 (No. 34, Takriza) he says that Mūsā was a son of Muḥammad Wa-n-Tagidda, originating from the Adrār-n-Īfōghās (see ibid. 489, No. 54, Tyések'). Descent from Sīdī Maḥmūd al-Baghdādī is claimed also for other Aïr Tuareg groups. Boubou Hama in his *Recherche sur l'Histoire des Touareg Sahariens et Soudanais* (Présence Africaine, Niamey,

1967), p. 390, remarks, though he cites no sources: '*Les Ishsherifen*—Au temps où Mokhammed ag Annor était chef des Temezguidda, Mohammed el Bagdad, arabe et chérif originaire de Bagdad vint dans l'Aïr avec sons fils Ahmed. Celui-ci épousa une femme de la tribu des Ikazkazan; il eut d'elle un fils at une fille; la fille épousa, également, un homme des Ikazkazan. C'est la souche de la tribu des Ishsherifen.

Le fils Ibrahim épousa une femme Tamezguidda, c'est la souche d'un tribu Ishsherifen qui serait dans l'ouest.

A la même époque un autre shérif ag Ahmed vint, lui, de Djanet, épousa une femme des Kel Takarat (Tamezguidda) et s'en retourna. Sa femme eut un enfant que Mokhammed ag Annor éleva et qui devint le chef des Tamezguidda: Mokhammed Nan Tiguidda, c'est lui qui vint de l'Aïr s'installer dans l'Azawak. Ses descendants ont formé tribu des Ishsherifen Tamezguidda et aussi celle des Ishsher Kel Gress.

54. Ibn Najjār al-Badrānī, in the text, is probably a copyist's error for Ibn (al-)Najjār al-Baghdādī, a famous Suhrawardī mystic who died in 637/1239. His full personal name was Muḥibb al-Dīn Abū ᶜAbdallāh Muḥammad b. Maḥmūd b. al-Ḥasan b. Hibatallāh b. Maḥāsin al-Baghdādī. See Richard Gramlich, *Die Gaben der Erkentnisse des ᶜUmar al-Suhrawardi* (*ᶜAwārif al-maᶜārif*) (Wiesbaden, 1978), p. 8.

5
Doctrines of the *Maḥmūdiyya*

Translation

Selected Folios of the Qudwa *that refer to the Doctrines of the* Maḥmūdiyya *as were recalled from the Words spoken by Sīdī Maḥmūd to his Followers*

1. Shaykh [Sīdī Maḥmūd]—may Allāh be pleased with him—used to say, 'The *fuqarā'* are upon the scales of the *sharīʿa*.' Whenever he took the oath from his novice he would say to him, 'This world is the abode of vanity and of deception. For the ritual ablutions, for prayer and for the *dhikr*, go to the *fuqarā'*. They will teach you the rules of the "Way".' He used to say to his companions when they perceived some failing in him who served, and they reported [this matter] to him, saying, 'It is [a] worthy [task] for him who is appointed,' 'Were he one amongst you then he would gather up all for your supply.' He used to be full of praise for him whom he saw to be worthy and qualified for this.

He said, for example, 'How blessed are the two men in this land, one the man and [the other] his in-law.' These two men were Shaykh Muḥammad b. Muḥammad b. Ibrāhīm[1] and Muḥammad b. al-Ḥājj, may Allāh be pleased with them both. He said, 'Were I to find seven upright men [then] how could one be sufficiently thankful?' He said to his *naqīb*,[2] Shaykh Tibardudāz,[3] who was sitting behind him and who was thinking about food which he had given to someone to eat, but the dogs had devoured it, responding to that thought which had crossed his mind, 'The alms of the wicked only enters into the belly of the wicked.'

He [Sīdī Maḥmūd]—may Allāh be pleased with him—used to show honour and respect to the children of the *fuqarā'* and of the *shurafā'*. He pressed upon his companions the need to strive with diligence and always to be ready to obey the will of Allāh. Whenever he wanted to express an opinion [on some matter] he would remark, 'the time is propitious'. Then the *naqīb* said, 'Assemble and be present'. Then all of them came until he had finished [his discourse]. He would terminate the gathering by reciting the *fātiḥa*. Whenever he engaged in discourse and in discussion, he said, 'Whosoever deserves it not is debarred.' He used to say, 'Is the land of Aïr one of the

Pls. 16–17. Folios in the *Qudwa* that exalt the *Maḥmūdiyya* as an orthodox and unique order that derives its rules and its teachings directly from the Prophet himself

Plate 17

countries of the Sūdān?'[4] They said to him, 'We are a part of the land of the Sūdān. We possess the place, now, where once the negroes lived.'[5] He said, 'Such is the land of fire.'[6] He likewise said, 'Were you dwellers in the land of Islam you would reach your destination in a very short time indeed. As for this country, the *faqīr* sleeps his night on one level and he awakens on a level below it.'[7] He—may Allāh be pleased with him—instructed them by question and by answer as was the custom of the Messenger of Allāh, His blessing and peace be upon him.

One of the *fuqarā'* said to him, 'My children write upon wooden tablets, what shall I recite for them from written books?' The *fuqarā'* said to him, 'It is enough for you [to teach] what is in the *Risāla* of Ibn Abī Zayd.'[8] Some of the opponents [of his teaching] said to the Shaykh, 'Your aim amongst us is the enjoyment of temporal power.' He answered them by saying, 'Poor fools, do you possess worldly goods which I could covet? Are you not aware that the doors of the Baghdād mosque number some three hundred or more? On Friday, at each one of them, a cow's skin is spread out and when the prayer is over you will find every skin covered with gold and with silver. All that I seek from you is that you will be the humble servants of Allāh, in all truth, not slaves of [your] fancy, nor of desire and of Satan.'

He used to instruct his companions in various ways. One of his companions was in the habit of praying, and [on one occasion] he forgot a pigeon [which had alighted] upon the top of his hooded cloak (*burnus*) and he put it in the fire, but the latter did not burn the pigeon. They mentioned what had happened to the Shaykh. He said to that man, 'Perchance you had prayed behind me?'[9] 'Yes,' he answered. One of them said to him, 'We are together, we and our holy companions. When a thief milks their she-camel it comes [to us] with the thief.' He [Sīdī Maḥmūd] said to him, 'Our (My?) miraculous power is made manifest in our [dumb] companions.' Due to that, one of them said, 'The act of a wise man is of more benefit to a thousand other men than the admonition given by a thousand men to another.' [*End of quotes from the* Manāhij?]. Another question similar to this was put to him by a questioner. He said to him, 'We, in our souls and in the personalities which we possess, are a miracle. Who is he who is able to understand what it is?'

When he made his testament to the *fuqarā'*, he said, 'Hold fast to what you have learnt from me. Omit nothing and add nothing to it. There is no doubt that he who holds fast to it will, on the morrow, place his hand in the hand of my ancestor, the Messenger of Allāh, His blessing and peace be upon him.' He [Sīdī Maḥmūd]—may Allāh be pleased with him—was apprehensive and fearful over the *fuqarā'*.

One day he left his house with the Qur'ān. He placed it before them and he swore by it that he would not conceal one *qīrāṭ*, one measure, from them. He—may Allāh be pleased with him—was possessed with an illumination, with an awe and a dignity. Sometimes, when a man beheld him, he was obliged to turn his head [aside], through Allāh's power. Some of them, when he went out to them and they looked upon his face, were smitten to the ground by the power of Him whose power it is.

He used to walk in front of the assembly at the foot of the [Aïr] mountains. The owner of the country said to him, 'I have been in this country since a bygone time, [yet] I did not know that this path [existed].' He said to him, 'I knew it when I was [still] in Baghdād.' He was a man who journeyed greatly and who saw many lands. When he arose, intending to journey forth, he recited the *fātiḥa* and he would open the *dhikr* with the words, 'There is no god but Allāh,' [this] on account of His words [in the Qur'ān], reports from his prophet, Noah, 'in the name of Allāh is its course'.[10] When they wished to halt, they similarly performed the *dhikr* on account of His words [in the Qur'ān], 'in the name of Allāh is its mooring'.[11] They would raise aloud their voices and they would exclaim, 'There is no god but Allāh.' When they had enjoyed their goodly portion of fellowship, they would terminate their gathering with the words, 'There is no god but Allāh,' three times, and 'truly . . .' up to 'Praise be to Allāh, the Lord of the Worlds.' They would recite the *fātiḥa* after praying for blessing upon the Prophet—the blessing and peace of Allāh be upon him—and he used to say, 'Camp at the waterhole, for your sustenance is from Allāh.'

Whenever he used to ascend [the Aïr mountains], high aloft above the land, he would halt to recite the *fātiḥa*. When he alighted upon graves and upon tombs, he would halt to recite the *fātiḥa*. Whenever he entered a village, or a town, the first thing he did was to visit the tombs of the godly. He knew the identity of those who were buried there due to the indication [that was given to him] by the lord of the Messengers. He would halt at that place and he would recite, 'Allāh . . . as He so wills,' and he would recite the *fātiḥa*.[12] Then he would sit down, take hold of his rosaries, and, having recited what Allāh so decreed of the *taṣliya* and the *tahlīl*,[13] and other than that, and reciting of the *fātiḥa*, he would arise and perform the *dhikr*, as Allāh decreed, and recite the *fātiḥa*. Then he would leave to go to the village mosque, whether the cemetery was known to the people or not, and when he entered the mosque he acknowledged its due [sanctity] by the *dhikr*, and the prayer. Whenever he spoke, he who was listening needed no explanation [of his words]. When one of them translated for him,[14] he who listened desired that his tongue might be stilled, so sweet was the utterance of the Shaykh and so pleasant was it in their hearts.

It was a rule enjoined upon those who believed in their *ṭarīqa*, and who adopted their attire, that he should discipline himself to their rules and to their moral practices, having been confronted with and presented with descriptions and demonstrations of the manner of their worship. He used to say, 'You must show a respect towards all Muslims and believe well of them, verily, Allāh Almighty will not ask a servant in the world to come, "Why did you better your view [you held] of your fellow men?" Because to think ill—even if you be a man of outstanding example amongst those most pious in our time; say, due to your being abstemious in this world, or being a filler of hours spent in Almighty Allāh's *dhikr*, or a doer of good deeds—that [in itself alone] does not enable a man to prevent his heart [and mind] from thinking ill, from harbouring hate and contempt. Such a thinker of evil is more deserving of a penalty than his opponents. If worship and devotion, during night and day, be weighed and placed in one pan upon the scales, and hatred and evil thinking be placed upon the other, then the latter would outweigh the acts of devotion. If the most pious amongst men of piety be like this then what is your view regarding those who are less godly than they are?'

He used to say, 'Never insult and abuse a man as a person, only the blameworthy act which he commits. You do not know what the final outcome will be for you, nor for him. Ponder upon the words of the Prophet—the blessing and peace of Allāh be upon him—regarding a bunch of garlic, "I loathe its smell."[15] He did not say that he loathed the very plant itself. Verily, its odour is but one of its properties.'

He used to say to his brethren, 'Be slaves of Allāh, the Almighty, not slaves of yourselves, nor slaves of your *dīnār* nor of your *dirham*. Verily, whenever your mind and your thought is attached to the love of it, whether it be praised or whether it be blamed, it will detract from your devotional act towards Allāh, the Almighty, to the extent of your attachment to it. You have not been created for the world, nor for yourselves, so do not flee from Allāh's presence. Verily, you are a sacred sanctuary unto yourselves. How comes it [not] about that you should not be declared a sacred territory, one which is inviolate, to others?'

He used to say, 'Those who follow the path are in three categories, the august (*jalālī*), that category which inclines the most towards the *sharīʿa* law, the beauteous (*jamālī*), that category which inclines the most towards the ultimate reality, and the perfectionist (*kamālī*). He who is in this last category combines the two [other] categories. He is superior and he is the most perfect of them all. May Allāh, the Almighty, have mercy upon you. Be on your guard lest you be the deceived, [namely] those who strive in their heart as little as is needful, although they have thought that they had disciplined themselves and that they had bettered their moral conduct and had dispensed with effort and with striving. That comes about solely due to ignorance dominating their self-awareness and the effect that it has. Some such [persons] have acquired the outward signs of moral conduct from the canonic law.' He said, 'If a man be greatly diffident and bashful, rare in any hurt which he does to others, much given to virtue, little in his inquiry, scrupulously honest in what he says, hard at his work, slight in his inquisitiveness, upright, very friendly, honourable and patient, full of gratitude, clement, tender, chaste, amiable, one who neither curses nor insults with abuse, nor is he a scandalmonger nor a backbiter, nor impetuous, nor hate-filled, nor miserly to excess, nor a great envier of others, but one who is cheerful and of joyful countenance, who shows love for Allāh's sake and, likewise, detests for Allāh's sake, these, then, are the marks and the signs of the moral standard set forth in canonic law. Such are its main features.'

He used to say, 'Restrain your anger from him who does evil to you, because it is with the permission of your Lord that he is given power over you. But, if your anger is aroused against him, then the power which he has over you will increase.' He used to say, 'Carry out all the canonic commands which have been appointed to you, in accordance with the command of the lawgiver, and not for any other cause. Forsake all causes and have naught to do with them, because of the saying of Allāh, the Almighty, "Allāh erases and establishes those things that He so wishes."'[16] He used to say, 'Do not rely on me in any matter and do not trust your own self in any matter. Do not treat with indifference Allāh's [apparent] waywardness in the way He acts; whether it be [done] for something, or [it would seem] for nothing. Never, arbitrarily, make some choice on your own account, so that you will have Allāh with you [on your side]. On the contrary, submit the matter to Him first of all, with obedience, before you see later that it is [in fact] His [will]. Assume [after acting thus] that what you have chosen for yourself is some circumstance in which Allāh will be next to you. You will not know whether you will attain what you have chosen, nor whether you will not attain it. When you do attain it, you will [still] not be aware whether your own good is in that circumstance. If the Real [*al-Ḥaqq*] denies you anything, then be thankful to Him for that denial, for verily He, the Almighty, has not denied it to you on account of parsimony. He has only done so in His wisdom.'

I have heard him say,[17] 'When the Ultimate Reality, the Almighty, gives you a choice in anything, then choose denial of the freedom to choose. Forsake it completely and then you will see that something will belong to you despite it. Be on your guard against grieving over the relinquishment of something, for verily, if it had been truly your own it would never have escaped you.'

He used to say, 'Be busied about what your Shaykh has commanded you to perform. Be not preoccupied in reciting what the people say without his counsel. All that the people say accords with [some] status. Such is not the business of a novice.' Muḥammad al-Shannāwī used to say,[18] 'It is a mark of a *faqīr* amongst the *fuqarā'*, in the *ṭarīqa*, that he will not be contemptuous of anybody who is in any way associated with it. Nay, rather, his duty is to extol him and to show him honour, just as he would do so to the mightiest of the princes.'

He [Sīdī Maḥmūd] used to initiate men, women, and children with the words, 'There is no god but Allāh' in any town he visited. He used to organize meetings for the *dhikr*, for men and for women, in the morning and in the evening. He used to say, 'O brother, perform the *dhikr* with your brethren, O sister perform the *dhikr* with the sisters who are your neighbours, for verily, all the assemblies of the *dhikr* which are in the Western land [*al-bilād al-gharbiyya*], now, are organized and made ready by the Prophet—the blessing and peace of Allāh be upon him.'

Once he said, 'We have set ablaze the fire of the Divine Unity in this country and it shall not be extinguished, if Allāh so wills, until the Day of Judgement.' Such were the Shaykh's very words. I have only intended by 'the words of the *mashāyikh*' [to mean] those men whose words accord with his own or whose way of life was his own way of life.

He said, 'Who is that one who imposes a condition upon him who calls [men] to Allāh, that he should be obedient in the giving of food to men, when they [on their part] give him no food to subsist?' Muḥammad al-Tūnisī[19] used to say, 'He who became famous, Abū'l-Mawhib, used to say, "To adore Allāh with a love for this world fetters the heart and fatigues the members. Though it be much, its worth is paltry, and it only appears to be much in the imagination of him who performs it. Such [outward] adoration is a sheer mannerism. It is devoid of any spirit. It is due to this that you may see many of the lords of this world fasting much and praying much and they perform their pilgrimage often, yet theirs is not the light of the ascetics, nor the sweetness of Allāh's servants." '

It is because of this that Abū Ḥāmid, al-Ghazālī,[20] said in his

Iḥyā' ᶜulūm al-dīn, 'another group are the lords of wealth who hoard possessions and who cling to them tightly, ruled by their cupidity. Then they busy themselves in their bodily adoration of Allāh, by works which do not demand their spending of capital; such as fasting in the day time and keeping awake at night and learning the Qur'ān by heart. Such men are deceived since an all-consuming cupidity has control of their inner being. Such men had need to restrain the expending of wealth at a time when they were pre-occupied in seeking for attainments which they could well have dispensed with.'[21]

Such a person in their company is like a man into whose garment there has crept a serpent. The man is on the verge of destruction, yet he is pre-occupied with the cooking of oxymel (honey and vinegar), in order to soothe his bile, and whom the serpent killed when it needed the honey and vinegar. Likewise, Bashīr[22] was asked, 'Verily, so and so, the wealthy one, is a great faster and he prays frequently.' He said, 'Poor man, he has left his state and has entered another which is different from it. On the contrary, the state of this man who is feeding the hungry and who is spending wealth for the sake of the poor, is better for him than in the increasing of his own hunger and in praying for himself as he amasses this world's wealth, yet he denies it to the poor.'

Sīdī ᶜAlī used to say,[23] 'The adding of wealth to the slave is like the adding of a province to the governor. Whoever claims the possession of riches in his hand, without his master, is disappointed and he is guilty of lying and of slander. It was a sin against him. But whosoever confesses that what he possesses is his master's, then that is not a sin, nor a presumption to his right, even were he to possess the entire world, because that only belongs to his Lord. His Lord, the Almighty, does not begrudge him anything nor does he reduce the entitlement of a saint of Allāh Almighty on account of the quantity of wealth which his hands hold, save for the one who is foolish. Ponder on the saying of the Prophet—the blessing and peace of Allāh be upon him—'I have been given the keys of the treasure houses of the earth.'[24] The Prophet—the blessing and peace of Allāh be upon him—was aware that Allāh's slave knows that whenever the property of his lord was great, then the favour of Allāh was bestowed upon him. He knew that the place of sin and temptation, through wealth, only existed in the claim of ownership to it.

He [Sīdī Maḥmūd] used to say, 'Whoever beholds men who are amongst the saints of Allāh, and who sees their [emaciated] bodies, will [thereby] only become increasingly indifferent to their status. His disfavourable view of them will be strengthened. It will deepen his lack of politeness towards them. Such a man [who reacts in this way] has [thus] been prevented, through the [mere] sight of the corporal body, from perceiving [the spiritual] realities.'

He used to say regarding the Almighty's words, 'In your midst are those who seek this world, and in your midst are those who seek the world to come,[25] meaning thereby, he seeks in this world for the world to come and he seeks the world to come for Allāh, the Almighty, whereas amongst you is to be found the believer who only seeks to follow me.' In the Qur'ānic verse there is therefore evidence for the believer who may seek the world though that does not in any way impair his faith.

He used to say, 'Whoever walks with one of Allāh's saints, seeking his happiness, Allāh will place his face at a distance of forty autumns from the fire of Hell.' He said, 'Verily hearts, when they distance themselves from Allāh, will loathe and detest those others which carry out His commands. Given that this be true of them at a time when scholars were in plenty, then mark well how it is even truer today, and more applicable, when he who has religious knowledge does not abstain from heinous acts of wickedness and even less so from minor sins and iniquities.' It is for that reason they have said, 'Do not keep company with a sinner who persists in his sinning and his offences. He who is not in fear of Allāh is not safe from His harm. If he were to fear Allāh, the Almighty, then he would not persistently sin as he does.' *See the pages of* [*the book called*] Tuḥfat al-Murīdīn.[26] [He said,] 'Those who have holy books in their hands but who do not understand the meanings of their content, and those who understand them but who do not agree to act upon them, then, these books are a token of separation [from Allāh] and of [His] abandonment, just as, in the same way, the Torah and the Gospel remained in the hands of the tribes of the people who received the first revelations. Verily we come from Allāh and verily to Him we are returning.'

As for the Ṣūfī [*faqīr*] and the jurist [*faqīh*], both have their origin in the messenger of Allāh—His blessing and peace be upon him. This is because the Ṣūfī and the jurist are two categories, though that which is described is [at the root], one and the same thing. Both categories were created by him [the Prophet]—the blessing and peace of Allāh be upon him. The same situation prevailed afterwards during the age of the Companions, and the age of those who followed them, in the moral conduct which they observed and which they practised. May Allāh be pleased with them all.

As the ages passed, and when ignorance had prevailed, and the ages came [wherein lived] those who professed to be jurists and Ṣūfī mystics, who were broad in their claims, amongst both categories of men there were likewise those who went much too far in their fancies. They were men without true guidance from Allāh. Each category alleged that it [alone] was rightly guided and that the other was upon the path to destruction, and in maintaining that the other had neither basis nor origin in the Qur'ān nor in the *sunna*. Each category began to view the other with a scornful eye, with contempt and with derision. The jurists alleged that they held an advantage over those others who claimed the [holy] poverty of Ṣūfism, due to the paucity of their jurisprudence, whereas the Ṣūfīs maintained that they held an advantage over those who claimed to be jurists, this due to the mere fact of their affiliation to the rules of Ṣūfī poverty. Each one of them was in error and led others astray. Satan toyed with them through their hearts. He became their master until division, opposition, and mutual envy occurred between them both. Know that the ways of the *ʿulamā'* [*sic*/*fuqahā'*] vary, and those of the Ṣūfīs vary likewise. Those who are members of the *ṭarīqa* [of Sīdī Maḥmūd] are betwixt the way of the Ṣūfīs and the way of the jurists. Beware lest you be an opponent of the jurists, due to some licence permitted by one of their schools, or that you oppose a Ṣūfī due to some licence permitted by one of the paths of the Ṣūfīs. Beware lest you oppose those who follow the *ṭarīqa*, and, more especially, if you do not follow deeply into their paths because ignorance about them has been the subject of admonition and of caution. So ask scholars who are the people of the reminder (*Ahl al-dhikr*)[27] if you do not know. They have declared it proscribed in both the Qur'ān and the *sunna*.

All of that induced them to seek for the leadership. They were those intended in the saying of the Prophet—the blessing and peace of Allāh be upon him—'Religious knowledge is a twofold science, the science of the tongue, and such is an argument against mankind, and the science which is learnt by the heart. The latter is the useful and the profitable science.' If each category, whether mystic or jurist, were to work with the heart that is given to it, then it would benefit and attain the standard of imitation which is commanded for each by our Prophet—the blessing and peace of Allāh be upon him—and what he forbade, in his saying, 'Do not be cut off, one from another, do not oppose one another and do not envy one another . . .' to the end of the *ḥadīth*.[28] ʿAlī b. Maymūn said,[29] 'By that means they destroyed the *sunna* of the Messenger of Allāh—His blessing and peace be upon him—Allāh curse them. They destroyed the *sunna* of [the Messenger of] Allāh and they revived the *sunna* of Satan,' until he said, 'the mischief of these two categories, which we have mentioned, is greater than that of the Jews and the Christians and the rest of the blind and the ignorant who are not an example which should be followed. As for these others, they are imitated by men and women, in both word and in deed and in circumstance, and it is believed that such is lawful, when [in fact] it is unlawful. What evil mischief is greater than this. In Allāh is to be found protection from it.'

[Chapter]

As for the people who have a knowledge of Allāh, they are to be divided into two groups. One group comprises those who are acquainted with His secrets and are governed by His wisdom and by His predestination. These he has appointed to offices amongst His creation in order to further its interests, and its welfare, and to ward off misfortunes, by a secret which He alone knows and by the *baraka* of the divine name and the attributes of Allāh revealed to Man. In them, Allāh bestows His mercy upon His creation. Many are their number and they are of many types.

There is also a people whom Allāh has appointed to show the way to Him, to offer guidance and to teach Allāh's creation the cause on account of which they were created from the divine unity, to fulfil His duties which were imposed upon them by the Qur'ān and by the *sunna*. This class of men is few in number at this time. They are called the people of the *ṭarīqa* of Sīdī Maḥmūd. They are the guides, the teachers, those who show the way to Allāh, that is to say, to the knowledge of Allāh, and who act as a guide and a teacher of Allāh's religion. He who is described thus is given the name of *shaykh* and *ustādh*. Such is the term used for the people in this occupation. The meaning of *Ahl al-ṭarīqa al-Maḥmūdiyya* is, 'those who call upon the people of Allāh to a clarity of vision'. A clarity of vision and of awareness is the gift which was brought by him [the Prophet]—the blessing and peace of Allāh be upon him—to teach Mankind about Allāh. It was his *sunna* and the word of his Lord. As for the *ṭarīqa* of Sīdī Maḥmūd, *it is the original path and the other paths have borrowed from it.*[30] It is the way of the sons of the world to come, in canonic law, in mystical discipline, and in ultimate truth. All else is but the following of a wayward fancy.

It is for this reason that the *shaykh* of our *mashāyikh*, Abū'l-Qāsim al-Junayd[31]—may Allāh have mercy upon him and be pleased with him—said, 'Knowledge is of two kinds, knowledge of Allāh, as Lord, and the knowledge of man's service as Allāh's servant. The rest is mere delusion of the soul.' Then he said, 'It is amazing to find one who seeks this path of ours and who has acquired the knowledge of its technicality whereby he derives thereby a knowledge of the meanings of the Book of Allāh and the *sunna* of His Prophet, that he does not occupy himself in Allāh's *dhikr*, turning aside from everything else so that He may pour into his heart the waters of mystically imparted knowledge (*al-ᶜulūm al-laduniyya*), for were he to study repeatedly the technicalities and their classifications and categories for a thousand years he would not smell its fragrance nor have seen that its effect was real and true.' May Allāh be pleased with him. This is true, proven, and attained by the perception and by vision, thanks be to Allāh.

The meaning of his words 'knowledge of Allāh as Lord' and 'knowledge of man's service as Allāh's servant' and 'the rest is mere delusion of the soul', takes note of all the sciences which Allāh has taught to His creation. Two things are here intended; that is, knowledge of Allāh, as Lord, and knowledge of man's service as Allāh's servant,—through the knowledge of Allāh, as Lord, the servant of Allāh is united as one with his Lord. He adores Him as he should and he [His servant] frees Him from such anthropomorphic concepts [as are due to] an imperfect belief in Him as deity, unworthy of his Lord in all the commandments and the prohibitions which are made manifest in the Qur'ān and in the *sunna*. It is by a knowledge appertaining to his heart, not a verbal knowledge, and it is a knowledge of the status of being a servant of his Lord. Likewise, the servant will be a servant who is freed from all that is unfitting and unworthy, on account of the state of his being one with his Lord.

When the Shaykh brought the *ṭarīqa* of Sīdī Maḥmūd, and it was his sole intent, it was all that he brought, it was the only thing in which he called upon them to accept. It was the only thing in which he gave them guidance. All he showed them was its rules. All he made them seek was the world to come and all that he made them reject was the [present] world and its vanity which is the mark upon him who is at a distance from the *umma* of Muḥammad—the blessing and peace of Allāh be upon him. [They] are those who shun [the world] turning their faces towards the world to come, except that he [the Prophet]—the blessing and peace of Allāh be upon him—only came and only ordained turning towards Allāh and turning aside from worldly things. Then they [who opposed him] rose up against him [Sīdī Maḥmūd] and they did to him what they did to his ancestor, Ḥasan b. ᶜAlī—*may Allah ennoble his countenance*[32]—and at that time the fire of the Prophethood was still burning amongst men.

The tomb of Sīdī Maḥmūd is still visible and it is still visited [on pilgrimage] at Aghalangha[33]—may the mercy of Allāh be upon him.

Pls. 18–19. Folios in the *Qudwa* wherein the jurists are castigated for their literalism in religion and the mystics are extolled

Plate 19

Shaykh Aḥmad al-Zarrūq said,[34] 'The saints of Allāh are Allāh's doors.' Their knowledge is the key to those doors and the teeth of that key is the safeguarding of that which is holy, of loyal service, constant humility, and a wideness of mercy. Whosoever treats men thus is open to Allāh's inspiration and is blessed. Otherwise, he is at risk and is in jeopardy. The Prophet said—peace be upon him—'A time will come when men will be the slaves of what they possess and they will disbelieve in the Merciful and will obey Satan.'

They will slay one another and they will despise their scholars. When they sit in their gatherings none will disclose his inner secret. Sahl b. ᶜAbdallāh al-Tustarī used to say,[35] 'When the evil of the age is imminent, no servant acts in the way that Allāh has commanded him. Allāh will decree that he be either a person who is followed and imitated, or else he will be a stranger in his age.' Amongst those sayings reported by the companions of Sīdī Maḥmūd are these, said by him, 'Our way is the *Maḥmūdiyya ṭarīqa*.' A man questioned him, saying, 'Are you one of the Ṣūfīs?' He said to him, 'The way of the Ṣūfīs is hard, but we are on the path of the lord of the Messengers, our footstep will follow his.'[36] He said, 'Those of the "Way" have concurred that it is founded and based upon solid foundations and upon a *sunna* which leads back to the greatest *Imām* of all, to Muḥammad—the blessing and peace of Allāh be upon him.' Sīdī Maḥmūd taught that whoever did not assemble with the *shaykhs* and learn the 'Way' from them should not be emulated in their *ṭarīqa*. All the pious amongst the predecessors made it a practice that whosoever had a lineage, linked to the *ṭarīqa* of Sīdī Maḥmūd, which was unsound, and who had not been given permission by his *shaykh* to go forth to guide the people in order to take their oaths of covenant, had no right to do the same.

Notes

1. On both these important Shaykhs of the *Maḥmūdiyya* see ch. 4, and in regard to Shaykh Muḥammad b. Muḥammad b. Ibrāhīm, the founder of the Tefis mosque, see n. 18, in particular.
2. *naqīb*: a superintendent and overseer. In a Ṣūfī *ṭarīqa* he is responsible for the conduct and the discipline of the *murīdīn*.
3. Tibardudāz is the name clearly vocalized in the text of the *Qudwa*. The *naqīb* in question was a Tuareg disciple of Shaykh Sīdī Maḥmūd. His name is connected with the Tamasheq, *berdeddez*, from the verb, *aberdeddez*, which Ghubayd says means, '*avoir la peau parsemée d'enflures*', *Lexique Touareg-Français* (Copenhagen, 1980), p. 9. My Tuareg friend Altinine Ag Arias informs me that *tabardaddaz* means 'pox-marked' or 'pimpled'.
2. Aïr, like many Saharan and Sahelian regions, Mauritania for example, lies on the border of the Maghrib and the Sūdān, and this provoked discussion between geographers. Aḥmad Bābā wrote that the scholar al-ᶜĀqib b. ᶜAbdallāh al-Anusammanī al-Massūfī was of the people of Akdas (Agades), 'a town near the bilād al-Sūdān'. Geographical uncertainty also

involved legal issues, see for example *El-Wasīṭ*, Études Mauritaniennes, no. 5 (Centre IFAN, St. Louis, Senegal 1953), pp. 10–13. According to al-ᶜUmarī, 'In the land of the Sūdān, there are also three independent white Muslim kings who are Berbers; the sultan of Ahīr [Aïr], the Sultan of [the town of] DMWSHH, and the sultan of Tādmakka', see Levtzion and Hopkins, *Corpus*, p. 274. This passage in the *Qudwa* is a curious statement, and, if authentic, is only likely to have been made by Shaykh Sīdī Maḥmūd when he had first arrived in Aïr, prior to his alleged differences with the Sulṭān in Agades.

5. The passage which tells of the conquest of Aïr by Berbers and Arabs from the negroes is not dissimilar to other passages which are found in the Agades Chronicle, an example being that cited in the opening chapter. Rennell Rodd discusses this whole question at some length in his *People of the Veil* (London, 1926), pp. 363–6.
6. The allusion to 'fire' in the text is not clear. Is Sīdī Maḥmūd referring to infidelity, is this the fire of Hell, and in what way were the negroes viewed in regard to it; was it the blackness of their skins? At least a handful of his followers were allegedly Fulani or Hausa. In this Sahelian belt it is sometimes the Arabs who are referred to as 'the fire' by negroes, see *al-Wasīṭ* by Aḥmad b. Al-Amīn al-Shinqīṭī (Cairo, 1378/1958), p. 283.
7. If this is a genuine saying, then it is clear that Sīdī Maḥmūd did not regard Aïr as *Dār al-Islām*. However, the anonymous writers of matters relating to Aïr, addressed to al-Suyūṭī (see the ch. on Geography of Aïr), specifically states: 'In the land of Aïr is the town of Agades. *It is a land of Islam and there are only Muslims within it.*'
8. A standard work of Mālikī *fiqh* widely studied and highly respected in West Africa. ᶜAbdallāh b. Abī Zayd al-Qayrawānī died in 386/996.
9. A belief widely spread in North Africa, and elsewhere in the Muslim World, see, by way of example, the reference of al-Bakrī to ᶜAbdallāh b. Yāsīn, the *Murābiṭ* in Levtzion and Hopkins, *Corpus*, p. 74.
10. A curtailed Qur'ānic passage, *Sūra II, Hūd*, verses 40–1 where Noah says to those believers who are with him: 'Ride ye therein [the ark], in the name of Allāh is its course . . .'
11. The same Qur'ānic verse is further continued '. . . and its mooring. Verily, my Lord is forgiving and merciful.' Other imagery derived from the story of Noah and the ark is to be found in ch. 3.
12. This verse is too brief in its reference to be identified within the Qur'ān.
13. The invocations: 'The blessing and peace of Allāh be upon him, the Prophet,' and 'There is no God but Allāh.'
14. An indication suggesting that Sīdī Maḥmūd was unable, with Arabic alone, to communicate with his African (Tuareg, Fulani, Hausa) followers without some assistance from interpreters.
15. References to garlic are found in a number of *ḥadīths*, though this specific one has not been located.
16. *Sūra 13, al-Raᶜd*, verse39, 'Allāh blots out what He will, or He confirms; and with Him is the Mother of the Book.'
17. The text nowhere makes it clear who is the source of this statement.
18. An unidentified *Ṣūfī* source.
19. Likewise unidentified.
20. Abū Ḥāmid al-Ghazālī (died 505/1111), the 'Proof of Islam', who came from Tūs. His *Iḥyā'* expounds theology and ethics from the viewpoint of the moderate *Ṣūfī* school.
21. The *Qudwa* follows the original; it shows that copies of *Iḥyā' ᶜulūm al-dīn* were extant in this region in the 17th century. See also *Ghazâlî, Iḥ'ya ᶜOuloûm ed-Dîn ou Vivification des Sciences de la Foi*, analysed and indexed by G-H Bousquet (Paris, 1955), pp. 309–10.
22. The Bashīr in the text has not been identified amongst the *Ṣūfīs*.
23. Sīdī ᶜAlī may be the Moroccan Berber mystic ᶜAlī b. Maymūn b. Abī Bakr al-Idrīsī al-Maghribī (died 1511) whose life spanned the latter half of the 9th cent. of the *hijra* (*c.*854/1450–917/1511) and who travelled extensively in the Muslim East and settled in Damascus. A short biography of him by Brockelmann, with an account of his mystical ideas, is to be read in the *EI*. There is also a detailed study by I. Goldziher, 'ᶜAlî b. Mejmûn al-Magribî und sein Sittenspiegel des östlichen Islam', in *Zeitschrift der Deutschen Morgenländischen Gesellschaft*, 28, (1874), pp. 293 ff.

24. This *ḥadīth* is cited, with variations, by al-Bukhārī (in several chapters), by Muslim, by al-Nasā'ī, and by Aḥmad b. Ḥanbal. It is entered by A. J. Wensinck and J. P. Mensing in their *Concordance et Indices de la Tradition Musulmane* (Leiden 1936–68), vol. xi, p. 28.
25. *Sūra 3*, *Āl ᶜImrān*, verse 152, 'Amongst you are those who love this world, and amongst you are those who love the next.'
26. A work insufficiently titled to be identified, possibly a local work of Ṣūfī practice known to, or written by, the author himself.
27. Those who know the history of the former peoples to whom God sent Messengers.
28. A *ḥadīth* of dubious authorship though one, it seems, current amongst Ṣūfīs, in the opinion of my colleague, Dr M. A. S. Abdel Haleem.
29. See n. 23, confirming a likely identification with ᶜAlī b. Maymūn al-Maghribī.
30. This statement suggests that the author of the *Qudwa* was in favour of the identification of his *ṭarīqa* with an original *Muḥammadiyya ṭarīqa*, a theory in vogue at a much later date, for example, it was the strongly held opinion of Aḥmad b. Idrīs al-Fāsī (d. 1837), who pursued such ideas in Arabia and the Middle East.
31. Abū'l-Qāsim b. Muḥammad b. al-Junayd, died 298/910, was one of the greatest exponents of the so-called 'sober' Ṣūfīsm. His *Rasā'il* have survived and his ideas deeply influenced later Ṣūfīsm, especially his views on the love of God, gnosis, annihilation of self, and the unification of the soul with God.
32. Ḥasan b. Alī Ṭālib, who allegedly died poisoned at the age of 45. A Shīᶜīte expression, 'May Allāh honour his countenance', is to be found in this passage.
33. Aghalangha is the *mashhad* of Shaykh Sīdī Maḥmūd. Unlike certain other sites in Aïr, al-Maghīlī has no especial associations with this important site.
34. Aḥmad b. Aḥmad b. Muḥammad al-Burnusī, al-Fāsī, (died 1493), was a widely travelled and saintly man who, according to the Timbuktu scholar Aḥmad Bābā, was the last of those who united within his person the mystic path and jurisprudence. His works are mentioned in Brockelmann, *GAL* ii, 253, *S* ii, 360–2.
35. Abū Muḥammad Sahl b. ᶜAbdallāh b. Yūnus was a *Sunni* theologican and mystic born at Tustar (al-Ahwāz) in 203/818. He died in Basra in 283/896. Attributed to him are his 'thousand sayings' which were collected and edited by his pupil, Muḥammad b. Sālim, (died 297/909). Some of his ideas foreshadow the notion of the *nūr Muḥammadī* of the later mystics (see the article on him in the *EI* under Sahl al-Tustarī). The source of the statement cited here has not been traced.
36. This statement may suggest that Shaykh Sīdī Maḥmūd did not regard his *ṭarīqa* (*ṭarīq* is often used in the text and translated as 'Way') as coming within the accepted pattern of any Ṣūfī 'order'; rather that his teaching offered a way of ascetic devotion which ran parallel to the strict rules of earlier existing *ṭuruq* or Ṣūfī 'Ways'. He appears to have turned the attention of his novices principally to the life of the Prophet himself as the ideal model (*qudwa*). See the comments to n. 30, and Conclusion.

The *Qudwa* also indicates that Sīdī Maḥmūd laid stress on an equitable balance between Ṣūfī practice and spiritual exercises and the demands of the *sharīᶜa*. At a far later date this was characteristic of the *Mirghāniyya*. Aḥmad b. ᶜAbd al-Raḥmān is cited as saying: 'Hold firmly, my brother, to the sharīᶜa, because you cannot approach the Reality (Ḥaqīqa) except through the "ṭarīqa" . . . "Sharīᶜa" is the root, "ṭarīqa" is the branch and "Ḥaqīqa" is the fruit. You cannot expect to find fruit except through the existence of [the] root, and [the] branch could not exist except through the root. He who sticks to the "sharīᶜa" and does not follow a Path is corrupt. He who follows a Path and does not stick to the "sharīᶜa" is a heretic.'

This passage is from the *Minḥat al-aṣḥāb*, by Aḥmad b. ᶜAbd al-Raḥmān al-Rūṭbī, quoted by R. S. Bhatnager, *Dimensions of Classical Sufi Thought* (Motilal Banarsidass, India, 1984), pp. 184–5.

Kissling has drawn attention to the danger that arose in the blind and unquestioning obedience of the dervish to the *shaykh*. It arose in the *Khalwatiyya*, and at a time close to Sīdī Maḥmūd himself: 'I am again referring to an example from the Halvatiyya. The following quotation, in which a well known sheikh of that order gives advice to a young relative of his who is inclined towards mysticism, speaks for itself:

"Do not follow the path of the Sufis, for there are no longer any real ones. *Tawḥîd* and *ilḥâd* are often difficult to distinguish, sometimes they cannot be told apart. Therefore, it is better for you to keep to the path of scholarship. But if you really desire to turn to Ṣufism, follow those sheikhs who stand firmly on the ground of the *sharīʿa*. If you meet a sheikh who, even in small matters, deviates from it, beware of him. For the fundament of *ṭarîqa* rests on the respect of all prescriptions and laws of the *sharīʿa*."

These remarks, uttered in 1526, indicate that, even then, the educational influence of the dervishes was not of the best. Although the insistence of many Sufis that they were remaining within the folds of the *sharīʿa* is well known, this quotation demonstrates a firm dissuasion which speaks well for the honesty and sincerity of the counselor.'

See Hans Joachim Kissling, 'The Sociological and Educational Role of the Dervish Orders in the Ottoman Empire', in G. E. Von Grunebaum (ed.), *Studies in Islamic Cultural History* (American Anthropological Association, vol. 56, no. 2, pt. 2, Memoir no. 76; April 1954), pp. 32–3.

6

Rules for the Hermitages in Aïr

A Chapter regarding their Assembling and the Appointment of some Companions of Shaykh Maḥmūd; Those who became Shaykhs and those who became Shaykhs from their Companions, may Allāh have Mercy upon them

When Sīdī Maḥmūd entered the land of the Maghrib he began to initiate, to appoint successors, and to give permission to [his followers] to go forth to [teach] the novices. He moved from country to country until he entered the land of Aïr. The people repented at his hand. Amongst them were the scholars (*ᶜulamā'*) and the students (*ṭalaba*), whilst others were the ignorant common-folk. Their number rose until it totalled almost one hundred. They were called the *fuqarā'* in this country.[1] They joined together in order to perform the *dhikr* of Allāh Almighty.[2]

It is reported from the Messenger of Allāh, His blessing and peace be upon him, that he said, in regard to the right hand of the Merciful—and both His hands are right hands—'They are men who are neither Prophets nor Martyrs. The whiteness [in colour] of their faces will strike the eyes [of those who behold them]. They will be made joyful and happy by the Prophets and the Martyrs in their seat and through their close proximity to Allāh, the Almighty.' He was [once] asked, 'Who are these men, O Messenger of Allāh?—His blessing be upon him.' He [the Prophet] said, 'They are a mixed company of strangers, from out of the tribes, who will gather together to perform Allāh's *dhikr*. They will let fall the sweetest of words, just as he who eats dates drips their choicest juices [from his saliva].' The word [which means] 'mixed company' (*jumāᶜ*) is spelt with a *ḍamma*, a 'u' vowel above the letter *jīm*. That denotes a confused crowd of men (*khilāṭ*), from varied tribes and from sundry places. The word 'strangers' (*nawāziᶜ*) is the plural form of *nāziᶜ* (*sic*, *nazīᶜ*?) This latter denotes a 'stranger'. What this means is that they did not join together due to any ties of kinship, nor on account of lineage, nor due simply to [a mutual] acquaintance. They only joined together for [the sake of] Allāh's *dhikr*, not for any other reason. As for his saying, 'the right hand of the Merciful', then you must know that 'the right hand', in respect of the Almighty, is a symbol of strength and of power. See the *Kitāb al-Lawāmiᶜ wa'l-asrār.*[3] His words—mighty and glorious He is—'the poor who have been detained in the path of Allāh are unable to make a journey . . .' to the end of the Qur'ānic verse. Also [addressed] to them are His words, 'Do not spurn those who call upon their Lord in the morning, and in the evening, seeking his face . . .' until the end of the verse.[4]

Ibn ᶜAbbās, may Allāh be pleased with him, said, 'The Messenger of Allāh, His blessing and peace be upon him, came upon "the People of the Bench"[5] and he beheld their poverty, their striving, and the goodness of their hearts. So he said, "Be glad O Companions of the Bench, whosoever from amongst my *umma* shall remain in the manner [of living] which you follow and is content with it, verily, he will be amongst my companions on the Day of Judgement." '[6] In al-Kirmānī it is said, 'They used to be few in number, or be many, and to increase in number due to those who came to them, and to grow less in number due to those who died or who journeyed away or who married, may Allāh be pleased with His Companions, all of them.'[7]

In the *Kitāb al-Jawāhir*[8] [it is reported that] a man said to Aḥmad b. Ḥanbal, 'These *fuqarā'* have forsaken their means of livelihood, their gains and their profits, and they have seated themselves in the mosques without any knowledge of learning.' Aḥmad said, 'It is knowledge that has made them sit in the mosques.' They said, 'Verily, they are preoccupied with eating crusts [of bread].' Aḥmad said, 'On the face of the earth I know not one who is more virtuous than such a people, who are sustained by Allāh by mere crusts of bread.'[9] [*This is continued*] *until he says* . . . 'Whosoever desires to follow in their path and to be one of their number, then his most important duty is to know the rulings of the *sharīᶜa* from the *uṣūl* of *fiqh* in regard to Allāh's obligations and what duties He has assigned, then he should be aware of what he cannot do without amongst those things which are connected with his livelihood. Then he should know the rulings of the science of theology and the gnosis of the mystics, then he should have a knowledge of the plagues of the soul which prompt evil thoughts and evil acts, then how to control his thoughts and how to purify his subconscious. Such is the science of gnosis. Then he should know the science of clairvoyance. Only he who has reached those stages (*maqāmāt*) can possess a knowledge of them.'[10]

It has been reported, quoting Abū Hurayra on the authority of the Prophet, the blessing and peace of Allāh be upon him, 'In regard to a knowledge of the awesomeness of that which is hidden and concealed, none possess an awareness [of it] save the gnostics of

Allāh. When they utter a pronouncement none denies it save those who have a meagre experience of Allāh.' *This is cited in the* Kitāb al-Jawāhir.

'The first of the "People of the Bench" were the *fuqarā'*. At the outset they were known as "the Guests of Allāh".[11] Amongst their number were to be counted one who was wealthy, another who was a prince, the trafficker (*al-mutasabbib*),[12] the independent trafficker, and the pauper. They expressed their thanks in time of prosperity just as they endured patiently when wealth was in scant supply. Those amongst them who were without wants did not depart from that [purpose] which their Lord had assigned them to carry out, namely that they should call upon their Lord in the morning and in the evening, seeking His will. Likewise, they were not commended for their living as paupers, rather it was on account of their desire to please Allāh, the Kingly Judge. The rule of the follower is identical to the rule of him who is followed in respect of the course which is followed, even if the one who is followed has a [clear] precedence.' *I have quoted here from the Qawā^{c}id of Shaykh Aḥmad al-Zarrūq.*[13]

A Chapter concerning the Rules of the dhikr

Amongst these rules, five precede the recitation of the *dhikr*. The first of them is [an act of] repentance (*tawba*). In order to accomplish this, the servant of Allāh forsakes that thing which is no concern of his, in word, in deed, and in desire.

The second rule is the washing, or the ritual ablution. Ritual ablution is the weapon of the true believer and the limbs of the body. If the ritual ablution is canonically valid and effective, then it removes the varied marks of Satan upon his members. The messenger of Allāh said, His blessing be upon him, 'The ritual ablution is [as] a light, let him who performs the *dhikr* go forth in purity, outwardly, inwardly, and observant of the word of Allāh Almighty, "I am seated beside him who remembers and recalls me." '[14]

The third rule is silence and stillness, so that the believer may attain truth and equity, betwixt the secret and the overt, because hearts are [as] vessels. When they are full of the truth they display an enhanced measure of their lights to the limbs of the body.

The fourth rule is that the believer hearkens with his heart when he commences the *dhikr*, through the zealousness of his Shaykh, since the heart of his Shaykh matches the heart of the Shaykh of his Shaykh, leading backwards to the Prophetic presence and to the heart of the Prophet [himself], the blessing and peace of Allāh be upon him. It is turned for ever in this way towards the Divine

Presence. He who performs the *dhikr*, when he pictures his Shaykh, and when he draws inspiration from his guardianship, then it is that the sustenance from the Divine Presence flows in its abundance upon the heart of the Lord of the Messengers, and from the heart of the Lord of the Messengers, the blessing and peace of Allāh be upon him, into the hearts of the *mashāyikh*, may Allāh Almighty be pleased with them, in turn, until his Shaykh is reached, and then into his own heart. He is strengthened by the words of the Almighty, 'If they seek for your help [in the religion], then to give help is an obligation which is imposed upon you in the religion.'[15]

The fifth rule is that he should regard the sustenance which he draws from his Shaykh as the drawing of sustenance from the Prophet, the blessing and peace of Allāh be upon him.

[This is] because he [the Shaykh] is his deputy, and it [that is, the sustenance] is from Allāh, the Truth—glory to Him—Almighty is His name. [It is] the *sunna* of Allāh, which, hitherto, was empty and vacuous. You will never find a substitute for the *sunna* of Allāh. This tie of the heart with the Shaykh is a major source [of spiritual power] in the spreading [of the divine presence], and you will find your inner soul turning to face him. By virtue of the [Prophet's] deputyship, he [the Shaykh] will become [a source of] mediation between the servant and the Lord.

What say you of a people whose task is to return runaway slaves to their Lord? Their principal task is to occupy the space between the servants of Allāh and their Lord. Almighty Allāh has said, 'They are the ones whom Allāh has guided aright so by their guidance be thou led.'[16]

Twelve [acts and positions] accompany the performance of the *dhikr*.

The first of them is that one should be seated upon a clean spot, just as one is seated during the statutory prayer, facing the direction of Mecca, if he who performs the *dhikr*, [the *dhākir*], is on his own. If a group comprise a company, then they should form a circle.

The second [condition] is that the *dhākir* should place both his hands upon both thighs, with his sleeves hanging down loosely, thereby they [in that company] may co-ordinate the communal movement of the individual heart [of each one of them].

The third [condition] is the scenting of the seating-place of the *dhikr* with a perfume which is pleasing to the brethren, because of the gathering there, and because of the presence of the angels, the believing *jinn* and the spirits of the saints. At times, the spirits of the Prophet and the Companions and the men of the divine secret and Shaykhs of the *ṭarīqa* [will attend]. This is the external act [of purification]. As for the internal act, it is the cleansing of that which is secret, and [in] the heart, from all that is not Allāh, following His words, 'O David, make a dwelling clean for me to dwell in, for neither my earth nor my heaven is sufficient for me. To suffice me, let it be the heart of my servant the true believer.'[17]

The fourth [condition] is the wearing of a fitting attire, in its loose fit and in its fragrance, on account of the saying of the Prophet, upon him be peace, 'cleanliness is of the faith'.[18] This is so that it can be of a lawful quality due to what has been reported of the Prophet, the blessing and peace of Allāh be upon him, who said, 'Whoever buys a garment for ten *dirhams* and in its price there be a single *dirham* which is unlawful (*ḥarām*), Allāh will not accept from him any sum in exchange, nor its requital (*ṣarf wa-ᶜadl*). His condition will be pure for his prayer to be valid.'

The fifth [condition] is the choice of a dark house, if it be possible, for it is there that the senses may be the most collected [for spiritual concentration].

The sixth [condition] is the lowering of the gaze, since this helps against external awareness, it blocks the paths of the external senses and so brings about an opening out of the inward senses of the heart.

The seventh [condition] is that he [the *dhākir*] should picture the form of the Shaykh before his eyes, and this is in view of the saying, 'the companion and then the road'.[19]

The eighth [condition] is [manifestation of] a candour and a sincerity which is [proof of] the attainment of an equilibrium between the secret kept within and the public expression [of it].

The ninth [condition] is an open frankness and the purifying of the act from every impurity. It is said, 'If by obedience to Allāh he [the *dhākir*] desires to come close to Him, glorious He is, then it is only by sincerity that he is saved from hypocrisy and by truth he is saved from pride and from self-admiration.'

The tenth [condition] is that he [the *dhākir*] should choose out of the *dhikr* the expression, 'There is no god but Allāh.'[20] With the maximum of force he should utter it aloud, making *lā ilāha* into a crescendo [of sound] above the navel from the space which separates the two flanks [of his body], and that he should link *illā'allāh* with the 'physical heart', which is situated between the two bones of the chest and the stomach, inclining his head to the left side in the presence of the 'spiritual heart'. Sahl b. ᶜAbdallāh said,[21] 'When you say *lā ilāha illā'allāh* prolong the words and look hard at the Eternal Truth. Cleave to Him, all else is worthless.'

The eleventh [condition] is that he [the *dhākir*] has the meaning of the *dhikr* ever present in his heart all the time.

The twelfth [condition] is for him [the *dhākir*] to banish all [dross] that is present from his heart by the words *lā ilāha* in order to facilitate the impact of *illā'allāh* in the heart, and so that it may pass through the members in accordance with the words, 'it is incumbent upon a man that when he says *Allāh* he should quake from the crown of his head to his toe. This is a state which indicates that he is one who is progressing upon the path, that there is hope for him, and that he will attain to one which is higher, if Allāh so wills it.'[22]

As for the three [four? conditions[23]] which follow the completion of the *dhikr*, the first of them is that he [the *dhākir*] when he is silent, should be still and be humble. He attends with his heart, watchful for the sudden inspiration of the divine influence in the *dhikr* (*wārid al-dhikr*), [namely] the prompting of a mystic state which perchance will evoke a response in him and which may enliven his presence in an instant in such a way that is not to be achieved by religious exercises, and by strenuous efforts, for over thirty years. The second [condition] is that he [the *dhākir*] should blame himself, and should do so repeatedly, since it is the speediest way for the enlightenment of his vision and for the disclosing of the hidden, in the severing of the thoughts of the self and of Satan, since he [the *dhākir*], when he blames himself, becomes like one who has died. He blames himself three times over or more. The second [condition, likewise] is a [total] stillness, so that nothing stirs, just like a she-cat when it hunts a mouse. The third [condition] is the banishment of thoughts. The fourth [condition] is that one of the names of Allāh flow upon the tongue [of the *dhākir*]. Perhaps He will respond to him and will enliven his heart at an instant when no effort or religious exercise has done this during more than thirty years, even if he observe and follow them scrupulously and repeatedly. The fourth [condition] is [also] that he should refrain from drinking quickly. This is because the *dhikr* leaves a burning [sensation], a feeling of longing and of excitement, for Him who is recalled, and [indeed] such is sought for in the *dhikr* [itself]. However, the drinking of water [hastily] after the *dhikr* extinguishes that and it has been condemned [likewise] on medical grounds.

The voices [of the participants] must be in unison. The words should be united together as they are uttered, because this is a factor in the manifestation of the spirit of the *dhikr*, which is the very life of the hearts of those who are participants in it. These rules impose upon him who takes part in the *dhikr* [some] elements of personal choice. As for him who is robbed of any choice, when his mind is no longer his own, then this is due to the unseen vision which [he who experiences] is vouchsafed. Indeed, he will become as one who is compelled [against his will], as one who cannot control himself, or who cannot grasp it, since he, on account of what he receives in responding to *dhikrs*, may experience a flow of words upon his tongue; *Allāh*, *Allāh*, or *Huwa*, *Huwa*, *Illā*, *Illā*, or :A:A:A with an extended *Alif* (*madda*), or AAA, with a shortening [to a] or to :Ah:Ah:A or *HāHā* or else a clamour, uttered without any [defined] letter. Some of them moan, and some of them cry aloud, and some of them utter [a statement] with an eloquent tongue. All of it is valid, uttered by a broken heart, some of them weeping and finding no rest save by acting so. Some of them clap their hands and cannot still their hearts except by acting thus. He who cannot attain the universal (*al-kull*)[24] says 'for shame!' (*uff*, *uff*, *tuff*, *tuff*) putting away his heart's wickedness and its baseness.[25]

It is his [the *dhākir*'s] rule that he should submit himself to the voice of the visitation of the divine meaning in the *dhikr*. According to Malik b. Dīnār, who said, 'In the Old Testament it is written, "We have prompted you by our caring, yet you had no longing, we have piped to you but you have not danced." '[26]

According to Wahb b. Munabbih,[27] 'When Allāh created Adam, peace be upon him, in the most perfect form, when He clothed him in the raiment of Paradise, gave him ten fingers on his hands and ten toes on his feet, placed ankle bangles around his legs, clad him in bracelets upon his forearms, placed a necklace around his neck, crowned him with a crown, or else with a garland upon his head and his brow, and He gave him an agnomen which He loved best of all, He said, "O father of Muḥammad, go around in Paradise and see if a little finger(?) equals yours or whether I have created another one who is superior to you?" So he went around in Paradise but he did not see one who was better than himself. He was proud and he strutted in Paradise. Allāh took a delight in his acting thus, and he called to him from His throne, saying, "Be proud, Adam, for it is fitting for you to boast that if you desire something then I shall create it exactly as desired. Your creation is unique, so let us say, 'to Allāh is due the pride which is to be observed in his descendants'." Amongst the ignorant it is the dance, amongst kings it is lordly pride, and amongst the saints it is ecstasy.'

Likewise, after that, his voice of visitation having ended, and he is at peace, so also it is his [the *dhākir*'s] duty to resign himself to tranquillity and to silence and, as long and as much as he can, also, to keep his attention centred upon his voice. Allāh is the One who grants the attainment of that which is true and correct. In the *Kitāb al-Jawāhir* it is said that Aḥmad b. Ḥanbal was asked [a question], 'These Ṣūfīs listen in the mosques, will they dance and take delight in a mutual ecstasy?' He said, 'Let them be full of joy in Allāh, for they have sorrowed long.' The *samā*ᶜ[28] is both *ḥālāl* and *ḥārām*. That which is meet to be considered unlawful is that [form of] *samā*ᶜ during which the women celebrate [it] with their verses. In it they evoke love poetry, they describe carnal love, and they call for amatory passion, they yearn after unlawful and carnal desire and [amatory] sport. Now this is *ḥarām*. That which is *ḥalāl* mentions Allāh Almighty, guides towards Him, longs for Him, and it stirs the hearts of believers to [heed] His words. Amongst the categories of *samā*ᶜ is joyous exclamation (*tahlīl*).[29] It produces a response.

What was ambiguous and was suspect was allowed and it evoked the *ḥarām*. Or what was *ḥarām*, yet prompted the truth, is *ḥalāl*. [It was made so] by the sincerity of the intention. The first [instance] is just like the *ḥarām* on account of the evil of the intention. Thus it is *ḥarām* [notwithstanding] because of his saying [in the *Kitāb al-Jawāhir*], 'I was told by the *faqīh* Aḥmad b. Muḥammad al-Tabbāᶜ [the follower], by word of mouth, that Mūsā b. ᶜImrān,[30] peace be upon him, when he went forth to Mount Sinai, was accomplished by Gabriel and by Michael. Both of them were performing the *tahlīl* and were raising their voices. That was mentioned amongst the miracles of his *mashāyikh*, and it was reported by Abū Mimshād al-Dīnawarī, that he saw the Messenger of Allāh, His blessing and peace be upon him, and he said to him, "Do you [O Prophet] disapprove of anything of this *samā*ᶜ?" He answered, "I disapprove of nothing, but say to them that before it [takes place] they should open with the reading of the Qur'ān and that, at its end, they should close it with the reading of the Qur'ān" . . . *until he says* . . . "It is heard (*samā*ᶜ) on account of three purports, love, hope, and fear. Ecstasy and goodness have three signs; dancing, clapping, and joyfulness. Fear has three signs; concealment, rootlessness(?), and shrieking. Yearning has three signs; much weeping, rising up, and gazing heavenwards. He who is the master of the situation needs three things; humbleness, gaiety, and generosity of heart" . . . *until he remarks* . . . "If a *khirqa*[31] should fall, then it is handed to the *naqīb*, and if its owner is present then he buys it [back] from the *fuqarā'*. He allows them to wear it and they divide it up just as the mantle of the Messenger of Allāh, His blessing and peace be upon him, was divided, or else they sell it, or it is given as alms for the sake of *baraka*. Know that the *dhikr* banishes Satan and subdues him and breaks him and curbs and deters him. It banishes care and grief from the heart and it brings joy and happiness. It removes sluggishness(?) and evil things. It strengthens the heart and the body. It restores the uppermost point of the back, it gladdens the heart and the face and it fills it with light. It gathers provision and it makes easy the latter. It clothes him who performs the *dhikr* in awesomeness. He is inspired by it in every affair. Whosoever has a tongue which is for ever moist with his *dhikr*, who fears Allāh, in what He commands and He prohibits, has cause to enter Paradise of the beloved, and [to enjoy] a close proximity to the presence of the Lord of Lords. The angels will seek the pardoning of the servant of Allāh when he cleaves to the *dhikr* and to praising. The valleys and the mountains are beautified by the one who remembers Allāh [standing] upon the top of them, be he a man or a woman. It is the *sunna* of the true believer who is thankful. The *dhikr* has delights which are sweeter than [the taste of] food that is savoured and drink which is enjoyed. The face of the *dhākir*, as well as his heart, will be clothed in the [physical] world with brightness, with beauty and with joy, and in the world to come it will be whiter than the moon and the light. The *dhākir* is quick though he be dead, whilst he who is neglectful is dead though he be living. Allāh is the One who bestows the knowledge of the true and the correct." '[32]

A Chapter concerning their wird

As for their *wird*,[33] it is the prayer which prays for blessings upon the Prophet, the blessing and peace of Allah be upon him (*ṣallā Allāhu ᶜalayhi wa sallam*). It is one thousand of such prayers, every Friday night, and one hundred every night, coupled to the *wird* of the sunset prayer. This is due to the saying of the Prophet, the blessing and peace of Allāh be upon him, 'Whoever prays a *ṣalāt* one thousand times on a Friday, saying, "O Allāh, bless Muḥammad, Your servant and Your Messenger, the illiterate Prophet" . . .*to its end* . . . verily, he will behold me at night in [his] sleep, or his abode and dwelling in Paradise, or else he will see his Lord . . .' *Here ends the quotation*[34] *from Ibn Hishām al-Qurṭubī.*[35] They recite a few verses from the *ᶜIshrīniyya*[36] and the *Witrāniyya*[37] and the last four verses of the *Burda*,[38] on Thursday night and Friday night and Monday night, and so too on the superior days [of feasting], such as the two *ᶜĪds*,[39] on the birthday of the Prophet.[40]

It is reported from ᶜAbdallāh b. ᶜĪsā[41] [who said], 'Whosoever recites the Qur'ān, blesses the Prophet Muḥammad—the blessing and peace of Allāh be upon him—and who prays to Allāh, expects good [to come to him] in the place where its presence is [to be] expected.' Most of their prayer for blessing is, 'The blessing and peace of Allāh be upon our lord, Muḥammad, your servant and your Messenger, the illiterate Prophet, upon his family and upon his

Companions.' It is quoted from Abū Huraya, may Allāh be pleased with him, that the Messenger of Allāh, His blessing and peace be upon him, said, 'Whosoever prays the *ᶜaṣr* prayer on a Friday, before he arises [from his place of prayer he should say], "O Allāh, blessings be upon Muḥammad the illiterate Prophet, upon his family and his Companions," doing so eighty times. He will be pardoned of his sins for eighty years, and worship for eighty years will be entered upon his record.' Whosoever so wishes it, then let him say what he wishes of the *taṣliya* at other than the hour of the *wird*, as [for example] their words uttered on a Thursday night, and on a Monday night, namely offering the *hadiyya*.[42]

The Wird *which they Follow in regard to the Fast*

They diligently keep their fast on Monday and on Thursday, and in the month of *Rajab*, and nine days out of the month of *Dhū'l-Ḥijja*, and as for him who wishes so, then he may fast as he wishes,[43] if such be ordered as a practice to be followed in their Way(?)

Following the 'Way'

Their 'Way' is the path of conformity. It is the business of none to add to it, nor should he subtract anything from it. Whosoever is guilty of the latter, if it be due to some incapacity, then his hope is that he be pardoned and it is to be sought for him. If it be on account of a shortcoming [on his part] or due to a weakness of will, then no blessing will be given to him in his activities and the Shaykh, or the *muqaddam*, or the companions, will command him to repent and to provide a sin offering; [that is], if he be amongst those who are firmly established amongst them and joined to them. They will command him to do one of three things: either he gives some of his wealth, or some service, or else he retires into a retreat, on account of that which was reported from Kaᶜb b. Mālik[44] who said to the Messenger of Allāh, His blessing and peace be upon him, 'My repentance will be that I divest myself of all my wealth and that I shall flee from the dwelling of my people wherein I committed my sin.' The Prophet, the blessing and peace of Allāh be upon him, said to him, 'One third will be your requital.' Thus it became a *sunna*, together with service of some kind or a retreat. Whosoever is not an established member amongst them, him they banish from their *ribāṭ*.[45]

If the Shaykh finds something wrong in the training of the novices and the instructing of the students, whosoever offends the sight, and if he has transgressed the divine statutes of Allāh, mighty and glorious He is, he [the Shaykh] is permitted to allow a flogging to be administered to him and a punishment, as a deterrent, because he is the *Amīr* over them. But if he does not transgress the bounds of Allāh, yet has something about a matter which is none of his business, or he has busied himself in that which is worthless, or he has blamed someone, or he has made mention of a missing person, or he has blamed one who is present, or he has forsaken a charge, or he has neglected his *wirds*, or who has been very noisy in his behaviour, or the like, then he orders him to repent seeking the pardon of Allāh Almighty on account of his [the Prophet's] words, 'They have wronged themselves, let them remember Allāh and seek His forgiveness from their sins.'[46] Let his chastening be in the presence of the brethren, facing the *qibla*, purposing with all his heart that he will never commit this sin again. In rectifying him it is the opinion of the Shaykh which counts most, in weight, in regard to the length [of chastisement] or its brevity, in accordance with the gravity of the misdemeanour [in question]. Then one of them approaches him [who is disciplined] and he remains standing [from a position] in the direction of the *qibla*. He advances his right foot, then his left, then the other follows his action with his right foot and then with his left. He takes him on the right and on the left because he is beloved of Allāh, since Allāh Almighty has said, 'Verily Allāh loves those who are repentant.'[47] The Prophet, peace be upon him, said, 'The repentant is beloved of Allāh.'[48] If the Shaykh is present, then it is the *naqīb* who acts in this way. If he is absent then the *naqīb* directs one of the brethren and he will take his place. Having finished this act [of repentance] they are filled with joy since he [the offender] had distressed them by his deeds.

What is Incumbent on those of the 'Way'

It is incumbent upon members of the 'Way' that they should adhere firmly to it. Know that the path of Allāh Almighty is remote from [the path of] disputes. Ostentation is [the cause of] argument and dispute. Contrition is called for since [dispute] cannot be tolerated. There is no dissent [between them], nor heresy [harboured], nor fashion in regard to what [offence] leads to an expulsion from their 'Way'. Any reproval amongst them is with the tongue. They avoid meddling in that [matter] which is not allowed by the canonic law (*sharīʿa*), though they show a tolerance in their rights in regard to that [issue] which arises amidst them alone. One of the conditions laid down by the people of this 'Way' is that they deal equitably and justly with their fellows. They do not rule like lords. They deal mercifully with men, by kindness and by showing care. In those matters which are of mutual concern they deal with them as their counsellors. One amongst their number does not give to his companion something that this 'Way' of theirs does not demand. If they are equal in their rank, yet one who is active and enterprising markedly surpasses another, then deference shown to the former, by the latter, is obligatory.

There is no hatred, no begrudging, nor mutual envy amongst them in regard to the gifts of Allāh Almighty. It is a condition made by them that they do not interrupt each other. They eschew an objection, unless he who objects be of a higher status, for in that situation politeness allows for it. But if he [the objector] is of a lower status, then he must be silent and he must ask to be pardoned. If he finds a fault and takes exception then he invalidates the basis of the obligation of his 'Way', for, verily, they are the people of truth. They only speak about what they perceive with their eyes. When a novice visits a Shaykh, then let him empty his heart of all his thoughts so that he may be receptive to what the Shaykh conveys, and so that no censure or disapprobation may occur. If what is unacceptable to him be offered, then he should blame himself [for it]. He ought to say, 'This is a situation that is none of my doing,' and the error should not be attributable to him.

If they see a sinner in an act of disobedience, they do not believe [him to be guilty of] the worst self-wilfulness. They say, 'Perchance he has repented secretly,' or 'Perhaps, he is amongst those whom sin will not taint.' They think ill of no-one. If they perceive in him but a glimpse of the supernatural they display no jealousy towards him nor do they deem themselves to be better than any other.

One of their habits is the purification of the self from all that is base, and its adornment by every noble trait of character. They tolerate an injury, they blame no other man, and they encourage those things which promote piety. They succour the aggrieved, they guide the stray. They teach the ignorant. All those who seek after them come to them. They deny not the beggar, they feed the guest, they show affection to the outcast. They give sanctuary to him who is fearful, they fill the hungry [with food], and they quench the thirst of the thirsty. They clothe the naked and they enrich the brethren with all that they possess, relying upon Allāh, alone, in all their affairs. They accept all unpleasantness which comes their way with a good grace, showing patience and fortitude in the face of pain, fleeing from humanity without believing ill of them, rather, preferring the Creator to the creation and endeavouring to fulfil the needs of men after emptying their hearts and their souls.

They resolve neither to shave a hair nor to shorten it, nor to clip a nail, nor do they divest themselves of any garment which they give to another, unless it be for the sake of purity. They are the people of contentment, which is true self-knowledge, having been filled without an excess of covetousness.

Another habitual practice of theirs is to behold their faults and their failings, to be preoccupied with [faults in] themselves, seeming blind to the faults of other men, keeping their silence except in regard to that which relates to the good. They avert their gaze from prying [into others' affairs]. They command the doing of good and the eschewing of evil. They are blameless in regard to the whole of the creation. They pray for Muslims within the depth of their hearts, they encourage the service of the *fuqarā'*, and they encourage care and mercy and the showing of it to all the servants of Allāh, even to animals. The Prophet, the blessing and peace of Allāh be upon him, said, 'The servant [*al-khādim*] is in the safe keeping of Allāh, as long as the servant serves the true believer, and for the servant in service will be the reward of him who fasts by day, and of him who arises to adore in the night, the reward of those who struggle in the way of Allāh, Mighty and Glorious He is, whose efforts will not relax, and the reward of the pilgrim, be he travelling in the month of pilgrimage, or at any other time to the holy places, the reward of him who is put to the test and the reward of all who are righteous in the earth. Blessed be the servant on the Day of Judgement and Resurrection! No debt nor punishment will face him. He who serves mankind will be granted mediation on that day, just like that granted to the tribes of Rabīᶜa and Muḍar.'

Anas said, 'I said, "O Messenger of Allāh, his blessing and peace be upon him, if the servant be a transgressor, what then?" He said, "O Anas, the bad servant is preferable, in the eyes of Allāh, to an adorer who is diligent, and to him who earns but who anticipates his reward in the hereafter. For the servant who labours there will be the reward of him whom he serves, with no diminution in his reward." '[49]

The Holy Ten

The Messenger of Allāh said, 'There are ten who will not be left in their tombs, but they will pray before Allāh, mighty and glorious He is, until the last trump is blown. [They are] the Prophets, the martyrs, the callers to prayer, those who die in the path to Mecca, the women who die in labour, those who repent of their sins and the servant of the Muslims in obedience to Allāh Almighty, those who pray at night when men sleep and those who show mercy and pity to the poor of my *umma*. The marks which show the fall of grace from the eye of Allāh are threefold: self-satisfaction, discontentedness with the will of Allāh, contesting the Truth by fatalism and predestination. The signs of closeness to Allāh Almighty are three: the forsaking of [belief in] luck and fortune and the following of the truth, humility before Allāh Almighty, amongst His creation. The signs of union with Allāh are three: an understanding mind in regard to Allāh Almighty, listening to Allāh, and submission in respect to him.'

Earning a Livelihood

Included in their rules is the earning of a livelihood for one of their number who supports a family and descendants. Their rule in this regard is that it should not be a preoccupation to distract them from the fulfilling of obligations to Allāh, Mighty and Glorious He is, at the hours laid down, but [one of them] tries to fix the hours of his activity from the hour of forenoon to the end of the hour of the noon prayer. He then returns to his companions and prays all the five prayers with them until the forenoon of the next day. If from his earnings there be anything left over from his familial maintenance, then he lays it on one side for his brethren and for those who are his companions.

The Chastening of the Brethren

Included within their rules is chastening of the brethren. Their purpose, thereby, is to eliminate entirely the element of an assuaging of one's individual and personal anger and wrath, nay, rather, the aim is to purify the heart [altogether] from rancour and from hate, and to accept the excuse of him who is blameworthy, for truly it has been said, 'Accept excuses from him who comes to you with an apology. He is cleared in your eyes over what has been said or in respect of an evil committed, for he who seeks to make you happy, openly, manifests his obedience to you while he, having disobeyed you in private, holds you in esteem.' It is also said, 'An open rebuke is better than a concealed hate.' Another saying tells of the manifestation of a joyous countenance to whosoever, in no circumstances, deserves it.

Their rule in regard to that should be that the aim sought is to seek for peace and for reconciliation, freed from all hypocrisy and deceit, because of the words in a *ḥadīth* of ᶜĀ'isha, may Allāh be pleased with her, when a Jew sought entry and permission to enter was granted to him, and the Messenger of Allāh received him with a smile. When he had departed. ᶜĀ'isha said to the Prophet, 'Why did you receive him with a smile?' He said, 'O ᶜĀ'isha, verily [among] the most evil of men is the one whom mankind honours and extols for fear of the obscenity of his speech.'[50]

Other examples may be seen in the consolation of the poets and of others like them. The rule which they follow in this respect is that they protect their honour from the poets' tongue, and the safety of the religion from them, giving to them what [favours] they ask. Some have even paid them money so that they would not slur them. The Prophet, the blessing and peace of Allāh be upon him, said, 'The sum given by a man to protect his honour should be accounted a charity.'[51] Another illustration of this is the suffering of fools for the sake of peace and for the warding off of injuries. The rule which they observe in all of this is that one amongst their number should make it his intention to protect his person and that he should have no other aim or motive in view. Al-Aḥnaf b. Qays said, 'Honour your fools, for, verily, they will guard you from Hell-fire and from disgrace.'[52] It has been reported of Ibn Sīrīn[53] that he said that Ibn ᶜUmar,[54] may Allāh be pleased with him, used to astonish him by the way he made a fool of his companion, thereby averting the levity of the foolish.

The Private Retreat (khalwa)

Amongst their rules is the entry into the cell of private retreat. This [practice] is based on the established tradition concerning his [the Prophet's] retreat, the blessing and peace of Allāh be upon him, in the cave of Ḥirā',[55] at the start of his mission, the blessing and peace of Allāh be upon him. Al-Suhrawardī said,[56] 'This is the origin behind the choice, by the *mashāyikh*, of the cell of private retreat for their neophytes and for their novices. Verily, when they devote themselves, fully and sincerely, to Allāh in their retreat, then He will bestow upon them that thing which will keep them company in their retreats as a compensation to them from Allāh.'

As for their saying, 'The cell [of retreat] is a constant [preoccupation], there is constancy in watching for Allāh Almighty and the vision of the heart [being one of] close proximity to Allāh until all else, other than Allāh, is forgotten.'

The Hour of Retreat

Amongst their rules is their entry into a retreat after the *ᶜishā'* prayer on a Tuesday night. They leave it after the sunset prayer on Friday night. For three days and nights they fast during the day-time until night falls, following the Qur'ānic injunction, 'He has revealed to them that they should glorify Allāh'—that is to pray—or 'extol' your Lord—'in the morning and in the evening.'[57] This is an absolute command to glorify Allāh; His people were [thereby] commanded to adapt it to the *dhikr* and to give thanks. In the book [called] *Tuḥfat al-murīdīn*,[58] [it is stated] that one ought to come forth from the solitary retreat and from meditation after the sunset prayer, unless the time of the solitary retreat should fall at the end of *Ramaḍān*. Then the inmate should stay in the place where he spends his retreat until he leaves it in order to celebrate *ᶜId al-Fiṭr* in accordance with their practice, and afterwards he should go from the common place of prayer to his house.

The Rules of Discipline in the khalwa

One of their rules is the seeking of the Shaykh's permission to come before his presence and to receive confirmation for an act of contrition and of repentence. The [token of] intention of him who seeks the same is that he performs an act of withdrawal and of humility whereby mankind will be relieved of his wickedness, and, at the same time, he asks for the protection of Allāh Almighty from the evil of the heart, sincerely and frankly before Allāh. In acting thus they may gather around the Shaykh and whosoever harbours a complaint against him in this respect will ask for his correction. Prayers will be said upon the point of entry, for success and for reconciliation and for the felicitation in this matter upon every one of them. Upon leaving the gathering, none of them utters a word. They pray two *rakᶜas* upon their prayer rugs. Upon entry every one of them says, 'O Lord, cause me to enter through a portal of Truth, Glory to Allāh Almighty. May the beneficient Lord of ancient might and dominion [convert him, the offender] from Satan the stoned.[59] O Lord open to us the gates of Thy Mercy.' They offer a recitation of the *fātiḥa* and they begin to speak. The *dhikr* continues, uninterrupted, except for the statutory prayer. When they hear someone reciting the *wird*, then they are content to hear it [said by him], but if he be at a distance from them, then they recite the *wird* [aloud to themselves]. If one who is resident in a retreat can have two pairs of sandals [with him], one of the privy, and the other for the mosque, then he has both [pairs] with him, so that if he desires to retire then he goes out with his staff and his leather bag for purification, on account of the saying of Yaᶜqūb (?), by his chain of authority going back to Anas b. Mālik[60] who said, 'The Messenger of Allāh, His blessing and peace be upon him, whenever he went forth for his ablutions, had water brought to him by me and he would wash with it.' ᶜAbdallāh b. Muḥammad[61] said, through a chain of authority, also, to Ibn ᶜAbbās, that the Prophet of Allāh, His blessing and peace be upon him, entered into the privy and I placed an ablution for him there. He asked who had done this and was informed, so he said, 'Oh Allāh, instruct him in the faith.' It is reported by al-Bukhārī,[62] 'No [inmate] also leans his back against a wall when in retreat, and keeps his silence, without recalling Allāh [in his mind].' They have said, 'In every word which is uttered, without necessity, spiritual light will go forth with it.'

Only the Shaykh or the *khādim* of the *fuqarā'* may speak to someone regarding his need or his requirement, and if they are at the corporate prayer, and especially if he be on his own, because should he miss the command to go forth then he may find none to join with him.

Let them not be lukewarm in their *dhikr* [of Allāh]. Let the eater [of food], who is a devout man, be neither one who eats to satiation, nor one whose hunger is unappeased. Let any grease which is used in his food be other than the fat of animals. Let him banish thoughts and fancies, be they good or evil. If the believers are beginners [in their devotions] and if, and when, they wish to go forth, then each one of them must say, 'My Lord, bring me forth through a portal of Truth, O Allāh, open to us the gates of Your favour.' They will leave between the prostration and the recitation of the Maghrib prayer *ḥizb*[63] with the shaking of hands. They will pass that night there and they will not utter a word.

Other Rules of the khalwa

[Here follow] other [rules] than those [mentioned above], together with a description of the *khalwa* and its affairs. As for the description of the cell concerned, it should have [a sufficient] height and a roof so as to enable you to stand upright with your hands stretched upwards. This measurable span applies equally to its length and to its breadth, but should it be a span above that which I have [just] mentioned then there is no harm in that [being so]. Something close to a [given] measure is deemed to be that measure. In the cell there should be neither aperture, nor orifice, nor niche, nor cellar [cave] where it is located, nor is it a place where you can be visited.[64] It should be remote from the dead. Its door should be short, firmly fixed and not elaborate.

You will be [a dweller] in a settled village, but you will be at a distance from its inhabitants so that none may pass the night at the door of the retreat. Be not on intimate terms with anyone, for, verily, the retreat is not the family retreat.

As for your situation in the midst of it, then, at the very outset, you should clean your garment, for there is no room for such an activity within the cell itself. You should increase the number of superogatory duties and habits and perform two *rakᶜas* at the time of every [act of] purification from the motion of the bowels or from the passing of the bladder. You must maintain your purity at such times as you face the *qibla*, constantly practising the *dhikr* and reciting the Qur'ān at night-time, when awake, and in the daytime always fasting. One should practise this persistently and one should not go forth [from the cell] unless it be for human need.

Your privy should not be [sited] far from your retreat. When you do go out, then guard yourself against [the inclination to drink from] the pool of water [there], for this will influence you [unhealthily], rather let your supply of water be, together with the privy, in adjacent surroundings at a point approximately half a mile from your cell. Make sure that your water does not change its texture and colour, that it does not become stagnant, nor turbid, nor undrinkable, for this [impurity] will cause you to suffer a disorder for some long while.

When you go forth to fulfil your [bodily] need then shut your eyes and close your ears. If you wish to take a morsel to eat then do so, but over it name its Creator, out of humility and need, watchfulness, and expectancy, until you know that it has settled at the mouth of the stomach. After that take another morsel and absorb it in a manner like the first. Continue in this wise until you have finished your meal. Let the water that you drink be sipped slowly. From time to time interrupt your draught. Do not suffer an immoderate hunger nor be satiated by heavy eating. Wear clothes which fit the size of your body and which, like your eating [habits], will leave [you] with no feelings of guilt. Do not slumber nor sleep except when you are overcome by drowsiness. Do not kill animals, kill not an ant nor a similar creature[65] and if you are fearful that vermin should be present at your head then you should shave it.

The Friday Prayer

Amongst the rules [of the *Maḥmūdiyya ṭarīqa*] is the Friday eve which is spent in prayer and other such rules, and that a member [of it] should pass the night and take his siesta in his place until he attends the Friday prayer.[66] If you wish to participate in it, wash with the statutory ablution for major sins which have been committed (*al-janāba*). Clean your clothes and make the close presence of Allāh Almighty your intention.[67] It is imperative that [a brother] should only appear, at times when it takes place, when his Shaykh commands him to appear there for some common benefit which will accrue to the other *fuqarā'*. The meaning of the happenings of the *dhikr* is only known to [the participants in] the *dhikr*, when it is performed, for he who is a mere deliberator is a one who is isolated. He is outside those who participate in it.

May Allāh Almighty have mercy upon you [all], know that prayer in seclusion has virtues which are purposed within the *sharīʿa*, namely the curbing of self-will, devoted attention paid to obedience, constant readiness to prepare for one statutory prayer after another, abandonment of a preoccupation with the affairs of this world, their avoidance, [and instead,] the fixing of one's vision upon the world to come and upon kindred matters. Such, then, are the fruits of solitary prayer and of meditation. Whosoever is solitary in a mosque, but his heart pursues those things which are not his concern in the affairs of this world, [then] how far is such a man from the reality of solitary prayer! This is especially so if he mentions the *dhikr* with his tongue, and he prostrates with his body in prayer, but he lacks the presence [of Allāh] in the [devotion] of his heart and of his mind, roaming at will amidst worldly matters, and their like, in all their futility. The heart is the pole (*quṭb*) upon which attention is fixed. It is the ultimate dependable source and the seat of human decision.

Visiting

One of their rules is visiting. For that reason Shaykh Abū Madyan,[68] may Allāh be pleased with him, said, 'O my brother, it is your duty to visit the *mashāyikh* wherever they may be, because in so visiting them there are to be found praiseworthy qualities and virtues. The first of these is the increase of faith and of assurance, an inward knowledge of the spiritual life, an increase and gain in moral character and the knowledge of the *ṭarīqa*, and a knowledge of reward and of recompense.' He said, 'Eighty Shaykhs agreed to visit the *mashāyikh* and to acquire a praiseworthy status from them. Whosoever visits a saint, although he does not acquire something of his state [of sainthood] he will not be free of his *baraka*.' They [also] cited what has been said by the *Imām* al-Shāfiʿī, 'There is no joy which compares with the companionship of the brethren and no distress that compares with being separated from them. Were it not for the discourse of the brethren I should not desire to remain in this [temporal] abode.'

Visiting Tombs[69]

One of their rules is the pilgrimage which they make to tombs. As was said by Shaykh al-Mashbaḥdhī(?),[70] 'The most beneficial experience for a novice is [to enjoy] the company of the pious, [in] the visiting of the tombs of the saints and [in] the service of kind and companionable masters.' Abū'l-Muhājirīn[71] went further in regard to this. He said, 'May Allāh have mercy upon persons who have visited the tombs of their brethren in their hearts. They are in their [Meccan-orientated] niches of prayer (*maḥārīb*) on account of it.' One of the men of love exclaimed, 'O company of those who love one another, how were you [ever] in a situation to endure [in your person], and to cope with, [the bidding of] farewells? Did you [too] suffer the pangs of the pain of separation or did you find the patience to endure the parting from [your] loved ones when the breeze of separation blew and the fires burned in the hearts of those who love and they lamented? When they mourned, [then] hearts absorbed from other hearts the odour of a burning fire. Hearts were impulsive, minds were intoxicated, and bitter was the weeping and the lamenting. You behold men who are drunk but they are not intoxicated. Because those who love one another, when they drink from the cup of the vision of a parting, are intoxicated by the spectacle of separation. This is because the sight of separation is [as] a draught. A lover has only to drink it and he will cast on one side all his shame' . . . *to where he says* . . . 'To be separated from loved ones is a misfortune. It has no consolation. It is a sickness that has no cure and its pains are only suffered by loving because the [pains at the] parting of lovers are [as] arrows which only fall into the hearts of those of mutual love for Allāh, Almighty. Parting is [as] an unsheathed sword. The only victims are virile youth amongst the free, and their wounds are suffered in the battlefields of [men's] hearts. None knows the qualities of separation, nor endures it and suffers it, but them; they, the lovers.' *Here ends the quotation from* [*his book*], Kanz al-asrār wa mustaqarr al-anwār.[72]

Constant Purity

Amongst their rules is constant purity. As one of them said, 'I hate to be impure.' When a brother arises in the daytime and he finds no water, he will strike his hands upon the wall and he will perform the dry ablutions (*tayammum*),[73] guarding his purity, until he finds water. They have said, 'The *faqīr* finds no sleep without having water at hand, and by his side, for his purification.'

The Eschewal of the Sinful

They make it a rule to forsake the company of [their] adversaries. Abū ᶜAlī says, 'The companionship of the wicked is a malady suffered and its medicine cures by separation from them.'[74] One of them said, 'Being a neighbour to the wicked is sinfulness.' Or as Abū Suᶜūd[75] said, 'Witnessing the presence of the heedless is a deadly poison, despite a compassion towards them, because one of the duties of the novice is that he remove his zealous concern far away from the base men of the world, nor should his hopes be placed on those who are most worthy of the same. Verily, their company is to be feared by him who takes the covenant. Do you not see that Allāh has commanded His Prophet, His blessing and peace be upon him, with the words, 'Be patient in your heart, together with those who call upon their Lord and do not obey the people of the world for they are people of indifference' . . . *to his words* . . . 'Do not obey him whose heart we have turned away from our remembrance.' Whoever you find to be godless, a follower of desire, do not be his companion. Speak not to him.'[76]

They have said, 'Whosoever is the bosom companion of another is the recipient of his character and his nature from a source which he cannot identify. Do not be a companion of the word of doubt, flee from him who utters it, for he is more ravaging than a wolf and know that his sins are malignant, just as the mange is malignant.'

They used to compare beguilement with women and the inclination [of men] towards them, until they said, 'The greatest destruction that may befall man is [a servile] obedience to their wives.' They said, 'In the time of impiety a woman has the entire world with her. She is rich in money because she is worldly. Dominating, she is not at a distance from it. If asceticism and piety were to be victorious then her faith would be bound to her desire. If she is satisfied, then she is a tyrant, and if she is sad, then she is disagreeable and she frets. If she is contented she wants [more].'

Do not keep company with anyone other than with him whom your Lord causes you to love. He is that one who will have you abstain [from pleasure] in this world and who will cause you to desire the [life of the] world to come. He will make easy for you those places which are hard and rough and he will tell you secrets. Men like these are those who are sought after. You will not be a companion of others who will oppress you. See where you can find a closeness to Allāh through one of His servants. Be a companion of that servant. That is the greatest of all matters of concern and it is the loftiest status of all. It is that which the Almighty caused us to have knowledge of by the mouth of His Prophet, the blessing and peace of Allah be upon him, in his *ḥadīth*, 'I am with those whose hearts are broken on account of me.'[77] You will arrive at the truth if Allāh so wills.

O my brother, you must disassociate your mind from absorption in that matter which is no concern of yours, because the foundation of their 'Way' is his saying, the blessing and peace of Allāh be upon him, 'It is the true and worthy Islamic religion of a man to forsake that thing which is of no concern to him,' and, about noble deeds of true morality, 'You should pardon him who wrongs you, give to him who deprives you, join with him who cuts you off, and forsake dispute and contention over religion. We have been told the report that a time will come upon mankind when, in it, they will stray from their religion and they will know it not' . . . *up to his saying* . . . 'It will rob the minds of many at that time. The first thing which they will lose is humility, then faith, then piety.' *He then goes on to say*, 'The first thing that men will lose is personal affection. In ancient times, whenever they met, one would say to his companion, 'What is your news?' and 'How is your health?' meaning, what news have you in regard to your person, about its strivings, its endurance, its patience in adversity, and, 'What is the condition of your heart?' [meaning] either, has [your] faith increased, or have you decreased, in your faith?

They used to tell each other mutually the circumstances of their hearts and they used to describe what good treatment Allāh had given to them. So that would be their thanks to Allāh for His favour and it would be an increase in the awareness of how to act. This is contrary to the custom of the people of this age. They question one another about the affairs of this world and about the causes of passion.[78]

Their Rules concerning the Addressing [*of Superiors*]

One of the rules to be observed by the *faqīr* is that when he has settled down and is seated after his arrival, he should not initiate a conversation without being asked [to do so]. When he comes to a Shaykh, or he visits him, then he must ask his permission if he wishes to leave. For there were, amongst men, some whose permission to visit was not sought after unless it be for some graver matter which was unavoidable. Rather, they used to sit at their doors, or in their mosques, waiting for them to come forth at the hours of prayer. This was out of respect and on account of the awe [in which they were held]. ᶜAbdallāh has related,[79] saying, 'The Messenger of Allāh, His blessing and peace be upon him, said, "When one of you pays a visit to his brother and sits with him, then he will not arise until he has asked his permission [to do so], and he will not go forth from the ribāṭ without his permission and he will not do anything without taking his opinion in it." ' See *Tuḥfat al-murīdīn.*[80]

Rules of Counsel, Comfort, and Consolation

Listed amongst their rules is the offering of sincere advice and [showing of] love and consoling with soft words to the best of their ability. This is on account of the words of the Almighty, 'Give to the kinsman his due of kinship according to a dual division; kinship by lineage and kinship in the faith, which is much the better.'[81] Consolation by soft words is most meritorious of all. Al-Junayd, when he was seen by Abū Ḥafṣ[82] in Iraq, stayed with him for a year, together with eight other persons, and every day he used to offer them new food . . . *until he said*, [*in the account quoted*], 'And when they wished to depart I [?] clothed him and I [?] clothed all of his companions.' This is quoted from *Kitāb Manāhij al-zāhidīn.*[83]

The Rules for Giving

Amongst their rules is that they should be just as he [the Prophet once] said, 'One who believes in the religion of Allāh is bountiful in what he gives.'[84] Because the rule for him who trusts Allāh is that he should not be timid in his giving, being aware that the moral deed of men, which Allāh has created, is an act that should be speedily performed.

Abū'l-Hudā [al-Sūqī] said,[85] 'Whosoever seeks the face of Allāh does a favour to those [relations to his who are] most distant. Allāh will restore goodness betwixt him and his distant relation, likewise betwixt him and his near relation who permits him to do good to his distant relation, for the sake of Allāh.'

Abū Ḥafṣ said, 'An [act of] insolence is to forsake spending [upon others].' When the *fuqarā'* come to you, then be with them, so that if you hunger, then they also hunger, or if you are satisfied, then they too will be satisfied, until their staying with you and their departing from you will be one and the same thing. See the *Manāhij al-zāhidīn.*

If a man is busy with his devotions, and not preoccupied by seeking his living, then what he has is faith and trust in his circumstance. To keep a close watch of his time requires that he manages his circumstance, to the extent that he is able to obtain some help in regard to obedience to that which his heart whispers inwardly to him in regard to news of his family. If the preoccupation of a man is one which demands the concern of his heart then his duty is the worthier, though it demands far greater examination and scrutiny. That is the good of those who seek the will of Allāh. The novice is he who gives to his duty towards Allāh a clear priority over any duty to himself. Hence, the priority of the brethren, amongst those who desire the will of Allāh, is more perfect than a concern for oneself. A believer's zeal to demonstrate bounty and charity to his relatives, and to the *fuqarā'*, takes priority over his view of himself and his family and what else concerns him which has a claim upon him. In the showing of priority and preference the saying of 'There is no god but Allāh' will continue to protect the servants of Allah, as long as they show no care for what they lack of worldly possessions. Phrased in another way, [this means] as long as they do not give any priority to the quality of their worldly life over and above that of their religion. If they do so and [yet] they proclaim 'There is no god but Allāh', then Allāh Almighty will say [to them], 'You lie, you are not truthful [in what you say].' But if he, [a novice,] has to leave on account of those needs which are the imperatives of his livelihood or for the pressing requirements of his family, or what he needs for himself, then let him depart and fulfil it in accordance with the recognized ruling. He should continue to perform his *dhikr* as he goes forth to carry out his duty and what is his legal obligation, actively performing it and seeking Almighty Allāh's help to do so, beseeching Him for the companionship of peace. He should not cease to bestow alms daily, as much as he can, be it only a date or a morsel, for, verily, much belongs to little in the eyes of Allāh, mighty and glorious He is, if the intention be good. See *Tuḥfat al-murīdīn.*

Companionship

Companionship [for one another] is amongst their rules. One of them said, 'Every believer has an act of mediation [to carry out].' Perchance you may enter into an act of mediation over your brother. He (?) used to say, that to pardon a servant [of Allāh] is to mediate between his brethren. This view was the view of Saᶜīd b. al-Musayyib, al-Ḥasan al-Baṣrī, al-Shaᶜbī, Ibn Abī Laylā and Ibn Shabrama(?), Hishām b. ᶜUrwa, Sharīḥ b. ᶜUyayna, Ibn al-Mubārak, al-Shāfiᶜī and Aḥmad b. Ḥanbal, may Allāh be pleased with them all.[86]

Amongst those who were inclined to an opinion that was inconclusive and who disassociated themselves [on this issue] were Sufyān al-Thawrī, Ibrāhīm b. Adham, Sulaymān al-Khawwāṣ, Abū

Sulaymān al-Darānī, al-Fuḍayl b. ʿIyāḍ, Dāwūd al-Ṭā'ī, Bishr b. al-Ḥārith al-Ḥāfī, Yūsuf b. Sibāṭ b. Qatāda, and al-Marqasī and others besides them, may Allāh be pleased with them all.[87] Their view was that preoccupation with the company of men, and close relationship with them, marked a severance from devotion [to Allāh] and its observance and personal attention paid to it, nay rather these [companions] would cast you into evil and [even] into perdition . . .

[Comradeship] is an intimacy which Allāh Almighty brings about. He causes [its presence] amongst human hearts. This is due to the sovereign power which belongs to Allāh Almighty. It is the joy of hearts when [human] breasts rejoice. It is the very ecstasy of joy. It marks an end to solitariness and to timidity. A friend is acquired by the dissolution of secrets. Every friend is a beloved although every beloved is not a friend. The scholars have said, 'There is no hypocrisy between two brothers and two friends though they behold one another with the eye. Their deeds possess the recompense for the secret and the solitary retreat. They are like people in a city and like companions on a journey. There is no hyprocrisy between a man and his family or between the voyager and his companions. There is no reputation which he needs to maintain nor has he to hide from them nor be in a solitary state. One must teach one's brother about that thing of which he exhibits ignorance, helping him with one's knowledge, for, verily, the poverty of ignorance is worse than poverty in wealth, just as one helps him with possessions, in one's person, with one's tongue and one's heart. Personal help is [offered] amidst the endeavour of life's vicissitudes and in concerns and matters of importance. Help with money, and through possessions, is to spend with due regard to the *sunna*, not out of fancy nor from desire, because if one assists another in his fancy outside [the bounds of] the *sunna* then one will do him an injury and one will perform a disservice.

One should not aid a brother in any way which will bring with it a dimunition in his [devotion to] religion. An example of help with the tongue is the mentioning made of his good qualities, and a rejection of those that are wicked. Help with the heart is to believe the best of him and to think well of what he does. In the *Tuḥfat al-murīdīn* it is said, and in some [other] reports, 'When Allāh Almighty wishes to do good to his servant, He bestows a pious friend upon him if he has forgotten to remember Him in his thoughts. If he recalls Him, then he helps and assists him.'

It has been reported that two brothers have only to meet together in frankness and in purity [of heart] whereupon Allāh Almighty will pardon them both. In *ḥadīth* it is said that whosoever befriends a brother in Allāh Almighty, then He will give him success and prosperity. He says that two brothers, if one of them is of superior power and capability in relation to the other, then the one will raise the other with him to that [higher] status which he enjoys and he will come up to his standard just as offspring join the company of their parents. On account of this it is said that none of all customary duties is deemed higher than the union of the brethren, for it is the equivalent of brotherhood from the wombs of their mothers. ᶜUmar, may Allāh be pleased with him, said, 'When one of you sees his brother's friendship, then let him take possession of it, for rare indeed is that thing which makes it a reality.' It has been said that 'Constant companionship is only to be found in noble people, and beautiful companionship is only to be found in people of good manners.'

Shaykh Abū Ḥafṣ was asked about the rules of the *faqīr*. He said, 'His rules are to keep the *mashāyikh* sacred, to keep good company with the brethren, to advise those who are junior to themselves, to forsake disputes between companions, clinging to preference and avoiding hoarding, avoiding the company of him who loves not the "Way" of the *fuqarā'*, helping the brethren in the sphere of their religion and the world to come.'

He who claims to be a *faqīr*, let him present these questions to himself. If he comes up to them, [their standards and demands,] then he is a *faqīr*. Shaykh Abū Turāb[88] used to say, 'When the heart becomes accustomed to avoiding Allāh, then it is accompanied by [feelings of] shock amongst the saints of Allāh, because a servant, when he turns to Allāh, mighty and glorious He is, knows the people of His presence. When he turns his back upon Him then he ignores them.' Allāh Almighty knows best. Shaykh Abū Madyan said, may Allāh be pleased with him, 'It is forbidden to the men of faith to tightly confine what is in store in the heart against those who are opposed to them.'

The Shaykh said,[89] may Allāh be pleased with him, 'The lords of this *ṭarīqa* have said, 'We used to spread the word of Allāh and the word of His Messenger. Whoever disbelieves us and denies our words is an infidel. Whoever believes us and wishes us to hold our peace in what we say is a hypocrite. He who believes us though he confesses to an inability to grasp what we declare, but who desires to really know some part of it, he is a sincere believer.' See *Talqīn al-murīdīn*.[90]

Abū'l-Ḥasan al-Shādhilī[91] said, 'Whosoever ends in his affair to the detriment of the *ᶜulamā'* and those who are pious, is an associate of the evil doers. The whole of Islam has escaped from him. Let not those external marks and learning and adoration, which he bears, deceive you, for verily they are [as] pictures which are devoid of souls. Truly, the spirit of Islam is love of Allāh and love for His Messenger and love of the godly. Al-Shaykh al-Shanbakī[92] used to say, 'He who eats of the food of a novice removes the "Way" from the *fuqarā'*. His heart will be hardened for forty mornings.' Shaykh ᶜAlī al-Marṣaᶜī(?) said, may Allāh be pleased with him, 'If a novice departs, counter to the rule of his Shaykh, and he begins to slander him and his companions, then it is unlawful for anyone to believe him, because he is in a state of apostasy from Allāh's "Way". He is accursed in that very spot.' He said, 'In this matter, rare it is that a novice who disobeys the decree of his Shaykh is safe from him. That is because hearts [of others] will have a hatred for him. He will find no escape [from his dilemma] other than to do an injury to the Shaykh and to his companions, openly or by implication [in some manner].' He said, 'That is a sign of the establishment of hatred in his heart, but if Allāh wishes good through that novice he will join him, after separation from his Shaykh, with somebody who loves his Shaykh and who arouses love for him. There the concern of the novice moves [back] to his Shaykh [once more] and he seeks to return to him again.' He said, 'When a novice learns the rule of his Shaykh and is cut off from his counsel, if the cause of that be shame in regard to his Shaykh or to his companions due to some humiliating action committed, or due to some weakness that has overtaken him, then it is as if a revocable divorce [has occurred]. It is for the Shaykh to accept him back when he returns because the honour of the Shaykh is in the heart and soul of this novice. It has not left him, especially when it determines what the novice says to the Shaykh when he turns off from the "Way". The Shaykh and his companions should be kind and pleasant to the novice, and be free of harshness and rudeness towards him, nor should they avoid him. Now they bind a compact with him due to the strength of the tie which exists between him and the Shaykh.

Shaykh al-Iṣbahānī[93] used to say, "Be not a companion of him who has no love of the 'Way'. As the days pass he will only increase in his back-sliding." He was asked, "What is the mark of love for the 'Way'?" He replied, "His love will distract him from food and from drink and from sleep, just as I tasted and experienced when I began it." Shaykh Abū'l-Qāsim al-Maghribī[94] used to say, "One of the mightiest of all trials and afflictions is the love which you suffer on account of one who does not agree with you and who will not leave you." Shaykh Abū ᶜAbdallāh[95] said, "I have seen none who serves the *fuqarā'* in truth who has not become mighty in this world prior to the world to come.

The Messenger of Allāh, His blessing and peace be upon him, passed by a man who was attending to [the baking of] a loaf of bread for his companions and he sank into it [as he baked] and the heat of the fire did him an injury. He said, 'The glow of the fire will never hurt him.' "[96]

Shaykh Abū Bakr al-Warrāq[97] used to say, "The people are of three categories, the *ᶜulamā'*, the *fuqarā'*, and the *umarā'*. When the *umarā'* are corrupt, the *fuqarā'* are made corrupt and when the *ᶜulamā'* are corrupt then obedience is spoilt, but when the *fuqarā'* are corrupt then the whole of humanity is corrupted." Once he was asked about the bulk of the people of the "Way". He said, "They are the ones whose hearts are sound, whose deeds are good, and whose tongues and private parts are pure. If they lack these qualities then they are the party of the Pharoahs and not from the body of the *fuqarā'*." One of them said, "Harm is diverted by half of the action of the *Bārakallāh*[98] and the other half by good deeds for Allāh, Mighty and Glorious He is." '

The Duties of the Shaykh

It is the duty of the Shaykh to protect the novice and to guard him within a firm fortress of strength, removing from him those things that break the rules and waylay him in the 'Way'. [This is done] in four different manners: by retreat, by prayer, by fasting, and by wakefulness. This will guard against sins that beset him in the 'Way'.

Verily, the goal of the novice is to restore his heart. As for fasting, it reduces the blood which pumps the heart. It makes it pure and white in the whiteness of his light. It removes the surplus fat of the heart. In the whiteness of its melting lies the softness and leanness of his heart. In the softness and leanness is found the key to the perception of the mystic's vision just as the hardness of the heart causes the veiling and the clouding of that vision. Whatever reduces the flow of blood to the heart, so the path followed by the eye is [thereby] narrowed in its vision. As for wakefulness during the night-time, it purifies and cleans the heart. It illumines it and it is joined to purity which comes into being on account of the fast. Hence it becomes like a pearly star and a mirror, so clear is it that the beauty of the Truth appears in it. In it, the highest stages in the next world are perceived and the novice despises the world in which he now tarries. To sleep not is also the result of hunger. To stay awake after satisfying one's belly is impossible. Sleep descends, it dominates and kills the heart unless the will is mastered by some necessity, and so it becomes the cause of an extra-sensory vision of the esoteric secrets.

It has been said that the quality of the *Abdāl*[99] is that their sustenance is present in their very wanting and sheer deprivation. Their sleep is mastery [of themselves] and their utterance is their compulsion. As for silence, verily it is made easy through withdrawal [from men] and by solitariness. But he who withdraws himself is not freed of the vision of him who brings him food and drink and arranges matters. So it is imperative that the novice should avoid speaking to him, unless he has to do this out of some dire need. The evil of speech is great. Silence calms, it penetrates the mind. It brings it piety and godliness so it learns the fear of Allāh. As for the retreat (*khalwa*), its advantage is the warding off of distractions, and in the control of listening, of vision, and of the sensations. These four things are [as] a shield and a fortress. They defend him [the novice] from the waylayers and they prevent those things which block his 'Way', by the grace of Allāh, glory be to Him.

Know that the self is the seat of blameworthiness while the spirit is the place of praiseworthy qualities. All the qualities of the self and its features are derived from two sources. One of them is recklessness and heedlessness, whilst the other is greed and covetous desire. The heedlessness [of the self] is due to its ignorance, and its greed is due to its cupidity. Reckless heedlessness begets haste and impatience, for patience is the essence of the mind whilst recklessness is characteristic of the self. Its passion may only be overcome by patience since the mind subdues passion. The latter is the master of the self and the mind is master of the spirit. The heart is to be found between the mind and the passion, and gnosis (*maᶜrifa*) is within the heart. For passion and mind, the two, dispute and compete. Passion is the lord of the army of the self and the mind is the lord of the army of the heart. Unity will . . . (?) . . . , the mind and [provoke?] an abandonment of the extent of the passion. Victory will come to him as it is so willed by Almighty Allāh. To him whom He wills comes happiness and to Him whom He wills comes wretchedness. . . .

One of them said, 'As long as the novice cleaves to Allāh Almighty, then his affairs will be joined to the Ultimate Reality according to the vision of the unseen world, either by faith or by knowledge, or by gnosis (*maᶜrifa*) or by the state of uncertainty (*yaqīn*). But if he returns to his own self in the planning of [his life] or in meditating upon his state by his forgetting the favour of his Lord, Mighty and Glorious He is, the condition is erased (*kashaṭa*) from him. He is hampered from comprehending his affairs to the extent of the darkness of his veil, and by his turning aside from his Lord, Mighty and Glorious He is, through his sin, and in an instant, moment by moment. Verily, your Lord is swift to punish. Verily He is pardoning and is merciful.'[100]

The Books and the Sunna

Know that the books and the *sunna* are the source which the saints of Allāh Almighty have shown to [His] servants. Whosoever forsakes both of them is in error, but he who follows them will be happy and fortunate. He who spurns them will perish and he who makes use of them will be saved. It is your duty to hold fast to them so you will be rightly guided, or if you are called upon to guide others. The messenger of Allāh, His blessing and peace be upon him, said, 'It is your duty to believe and to beware of raising an objection,' and Abū ᶜUbaydallāh, may Allāh have mercy upon him, said,[101] 'To believe is to show loyal obedience and to object is to commit an offence. If you know, then follow, and if you are ignorant, then submit.'

Aḥmad b. ᶜAṭā'allāh said in his *Ḥikam*:[102]

'Glory be to Allāh, glory to Him who has only created the evidence which reveals who his closest followers are, by evidence which permits an awareness of His own divine essence. He [Allāh] has only permitted them to be known to one whom He, the Almighty, desires should know the very essence of His being. Sometimes, He has informed you about the secrets of His unseen kingdom, yet He conceals from you the awareness of the secrets of His servants.'

What their inner hearts contain is either loyal trust or else it is error or deceit, because only he who is trustworthy, exclusively and uniquely, namely he who possesses the breadth of faith in Allāh's omnipotence, and such is a grace which is bestowed by Allāh Almighty, is truly in a position to know them. For that reason one of them said, 'Belief in this *ṭarīqa* of ours is to follow closely in obedience to Allāh. Let not a doubt enter into your heart on account of what has befallen Allāh's servants due to the power and the authority of men, and the devil and the hostility which they received [from others]. Verily, [both] the blame of the godless and the heedless and their praise is ineffectual, their acceptance and favour and their rejection is one and the same, because many of them do not praise those who merit praise in the eyes of Allāh, nor do they reprove him who merits reproof in the eyes of Allāh. Their action is to the contrary. May Allāh guard us from behaving like them.

Colophon

O Allāh, to Thee come all our wishes. O Master of pardon and of health. My Lord, accept my repentance. [Gap] O Allāh, the blessing and peace of Thine be upon our Lord Muḥammad [in] the night [?] and at every hour and every time. The blessing and peace of Allāh be upon [him?] [gap] until the Day of Judgement and blessing and peace be upon all the Prophets and the Messengers and upon thine angels and those who are brought nigh unto Thy presence, all the people of Thy obedience, the company of the heavens and the company on earth. May Allāh, glory be to Him, be pleased with the lords of men and with the Companions of the Messenger of Allāh, with us all and all Muslim believers, and upon those who were their followers, bestowing His favour and His grace until the Day of Judgement. O Lord, gather us together with them in their body of men and beneath their banner, in Thy mercy, O Most Merciful of the merciful. So [I shall now conclude] my book which bears the title of *The example for the believer to follow among the biographies and histories of the excellent amongst men.*[103] It is a book by the Shaykh al-Sayyid, the *Imām* of the elect and the common people, the guide in the path wherein he sets forth to [follow] the truest and the straightest of paths. None who recounts his qualities will recall them without there appearing the mark of that [their virtue]: Abū Ḥammād (Aḥmād) al-Ṣādiq [b.] al-Shaykh Uwāyis [al-Lamtūnī], may Allāh be pleased with him, and with us all, by His *baraka*. He is able to do that and it behoves Him to answer our prayer. So be it.

Notes

1. *fuqarā'* (singular *faqīr*), literally 'poor men', those who observe the rules of poverty, a term also used for ordinary Ṣūfīs, some of whom do not observe this rule of poverty but who supply donations. Hence the term is sometimes used to mean 'lay members', see E. W. Lane, *The Manners and Customs of the Modern Egyptians* (London, 1860), pp. 251–2.
2. *dhikr* see *EI*. An assembly of Ṣūfīs who are dedicated to the recitation of Allāh's name. These rituals will vary between each Ṣūfī *ṭarīqa*. In the *Maḥmūdiyya*, as in most other *ṭuruq*, the ritual is confined to the repetition of divine names and phrases though it does not apparently exclude musical accompaniment or ritual dancing, see n. 28.
3. One or two Ṣūfī works are known by this title or by one similar. There is no mention of the author's name in the *Qudwa*. Another comment on the references to the 'right hand of Allāh', and its duality, is to be found in Clément Huart, *Textes Ḥouroûfîs*, E. J. W. Gibb Memorial, vol. ix (Leiden, 1909), pp. 102–3.
4. *Sūra 2*, *al-Baqara*, verse 273, and *Sūra 6*, *al-Anᶜām*, verse 52.
5. *Aṣḥāb al-Ṣuffa*, a term used to describe the devotees who seated themselves on the bench of the Mosque of Medina in the time of the Prophet. According to Lane, under *Ṣuffa*, this

term was applied to certain persons who were the 'guests' of al-Islam and who were supported by the charity of the Muslims. They consisted largely of poor refugees and homeless men who passed the night in the *Ṣuffa* of the mosque of the Prophet, a covered place attached to the mosque, covered in and roofed over with palm-sticks.

6. An unidentified *ḥadīth*.
7. Possibly Abū'l-Fawāris Shāh b. Shujāᶜ al-Kirmānī, amongst the early Ṣūfī authors, who came from a princely family. He died some time after 884. See A. J. Arberry, *Muslim Saints and Mystics* (London, 1966), pp. 183–4.
8. This title is variously spelt, *Kitāb al-Jawhara* and *Kitāb al-Jawāhir*, even, incorrectly, *Kitāb al-Jawāhira*, in the *Qudwa*. The passages cited are so varied and so devoid of context that it has not been possible to identify the title with any of those works which have a similar title listed in Brockelmann, *GAL*, and elsewhere.
9. In this context, 'the integral and permanent realization of a spiritual degree'. Sometimes referred to as a 'station' in a Ṣūfī 'Way', see M. Milson, *Kitāb Ādāb al-Murīdīn* (Harvard Middle Eastern Studies; Cambridge, Mass., 1975), p. 43, para. 68.
10. Abū Hurayra. One of the Companions of the Prophet, died *c.* 676–8, to whom are attributed some 3,500 *ḥadīths* many of them of dubious authenticity.
11. *Aḍyāf Allāh*. Ḍayfallāh occurs as a proper name amongst holy men in the Sūdān.
12. Lane says *tasabbaba* is used as meaning 'he trafficked', a term applied to a man who employs means to procure his subsistence.
13. Shaykh Ahmad Zarrūq al-Burnusī al-Fāsī, 1442–93, was described by Aḥmad Bābā of Timbuktu as 'the last who united in himself the mystic way and *fiqh*'. On the most famous of his works, see Brockelmann, *GAL*, ii, 253. Studies in Arabic on his life and his works include ᶜAbdallah Gannūn's *Aḥmad Zarrūq*, in the series *Mashāhīr rijāl al-Maghrib*, and the edition of *Kitāb Ṭabaqāt al-Shādhiliyya al-Kubrā* by al-Ḥasan b. al-Ḥājj Muḥammad al-Kawhan al-Fāsī, (ᶜAlāmiyya Press, 1347 AH), pp. 123–6. His most famous works were a Qur'ān *tafsīr*, his commentary on the *Risāla* of Abū Zayd al-Qayrawānī, three commentaries on the text of *al-Qurṭubiyya*, thirty-six commentaries on the *Ḥikam* of Ibn ᶜAṭā'allāh, a commentary on the Beautiful Names of Allāh, a commentary on the *Dalā'il al-Khayrāt*, a book on good counsels, and his book entitled *Kitāb Qawāᶜid al-Ṣūfiyya*, referred to here. One of the outstanding writers on Ṣūfism, he is especially honoured by the *Shādhiliyya ṭarīqa*, to which he belonged.
14. Unidentified.
15. *Sūra 8, al-Anfāl*, verse 72. The expression *fi'l-dīn*, 'in the religion' is misplaced in the quotation.
16. *Sūra 6, al-Anᶜām*, verse 90.
17. Unidentified.
18. A well-known proverb but unidentified, specifically, in any *ḥadīth*.
19. Part of the proverb 'the companion before the road and the neighbour before the house'.
20. *al-takbīr*, the formula of exhortation, 'Allāh is greater than any other,' *Allāhu Akbar*.
21. Abū Muḥammad Sahl b. ᶜAbdallāh al-Tustarī, whose pupil, Ibn Sālim, founded the *Sālimiyya ṭarīqa*, was born at Tustar (Ahwāz) about 200/815. He studied with Sufyān al-Thawrī and Dhū'l-Nūn al-Miṣrī and he died in Basra in 282/896, see Arberry, *Muslim Saints and Mystics*, pp. 153–60. To him is attributed the saying, '*Taṣawwuf* is to eat little, to take rest with Allāh and to flee from men.' He favoured self-mortification for the furtherance and success of spiritual discipline.
22. The sense is not sufficiently clear from the context whether a quivering motion to the right and to the left is intended, or whether the participant became excited, and his heart was moved by joy, or whether he simply lost his balance.
23. The precise numbering became slightly confused in the author's mind. It has been left unchanged in the text.
24. *al-Kull*, the attainment of the Universal, the passing away of human attributes to God.
25. Seemingly the Arabic expressions, *uff*, *tuff*, etc., indicating interjections (*aṣwāt*) of disgust and displeasure, though this is not certain. For sarcastic comment on these exclamations and utterances by Ṣūfīs in a state of ecstasy, see Kātib Chelebi, *The Balance of Truth*, trans. by G. L. Lewis (London, 1957), pp. 43–6. His comments were particularly directed against the practices of the *Khalwatiyya ṭarīqa*.

26. Mālik b. Dīnār was the son of a Persian slave from Sijistān who became a disciple of Ḥasan al-Baṣrī. He achieved fame as a traditionist, transmitting *ḥadīth* from Anas b. Mālik and Ibn Sīrīn, amongst others. He died about 748, see Arberry, *Muslim Saints and Mystics*, pp. 26–31. ᶜAyn al-Quḍāt al-Hamadhānī described him as 'one of the greatest ascetics and preachers of spiritual realities'. The Bible passages cited are from Matt. 11: 17, and Luke 7: 32.
27. Wahb b. Munabbih, who died in 728 or 732 AD, was a Yemenite of Persian origin. His father was probably a Jew. He was famous for his knowledge of the Jewish and Christian scriptures. He, it is said, composed works on Arabian lore and early history, some of it indebted to models from Pseudo-Callisthenes. Noted works attributed to him include the *Isrā'īliyyāt* and his *Kitāb al-Mubtada'*, which is the source of Muslim versions of the lives of the prophets and biblical stories of all kinds.
28. *samāᶜ*, a Ṣūfī audition, sometimes accompanied by music and dancing, wherein passages from the Qur'ān are read and recited, and the atmosphere is one conducive to a feeling of ecstasy and spiritual enlightenment. On the merits of this Ṣūfī audition in the *Suhrawardiyya ṭarīqa*, see Milson, *Kitāb Ādāb al-Murīdīn*, pp. 61 ff.
29. *tahlīl*. A loud exclamation of the confession of faith, 'There is no god but Allāh,' *Lā ilāha illā' allāh*.
30. Aḥmad b. Muḥammad al-Tabbāᶜ is possibly a son of Muḥammad b. ᶜAbd al-ᶜAzīz al-Tabbāᶜ who was a well-known figure amongst the Ṣūfīs.
31. *khirqa*, the coarse woollen robe, though sometimes decorated, worn by Ṣūfī mystics. It is an outward sign of the vow of poverty. According to the article in the *EI* (*khirḳa*): 'The investiture of the *murīd* with the *khirḳa* by his tutor (*shaikh, pīr*) had a ceremonial character. "The donning of the robe", says Suhrawardī in the *ᶜAwārif al-maᶜārif*, "is the tangible sign that the man is entering upon the way of truth, the symbol of his entrance upon the mystic path, the sign that he is abandoning himself and putting himself entirely in the hands of the shaikh." '

    Milson, *Kitāb Ādāb al-Murīdīn*, pp. 64–6 (section 149) describes the practice followed by the *Suhrawardiyya tarīqa* for the division of the *baraka*-filled *khirqa* which is thrown off during the *samāᶜ*. The 'redemption' of the *khirqa* by payment of money before its return to the Ṣūfīs is conditionally justified by al-Suhrawardī, and his view is also found in the *Qudwa*, although it is disapproved of by Jīlānī and by some other Ṣūfīs.
32. The sentiment in this passage can be paralleled in the Psalms and in passages in the Gospels, for example *John* 11; 24–6. It can be matched in many passages amongst the great Ṣūfīs concerned with the 'death of the Self'. Junayd, cited in al-Ghazālī's *Iḥyā' ᶜulūm al-dīn*, remarks in connection with the gnostics' beholding of the Divine Essence, 'life becomes death, explanations come to an end, signs are effaced. Mortality (*fanā'*) is ended and immortality (*baqā'*) is made perfect.'
33. *wird* (plural *awrād*), in theory denotes, to cite Sharqāwī, 'all kinds of acts of devotion (*ᶜibādāt*) such as prayer, fasting, the *dhikr*, where the believer has the initiative' (see Paul Nwyia, *Ibn ᶜAṭā' Allāh (m 709/1309 et la naissance de la Confrérie Šāḏilite* (Beirut, 1971), pp. 258–9). L. Massignon in his article *wird* in the *Shorter EI*, p. 634, says that it means both the time of private prayer of the pious believer and also the formula of prayer recited, the *ḥizb*. Each Ṣūfī *ṭarīqa* has its formula of prayer used in initiation, its *wird*, together with the *isnād* of the transmission of the initiation. The *Maḥmūdiyya* had its individual *wird* which consisted of an extended repetition of the *taṣliya*. Here the *Maḥmūdiyya* approaches the practices of the *Khalwatiyya*, see Louis Rinn, *Marabouts et Khouan* (Algiers, 1884), pp. 295–6.
34. Unidentified. See Paul Nwyia, *Ibn ᶜAṭā' Allāh* . . ., p. 270. On the mystical experiences of the Shehu, which included a vision of the Prophet as well as ᶜAbd al-Qādir al-Jīlānī, see M. Hiskett, *The Sword of Truth* (Oxford, 1973), pp. 63–9. Also see Louis Rinn, *Marabouts et Khouan*, p. 296.
35. Text and author unidentified.
36. The *ᶜIshrīniyyāt* of al-Fāzāzī are widely studied in the South Saharan and Sahelian region. Their author, Abū Zayd ᶜAbd al-Raḥmān b. Yakhlaftan b. Aḥmad al-Fazāzī, entitled his work of praise to the Prophet, *al-Qaṣā'id al-ᶜishrīniyyat fī madḥ sayyidinā Muḥammad*. He died in *Dhū'l-Qaᶜda*, 1230. See Brockelmann, *GAL*, *s i*, 482. Also see M. Hiskett,

The Sword of Truth, pp. 35, 37, and 115. It is this work, 'the twenties', which was the inspiration of one of the finest compositions of Muḥammad al-Najīb al-Anuṣammanī 'al-sayf' who was, allegedly, amongst the leading supporters of Sīdī Maḥmūd al-Baghdādī.

37. Unidentified. I suggest that *Witrāniyya* should read *Witriyyāt*, the full title of his work being *al-Witriyyāt fī madḥ afḍal al-makhlūqāt*, poems in praise of the Prophet by Muḥyī'l-Dīn Jamāl al-Islām Muḥammad b. Abī Bakr al-Rashīd al-Wāʿiẓ al-Baghdādī al-Witrī, d. 662/1264. See *GAL S* i, p. 444. A pentastich (*takhmīs*) on this work was composed by Muḥammad b. ʿAbd al-ʿAzīz b. al-Warrāq al-Lakhmī (d. 680/1281).
38. The *Burda*, or *Mantle Ode* of Sharaf al-Dīn Abu ʿAbdallāh Muḥammad b. Saʿīd al-Dalāṣī al-Būṣīrī (1212–c. 1296) is a panegyric in praise of the Prophet, composed by him in thanks for a miraculous cure from paralysis following a vision which he had that the Prophet had cast his mantle upon him. The poem itself is credited with miraculous power. Less Ṣūfī than hagiographic, this was one of the principal works of meditation studied by ʿUthmān dan Fodio. See Brockelmann, *GAL*, i. 265; *S* i, 467.
39. Specifically ʿĪd al-Fiṭr (*al-ʿīd al-ṣaghīr*) at the end of *Ramaḍān* and ʿĪd al-Aḍḥā (*al-ʿid al-kabīr*) celebrated on the tenth of Dhū'l-Ḥijja.
40. The Birthday of the Prophet, celebrated on the twelfth of *Rabīʿ I*.
41. A minor transmitter of *ḥadīth*.
42. Nowhere is it made clear in the text what gift is intended, but see Louis Rinn, *Marabouts et Khouan*, pp. 96–7, for one possible explanation.
43. On this voluntary fasting (*ṣawm al-taṭawwuʿ*) see *Ṣawm* by C. C. Berg. in *The Shorter EI*, pp. 505–6.
44. Kaʿb b. Mālik al-Anṣārī, the poet, was involved in the slandering of ʿĀ'isha, the famous *ḥadīth al-Ifk*, see the article by Sahair El Calamawy, 'Narrative elements in the *Ḥadīth* literature', in *Arabic literature to the end of the Umayyad period*, vol. i of the *Cambridge History of Arabic Literature* (Cambridge, 1983), p. 313. There are numerous references to Kaʿb in A. Guillaume, *The Life of Muhammad* (Oxford, 1955).
45. *Ribāṭ*. See *EI*. A Ṣūfī convent, synonymous at times with a *Zāwiya*. One such convent was founded by Abū al-Najīb al-Suhrawardī on the Tigris. The form of the *ribāṭ* in Aïr may well have retained some elements of the Saharan forms of *ribāṭ*, exemplified by the concepts of the Almoravids in the Western Sahara. Several leading members of the *Maḥmūdiyya* were of Lamtūna or Massūfa origin. This is the only place where a *ribāṭ* appears in the life of the *Maḥmūdiyya* in the *Qudwa* and there is no clear picture there of what building or organization is intended.
46. Unidentifiable from the context.
47. *Sūra* 2, *al-Baqara*, verse 222.
48. Unidentified.
49. Anas b. Mālik, Abū Ḥamza (died 711/12) staunchly defended written *ḥadīth* and transmitted it, principally from the Prophet, his family, and a few leading Companions.
50. Unidentified.
51. Unidentified.
52. Many wise sayings and proverbs which are attributed to ʿAlī are given to his lieutenant, al-Aḥnaf 'the bandy-legged' b. Qays, who died after 687. His sayings are extensively cited by al-Jāḥiẓ.
53. Ibn Sīrīn. Abū Bakr Muḥammad Ibn Sīrīn, who is cited in the spiritual chain of the *Shādhiliyya* between Anas b. Mālik and Ḥabīb al-ʿAjamī, although only in some. He was a commentator of Ḥasan al-Baṣrī. See Richard Gramlich, *Die Gaben der erkenntnisse des ʿUmar al-Suhrawardī* (*ʿAwārif al-ma ʿārif*), vol. vi (Wiesbaden, 1978), 23, 8.30, 49, pp. 179 and 234.
54. ʿAbdallāh b. ʿUmar b. al-Khaṭṭāb (died 673) was an opponent of written *ḥadīth*.
55. The cave of Ḥirā', outside Mecca, where the Prophet used to seclude himself and where he heard a voice commanding him to recite; by tradition this occurred during *Ramaḍān* in 610. The text of the *Qudwa*, in line with the teachings of ʿUmar al-Suhrawardī in his *ʿAwārif al-Maʿārif*, see this practice (*sunna*) as the original inspiration of the significant rule of *khalwa* in the *Maḥmūdiyya*, as in other *ṭuruq*. Compare this passage with the retreat for forty days advocated by Suhrawardī in Richard Gramlich, *Gaben* pp. 193–7.

56. Ibid. 15 p. 197, where ᶜUmar al-Suhrawardī is cited.
57. Unidentified.
58. Possibly from *Tuḥfat al-murīdīn wa-raghbat al-sālikin* by ᶜAbd al-Wahhāb b. al-Ḥusayn al-Tamīmī al-Qaysī, see Brockelmann, *GAL*, *S* ii, 998, 26.
59. The stoned Satan. The stoning of Iblīs is one of the rites prescribed for the ceremonies around Mecca, at Muzdalifa where three stone cairns are lapidated during the height of the pilgrimage. The following passage from Peter J. Awn's *Satan's Tragedy and Redemption: Iblis in Sufi Psychology* (Leiden, 1983) p. 38, furnishes an example of the cosmic extension of this theme: 'Iblīs' sinful pride brings about a complete transformation, internal as well as external. The name change from ᶜAzāzīl to Iblīs dates from this change in character and points to the depth of his conversion to evil. His corrupt nature manifests itself now as Ash-Shayṭān, Satan. "And He said, 'Be gone from this place (Paradise)! For you are stoned' " (Qur'ān 15:24). Iblīs is henceforth a pariah laden with the contagion of evil; his lot is to be reviled, cursed, and driven away by the stones of the faithful.

    The image of stoning is preserved even on the cosmic plane, for when the faithful look up into the heavens at night and see shooting stars flash across the sky, they are witnessing the ceaseless battle between the spirit world and Iblīs. Every time Iblīs and his armies assault the heavens to secure a foothold in the land of his former glories, hosts of angels shower them with meteorites. Iblīs and his followers are driven once again to the lower regions of darkness.'
60. Probably Yaᶜqūb b. Ḥumayd b. Kāsib al-Madanī, see Richard Gramlich, *Gaben*, para. 30, 59–61, pp. 236–7.
61. Uncertain identification, possibly the grandfather of ᶜUmar al-Suhrawardī. Several leading Ṣūfīs are named thus.
62. Unidentified.
63. See the article on *ḥizb* by D. B. Macdonald in *The Shorter EI*, p. 139.
64. The man-made *khalwa*, as the preferred place of meditative retreat, figures prominently in the *Maḥmūdiyya*, furthermore it must be a structure of specific dimensions. This is one of the details in the *Qudwa* which superficially suggests similarities, even borrowings, or common rules, shared between the *Maḥmūdiyya* and the *Khalwatiyya* in particular. Martin Lings draws attention to it in his *A Sufi Saint of the Twentieth Century, Shaikh Amad al-ᶜAlawi* (London, 1971), p. 85: 'In some Sufic brotherhoods—the Khalwatī Tarīqah, for example—it was the tradition to make retreat in a special hermitage. But in the Shādhilī Tarīqah and its branches, the spiritual retreat had usually taken the form of withdrawal to the solitudes of nature, after the pattern of the Prophet's retreat in the cave of Mount Hira, and though inevitably the *khalwah* must have been used on occasion, to introduce it as a regular methodic practice was something of an innovation for the descendants of Abu'l-Hasan ash-Shādhilī.'

    This, together with other borrowed rules of the *Maḥmūdiyya*, will be discussed later in this book (pp. 152–5 and 163–5). It is too easy to assume that the *Khalwatiyya* was the source for the practice of the *khalwa* in Aïr. The relevant passages in the *Qudwa* appear to be drawn from several sources. The *khalwa* was central to other *ṭuruq* which pre-dated the *Khalwatiyya*. One such example is the *Kubrawiyya*. M. I. Waley, in his paper presented at the Second European Seminar of Central Asian Studies, held at SOAS, London University, April 1987, showed that a dark and confined *khalwa* (*khalvat*) was an important doctrine of the *Kubrawiyya*, as formulated by Najm al-Dīn Aḥmad b. ᶜUmar Kubrā, and by his disciples, and other Kubrawī followers, for example, Najm al-Din Rāzī Daya, in particular, and ᶜAzīz al-Dīn Nasafī. It was based on the eight principles of Junayd. Others of these principles are clearly to be seen in the *ādāb* set forth in the *Qudwa*, for example, devotion, obedience, and imitation of the *Shaykh*, the fast, the detailed hygienic rules within and without the *khalwa*, prayer, bodily purity, and nocturnal wakefulness. One is struck by the debt owed by the author of the *Qudwa*, and, it would seem, Sīdī Maḥmūd himself, to such rules and recommendations formulated by these Central Asian Ṣūfīs of the 13th cent.
65. Care in protecting animal and insect life is a peculiarity of the *Maḥmūdiyya*, at least to this extent, and it probably was a feature of the teaching of Sīdī Maḥmūd himself. This

most closely resembles certain practices associated with the *Bektāshiyya ṭarīqa*, see John Kingsley Birge, *The Bektashi Order of Dervishes* (London, 1937), p. 130.

66. Another peculiar feature of the *Maḥmūdiyya*. The Friday prayer has featured prominently in the duties imposed upon devout Muslims in the region of Aïr. Al-ᶜĀqib b. ᶜAbdallāh al-Anuṣammanī al-Massūfī, one of the circle of al-Maghīlī, wrote a work on this subject specifically, *Wujūb al-jumᶜa bi-qaryat Anuṣamman*.
67. See the article *Djanāba* in the *Shorter EI*, by Th. W. Juynboll, pp. 87–8.
68. Abū Madyan Shuᶜayb b. al-Ḥasan al-Maghribī al-Anṣārī al-Andalusī, died *c.* 1193, who enjoyed in the West a status amongst Ṣūfīs which rivalled that of ᶜAbd al-Qādir al-Jīlānī in the East. See the article 'Abū Madyan' by A. Bel in the *EI*, Brockelmann, *GAL*, i, p. 438. He taught Ibn ᶜArabī and had a profound influence on the writings of Abū'l-Ḥasan al-Shādhilī.
69. A marked feature of Maghribī Islam, as elsewhere, and very common in Aïr and Azawagh, including the tomb of Sīdī Maḥmūd himself at Aghalangha.
    On the subject of 'pilgrimages to tombs' and 'visiting tombs', see Kātib Chelebi, *The Balance of Truth*, pp. 92–6.
70. Unidentified. The name is probably corrupted in the text. Perhaps it should read quite differently.
71. An unidentified Ṣūfī.
72. An unidentified Ṣūfī text, 'The treasure of secrets and resting place of lights.'
73. *Tayammum*, the recommendation, or permission, to perform the ritual ablution of the face and the hands with sand instead of water in certain circumstances, more especially when water is scarce or totally lacking.
74. Abū ᶜAlī is a common name amongst famous Ṣūfīs. It was an honorific name of al-Ḥasan al-Baṣrī. One possibility is Abū ᶜAlī al-Ribāṭī, see Richard Gramlich, *Gaben*, 17, 9, pp. 131–2.
75. Abū Suᶜūd/Saᶜūd is probably Aḥmad b. Muḥammad Abū'l-Saᶜūd b. al-Shiblī al-Baghdādī.
76. Cited in part from *Surā 18, al-Kahf*, verse 28.
77. Unidentified.
78. Unidentified.
79. Not clear, although possibly the grandfather of Abū Ḥafṣ ᶜUmar al-Suhrawardī, see Richard Gramlich, *Gaben*, p. 2.
80. This Ṣūfī work, cited in a number of places by the author, cannot, in view of its vague title, be identified with any specific manual.
81. Unidentified.
82. Probably Abū Ḥafṣ ᶜAmr b. Salama al-Ḥaddād, who was a blacksmith of Nishabur. He visited al-Junayd in Baghdad, also al-Shiblī and other Ṣūfīs. He returned to Nishabur to resume his occupation and died there in 265/879. See Arberry, *Muslim Saints and Mystics*, pp. 192–8.
83. Unidentified.
84. Unidentified.
85. A passage where the leading follower of Sīdī Maḥmūd is quoted verbatim.
86. Abū Muḥammad Saᶜīd b. al-Musayyib b. Ḥazn b. Abī Wahb al-Qurashī al-Makhzūmī. ᶜĀmir b. Sharaḥīl al-Shaᶜbī. Abū ᶜAbd al-Raḥmān ᶜAbdallāh d. al-Mubārak al-Ḥanẓalī al-Marwazī (736–797).
87. Abū ᶜAbdallāh b. Saᶜīd b. Masrūq al-Thawrī. Abu Isḥāq Ibrāhīm b. Adham (died 782). Abū Sulayman ᶜAbd al-Raḥmān b. Aḥmad b. ᶜAṭiyya al-Dārānī (died 830). Abū ᶜAlī al-Fuḍayl b. ᶜIyāḍ al-Tālaqānī (died 803). Abū Sulaymān Dāwūd b. Nuṣayr al-Ṭā'ī of Kūfa (died 777/782). Abū Naṣr Bishr b. al-Ḥārith al-Ḥāfī (767/841). Yūsuf b. Asbāt is more correct. Al-Marqasī is unidentified. His name may be misspelt in the text.
88. Abū Turāb al-Nakshabī.
89. Unclear as to who the Shaykh is. Is he Abū Turāb?
90. Unidentified.
91. The founder of the *Shādhiliyya ṭarīqa*. See the article by D. S. Margoliouth in *The Shorter EI*.
92. Neither Shanbakī nor Marsaᶜī can be identified for sure, though the former may

be the Agades scholar and saint Muḥammad Shambakī who lived in the city about 1500.

93. Possibly the teacher of Ibn ᶜAṭā'allāh, Shams al-Dīn al-Iṣfahānī (died 1289) who taught *kalām* and philosophy in Cairo.
94. Unidentified.
95. Unidentified.
96. Another example of protection from burning due to *baraka* is found in ch. 5 (1).
97. On Abū Bakr Muḥammad b. ᶜUmar al-Warrāq, author of *Khatm al-Awliyā'* (died after 930), see *Sezgin* i, 653.9. and the *Kashf al-maḥjūb* of al-Ḥujwīrī, pp. 142–3, and the *Ṭabaqāt al-Ṣūfiyya* by Abū ᶜAbd al-Raḥmān Muḥammad b. al-Ḥusain al-Sulamī (Cairo, 1953), p. 221.
98. An Arabic expression which signifies a blessing; an invocation of divine blessing either on an individual or else a specific blessing upon Muḥammad and his family, see Lane under *bāraka.*
99. The *Abdāl* are the hierarchy of Ṣūfī saints, see R. A. Nicholson, *The Mystics of Islam* (London, 1914), pp. 123 ff. However, the author of the *Qudwa* seems to have another sense in mind, namely 'dervishes' in general. Here he comes close to the use of *Abdāl* amongst the Bektāshis, for example, as the following definition of John Kingsley Birge in his *Bektashi Order of Dervishes*, p. 251, makes clear: 'It is also used in the sense merely of dervish, and in that meaning is synonymous with *Kalender* and *isik*. There appears to have been in the thirteenth century a group more or less organized who were called the *Abdalan* or the *Rum Abdallari. Kaygusuz Abdal* belonged to this group. The term is used frequently in Bektashi verse. The word is frequently used in Bektashi names, *Abdal Musa*, *Derun Abdal*, *Genc Abdal*, *Kalender Abdal*, *Kazak Abdal*, etc. *Fuat Bey* in his *Ilk Mütesavviflar*, p. 376 says the *Abdal's* were a branch of the *Babai* sect. See *Köprülü's Halkedebiyati Ansiklopedisi* for a thirty-three page important article on the word *abdal.*'
100. *Sura 6, al-Anᶜām*, verse 165.
101. Unidentified.
102. The Arabic text of the *Qudwa* quotes the *Ḥikam* of Ibn ᶜAṭā'allāh faultlessly in this passage. Victor Danner in his Ṣūfī Aphorisms, (Leiden, 1973), renders the passage as: 'And he said (may God be pleased with him!):

    156. Glory be to Him who has not made any sign leading to His saints save as a sign leading to Himself, and who has joined no one to them except him whom God wants to join to himself.

    157. Sometimes he reveals to you the invisible domain of His Realm but veils you from knowing the secrets of servants.'
103. The author's name is spelt Uwāyis in the text. This name is honorific and is undoubtedly borrowed, despite the spelling, from that of the famous early Ṣūfī saint, Uways al-Qaranī, whose name was particularly revered by Aïr *Ṣūfīs*, see the *silsila* of the *Maḥmūdiyya* in the Conclusion where this matter is specifically discussed, likewise J. P. Brown (ed. by H. A. Rose), *The Darvishes or Oriental Spiritualism* (London, 1927), p. 447.

7

The Martyrdom of Sīdī Maḥmūd

F. Nicolas, in his study of Islam in Aïr, says about Aghalangha, the burial place of Sīdī Maḥmūd:[1]

He is enterred at Aghalangha, together with Shaykh al-Muṣṭafā. Pilgrims who are at the place of his tomb insert a stick in a hole which is situated near to the head of the supposed body, and from it they draw *baraka*. During the period when Sīdī Maḥmūd passed three years in the country of Aghalangha, the Kel-Away were already in the Temgak mountains.[2]

Neither the date of his stay, nor holy places other than his tomb, are fixed in the local histories and hagiographics. They are occasionally confused with the sites which are associated with ᶜAbd al-Karīm al-Maghīlī and his son. Nor is there unanimity as to who was directly responsible for his death. Ghubayd maintains that a battle was fought at Aghalangha, when many of the Kel-Away followed Sīdī Maḥmūd.[3]

Spencer Trimingham, on the other hand, believed that Sīdī Maḥmūd was killed by the Kel-Away about 1640. There are other accounts which tell of the martyrdom. Few are compatible.[4]

The *Qudwa*, however, describes the tragic events differently. The text says that the saint was martyred at Aghalanga, but it charges the Sulṭān of Agades and his jurists for the events which led up to the martyrdom. So scant is the information that it is barely possible to fill in further details as to why the Sulṭān's wrath was aroused: was it settlement by the *fuqarā'* on land which the Sulṭān maintained was his own estate in the Massif?[5] Was it the interruption of the commercial routes to the north of Agades? Was it fear of a coup in Agades itself, or objections to the Tuareg system of succession and government?[6] The text draws attention to two specific factors which determined the Sulṭān's actions: a hostility on the part of the jurists of the Sulṭān to oriental mysticism of the kind which Sīdī Maḥmūd had introduced, and secondly, that the Sharīfian status of Sīdī Maḥmūd—with the possibility that the Sulṭān himself may have claimed this status[7]—put him in a peculiar and hallowed category in Aïr society at that time, giving him a protection and freedom of action denied to others. The contravention of this holy and inviolate status led to a crisis in the heart of the Agades Sultanate. The account is plausible but it cannot be corroborated from any other sources and it may well suffer from retrospective interpretation by the author of the *Qudwa* whose purpose was to plead the cause of his mystic order in the Sahara and to praise the saints of the *Maḥmudiyya* in particular.

Nevertheless, there is a passage in the *Qudwa*, citing practices in the days of Sīdī Maḥmūd himself, which suggests that the *ṭarīqa* founded by him both transcended, and at the same time preserved, the traditional social order and family life of Aïr. At some point a conflict between the Sulṭān and his subordinate chiefs, his jurists and administrators and the followers of Sīdī Maḥmūd, and ultimately himself, must have been inevitable. This passage states that:

> It is a rule of theirs to give the *fuqarā'* a preference over the rich, and the sons of the world to come a preference over the sons of this world, but it is not a condition of theirs that there should be no status between them, nay rather, there is found amongst them he who lives independent of others, he who seeks his livelihood as a trafficker, he who is married, and he who is a bachelor. This is what we have transmitted of that which is in line with the rules of the members of the 'Way'.

Bearing this in mind, and allowing for the fact that the numbers of his followers slowly grew, the following somewhat naïve and incoherent account of the events that transpired subsequently in Agades and the Masif has an authentic ring. It is a classic example of a petty Muslim head of state, claiming his appointment by an agreement from the Caliph, locked in conflict with a dynamic or a better educated religious leader whose other-wordly goals and priorities were directly opposed to the interests of his local Sultanate. Agades and Aïr lay on a major route for African commerce and trade, and, in any case, the Sultanate had been founded as an institution in order to resolve conflicts, incompatible rights and the commercial interests of a number of Tuareg tribes.

When the people of belief and sound character believed in Shaykh Sīdī Maḥmūd—Allāh be pleased with him—and when his cause was made manifest and men benefited from him in knowledge and religious learning, in conduct and the rules for *Ṣūfī* living (*ādāb*), and when his followers amongst those who were repentant multiplied in number, then it was that the Devil was envious of them and he, the Accursed One, arose in order to extinguish that [movement]. He worked in the hearts of some of the jurists (*fuqahā'*), through envy, and they proceeded to obey the Devil's calling, Allāh curse him.

They brought the Shaykh before the Sulṭān of Agades. They said to

Pls. 20–2. Folios of the *Qudwa* where the circumstances of the martyrdom of Sīdī Maḥmūd are discussed and where the Sulṭān and his jurists are blamed

Plate 21

Plate 22

the latter, 'This Arab Shaykh has only come in order to usurp your position.' They had no love of him because he diverted the attentions of the people away from them towards himself on account of the way that he was accepted and the power which he had acquired amongst them. It meant the decline of their own power and status. They said to the Sulṭān of Agades, 'Do not show slackness in this matter or be remiss in dealing with this man, otherwise there is no way of avoiding his coming to you and his unseating you from the Sultanate.' So the Sulṭān of Agades sent troops against him and they killed him on account of these jurists.

After that, the Sulṭān saw his [Sīdī Maḥmūd's] book, in which there were proofs of his Sharīfian status. He perceived the authenticity of his lineage going back to the Messenger of Allāh. The Sulṭān of Agades said to them, 'You have betrayed me. You had said that he was but a rude bedouin Arab and not a *Sharīf* in his status.' Poor wretches, they were only made to act in this wise on account of their love of the world, their revival of the ancient *sunna* of the Devil and the injury and destruction of saints and of scholars. Every deed that is committed has a follower of him who commits it. These men were misguided wretches who had forsaken the path of just Sultāns and scholars. Had they been amongst the latter they would have risen up against him only after much scrutiny and research, discussion and enquiry, until they had silenced and convinced him, lawfully, and with conclusive evidence of proof, so that it could not be said of them that they had slain him wrongfully. But they could not act in this way, nor had they the power to do it because he was the paramount scholar in his land which had been noted for learning since time immemorial. There was none in his time who could argue against him since he had insight and knowledge in the four schools (*madhāhib*), whereas they had no knowledge save in what they had read of the [works of the] school of the *Imām*, Mālik b. Anas.

We have only spoken of envy (*ḥasad*) because when they had outward authority with the governors and the princes, through their power to exercise the canonic law and to issue legal rulings and to teach, inordinate desire for worldly things was a necessity for them. If they were aware, they believed themselves to have sole dominance. When a scholar, or a servant of Allāh, brought a summons to [obey] Him, then envy took hold of them. He was not a competitor of theirs over the privilege enjoyed by witnessing to the Faith, by the office of *Imām*, the post of *Qāḍī* or in the status of *Muftī*, and in all such circumstances of theirs. However, the mass of folk, when they are called upon to repent to Allāh, are softened in their hearts, they are humble and repentant and they eschew their evil ways. When the people hear of that, they will hasten to him, for love of Allāh, because of the Almighty's words [in the Qur'ān], 'Verily those who believe, and who perform righteous works, the All Merciful will bestow tenderness and affection upon them.'[8] It is said 'betwixt Him and them', and 'betwixt them and the creation'. All is sound and true.

When Satan sees this, he seeks for one who will help him to extinguish that light. The only ones whom he can find in this affair are amongst the jurists who enjoy no portion of grace from the illumination of spiritual knowledge. They are the first of those from whom, by ruse and guile, he seeks to extinguish the [little] light they have.

Now this is what occurred in the time of al-Junayd.[9] Learning protected him, because the Sulṭāns were just men at that time and a little after it. When he brought them this learning in the time of the Sulṭān al-Mutawakkil [the latter] said to them [the jurists], 'Oh enemies of Allāh, you have determined to banish Allāh's saints and you have resolved that you will not leave a single one of them on the earth from amongst them. You did not heed a warning, nor were you restrained when you killed al-Ḥallāj, though, every day, you beheld a moral example from him, until it has moved your hearts to slay al-Junayd [also]. By Allāh, you have no means of doing this to him until you master him with a valid argument. You have all conspired together to oppose Shaykh al-Junayd. If you better him, then it is fit for him to die by the sword, but if he betters you in the argument then it is most meet that you should perish by the sword.'

When they were present at court, after eight months, and they were ashamed to face him, they began to oppose one of his companions in their argument. The Shaykh was guarded from them by his learning and his knowledge. The Sulṭān said to him, 'If you do not show your disregard for these men, then my sword will administer my recompense to them.' They numbered eighty jurists and one hundred students. The Shaykh said, 'Allāh forbid that anyone should endure torture on my account.' The Shaykh arose and left them for Allāh's sake. This was after they had killed al-Ḥallāj. The Sulṭān said to them, 'I am innocent of his death. It is they who carry the burden of the sin committed against him, not I.' Then they desired to kill al-Junayd and then took place that episode which involved him and them.[10]

See [*Kitāb*] *Tamām al-Qimma*(?) and refer to the book of the tales of the prophets and the saints and to the book of Muḥammad al-Zawāwī al-Farāwiṣī. [*Sic*].

Such is the way of just Sulṭāns amongst the Ṣūfī *fuqarā'* and amongst the jurists. Whosoever forsakes it and follows the sayings of the envious ones must needs be repentant.

Notes

1. According to the map of Niger in Ghubayd's book, Aghalangha lies some 90 km. to the north of Agades on the western fringe of the Aïr Massif.
2. F. Nicolas, 'Etude sur l'Islam, les confréries et les centres maraboutiques chez les Tuareg du Sud', in *Contribution à l'étude de l'Aïr* (Paris, 1950), pp. 484–5.
3. See pp. 20–3 of Ghubayd, and ch. 8 (*III*).
4. J. Spencer Trimingham, *A History of Islam in West Africa* (Oxford, 1962), p. 133, n. 2. The late date for the martyrdom, together with the involvement of Khadākhadā in the event, has been reiterated by Dominique Casajus in his *Tente dans la Solitude* (Cambridge / Paris, 1987), pp. 120 and 338–9. On p. 338 he remarks:
   'Nous avons vue que les avis divergeaient sur la date de l'arrivée des Iberkorayan dans l'Ayr. Elle n'est pas postérieure en tout cas à celle des Ilisawan et des Itesen. On peut retracer avec assez de précision les événements qui, au début du XVIIe siècle, les ont amenés à quitter la mouvance du sultan (voir Ghoubayd Ag Alawjaly 1975: passim). Un conflit éclate à cette époque entre les Kel Ewey et les Itesen d'une part, les Ioulimmedan et les Iberkorayan d'autre part, les Iberkorayan se ralliant aux Ioullimmedan pour la circonstance. Il s'agit d'une des guerres saintes dont nous avons parlé au chapitre 3. Sidi Makhmud Al Baghdadi, le mystique arabe qui avait appelé les Itesen à la guerre, appartenait à la confrérie soufi de la Qadiriya. Les Iberkorayan étaient guidés par Khadakhada, un membre de la confrérie soufi de la Khalwatiya. Nous avons dit au chapitre 3 que le role joué par le sultan de l'époque, Mokhamed Attafridj, était controversé. Pour certains informateurs, il ne fut pas étranger à l'assassinat de Sidi Makhmud. Pour d'autres informateurs et pour Ghoubayd, Sidi Makhmud a été assassiné par les Kel Ewey.'
5. The anonymous set of questions sent from Agades and Aïr to al-Suyūṭī in the middle of the 15th cent. (see the ch. on Geography of Aïr) makes it clear that herders might have access to fresh herbage in the Sulṭān's estate in the Massif, provided it be uncultivated 'dead' land. Notwithstanding this, if it can be proved that land in the region of Agades and Aïr is land owned by a lord then he is under no obligation to give it up and he can sell it as he so wishes. If a Sulṭān has assigned land into 'estates', if it is 'dead land' he has no business to do so since such land is a *ḥimā*, sacrosanct territory, but if the land is not 'dead' and is part of the land of the Public Treasury (*bayt al-māl*), divided into estates by the Sulṭān, then the latter has the exclusive possession of the herbage. Al-Suyūṭī, at a distance, was of the opinion that such was the situation as prevailed in Agades region and Aïr. See my *Tuaregs* (Warminister, 1972), pp. 49–51. See also pp. xxvi and xxvii in this book. It is not clear as to how much of Aïr was in *de facto* possession of the Sulṭān of Agades, nor is it clear whether the land cultivated by the *Maḥmūdiyya*, or used as sites for its mosques, cells, hermitages, and retreats, came within the scope of this ruling of al-Suyūṭī.
6. Both al-Maghīlī and his successors, Bello included (see *Infāq al-maysūr*), were strong opponents of the succession of sister's sons to the Sultanate. There is no evidence from the *Qudwa* that the *Maḥmūdiyya* took any stand on this social issue, or felt that its Ṣūfī teachings conflicted in any way with local practice, or with those rules which al-Maghīlī had taught to the Sulṭān's predecessors and to his advisors.
7. According to the Kel Es-Sūq the house of Muḥammad Ṣaṭṭafan claimed to be of Sharīfian origin from ancestors in the region of the Adrār-n-Īfōghas. According to the *Tārīkh al-Fattāsh* by Maḥmūd Ka^{c}ti (see O. Houdas and M. Delafosse, *Tarikh El-Fattash*, French trans. (Paris, 1913), pp. 212–14), the 16th cent. was an era when the deliberate, or accidental, slaying of a *sharīf* was a most grave offence in the Sahelian Muslim communities. In the thirty-third year of the reign of the Askia Dāwūd (1549–82), the latter accidentally slew the *sharīf*, Muḥammad b. Muzāwir. Full of grief and remorse and in fear of being chastised by God because of his misdeed he wept profusely and decided to fast. He consulted his leading *^{c}ulamā'* and *fuqahā'*, amongst them Muḥammad Diaghité, the *khaṭīb* of Gao, the *alfa* Ka^{c}ti, the *askia-alfa* Bukar Lanbār and the *sharīf*, ^{c}Alī b. Aḥmad. These counselled him to seek God's pardon and protection and to visit the grave of the deceased

sharīf. Unless some such penance was performed then the blood debt would need to be paid in accordance with Islamic law, 'since *sharīfs* enjoy great consideration and regard in God's eyes, in what esteem should they not be held amongst mankind?' Ill treatment of a *sharīf* was deemed to be an insult to the Prophet himself.

A possible influence of Ka^{c}ti on the thinking and the interpretation of the author of the *Qudwa* in regard to these matters cannot be excluded. Shaykh Aḥmad al-Ṣādiq died between 1670 and 1680. The *Tārīkh al-Fattāsh* was completed about 1665.

8. Qur'ān, *Sūra 19*, *Maryam*, verse 96.
9. On the circumstances surrounding the martyrdom of al-Ḥallāj, see the article on the latter in the *EI*, and in particular L. Massignon, *La Passion d'al-Ḥallāj, martyr mystique de l'Islam* (Paris, 1922).
10. The accession of the Caliph al-Mutawakkil took place in 847 AD. According to R. Nicholson, *Literary History of the Arabs*, p. 376, 'He persecuted impartially Jews, Christians, Mu^{c}tazilites, Shī^{c}ites and Ṣūfīs.' Al-Junayd died in 298/909–10. Since al-Ḥallāj was executed in Baghdad on Tuesday 24 *Dhū'l-Qa^{c}da* 309/26 March 922, twelve years after the death of al-Junayd, this whole passage is unhistorical. It is, however, not unique in its chronology of events, since it is found in the well-known legend of Junayd's condemnation of Ḥallāj, made familiar in Farīd al-Dīn ^{c}Aṭṭār's version where Junayd is made to be the spokesman of the jurists who had condemned Ḥallāj. His role was ambiguous, though here, in the *Qudwa*, the jurists are openly condemned, see Carl W. Ernst, *Words of Ecstasy in Sufism* (Albany, 1985), pp. 130–1 and 140–2.

8

The Later History of the *Maḥmūdiyya*

I
The Relationship between Shaykh Jibrīl, ᶜUthmān b. Fūdī, Muḥammad Bello, and Sīdī Maḥmūd

That there was a powerful, if subordinate, influence, in thought, teaching, and mystical practice, of Shaykh Sīdī Maḥmūd on the leaders of the Sokoto *jihād* can hardly be doubted. Unfortunately, it is difficult to identify in detail from the documents which have survived. If it is hard to identify, it is even harder to assess. Much of what is known about Sīdī Maḥmūd has been derived from the traditions of the *Khalwatiyya* Ṣūfī order which inherited his mantle in Aïr. Because of the known connection between Jibrīl and ᶜUthmān and this Ṣūfī order, one is likely to arrive at the conclusion that all that is known about Sīdī Maḥmūd came late to Hausaland, via recent *Khalwatiyya* teachings and devotional works. We cannot accept this explanation despite the meagre documentation. The *Khalwatiyya* case rests on the work known as *Ṣifat al-wird* which is attributed to the recent compiler, Mūsā Abatūl, who gleaned the *Qudwa* for almost all of his biographical material.[1] References to Sīdī Maḥmūd in the noted work *Infāq al-maysūr*, by Bello, were written earlier than *Ṣifat al-wird*. Hence, on chronological grounds, the latter text has to be entirely excluded as a source for his information.

Apart from *Infāq al-maysūr*, with which I am particularly concerned, and through initiation, I would detect four other principal sources whereby ideas of Sīdī Maḥmūd, his main doctrines, and certain biographical details about him reached Hausaland, Sokoto in particular:

The Life and Teachings of Shaykh Jibrīl b. ᶜUmar al-Agdasī

In Ṣūfism, according to B. G. Martin, 'Jibril initiated Usuman, Abdallahi, and Muḥammad Bello into three Ṣūfī orders, the Qadiriya, Khalwatiya and Shadhiliya.' Martin also cites a poem of Bello where the dazzling light of Jibrīl is given a particular emphasis:

Jibril, *Shaykh* of *shaykhs* in our country
Blessings are what he confers in great number
He disperses the gloom of error
Like a lamp shedding light over the land[2]

The light of Jibrīl is a quality shared between him and his illustrious Ṣūfī predecessor in Aïr. In short, Jibrīl inherited the Ṣūfī legacy of Aïr and Agades which had flourished in the Asben Massif since the sixteenth century.

Sīdī Maḥmūd claimed a Spiritual Silsila, *through to ᶜAbd al-Qādir al-Jīlānī*

It is also reported that he was a blood descendant of Jīlanī.[3] The spiritual and intimate relationship between ᶜUthmān and Jīlanī is well known and has been given a strong emphasis by Mervyn Hiskett in his biography, *The Sword of Truth.* It was Jīlanī who girded ᶜUthmān with the 'Sword of Truth':

When the period was complete the Lord of Creation led him to the Merciful and all the angels of the Merciful were present and the Shaikh, the pole of the Qadiriyya order, the Chosen One, was present—and the words that testify to the presence will come in due course—and the Shaikh ᶜAbd al-Qadir took our Shehu by the hand and sat him in front of him and said: 'This man belongs to me,' and for this reason the Shehu Usuman said in his *al-Qasida al-sudaniyya* (The Sudanic Ode): 'Our intermediary to Muhammad is the Shaikh ᶜAbd al-Qadir.'[4]

The Theme of a Hierarchy of 'Baghdād Saints' exerting some kind of Spiritual Hegemony within Hausaland occurs elsewhere in Hausa Literature

One such example is the 'Song of the Shaihu's miracles' from Sokoto. The particular instance seems to be directly influenced by stories which had come south from Aïr:

Another miracle concerned holy men from far away
In Baghdad. They watched out for his light from afar off
There in the west, in the direction of Syria; they sent a single man
That he should go and see. When the holy man came near,
Upon a *danya* tree he alighted.
Kwairanga sent someone to go and tell the Shaihu,
Our Shaihu went to meet him there, he said,
'It was explained to us that you saw a light there.'
The holy man did not alight on the ground because this Hausa country
Was a land of paganism. When the Shaihu had spoken,

Then they greeted each other and Shaihu joined him up there (in the tree);
He and Kwairanga, his good friend who loved him.
Then they bade (the holy man) farewell, wishing him a safe journey;
As far as Tambagarka they escorted him.
Every day (the Shaihu) would see the students of the *Shaikh*, that is Shaikh Abd al-Qadir al-Jailani at his door.[5]

Several details from the above show some resemblance to those which are to be found in the biographical works about Sīdī Maḥmūd. These include:

(*a*) the light emanating from a holy man's person.

(*b*) the mention of Baghdād, specifically, as the city from which the holy man came.

(*c*) the meeting between the Shehu and the holy man at a tree. Among the sayings in the *Qudwa* is the following:

> Among them was the saintly scholar, Muḥammad b. Muḥammad, who was nicknamed Amezdennig, the son of the saint known as Inzakrīn. He was a companion of Shaykh Maḥmūd. The latter ordered him to guide the disciples and the novices. He used to say, 'Whosoever from amongst the novices sits with me for a period of forty days beneath this tree will have his need fulfilled by me if Allāh wills it.'

Other references to arboreal associations between Sīdī Maḥmūd and his disciples are to be found elsewhere in Aïr legends and miraculous tales.

(*d*) the ground upon which Sīdī Maḥmūd trod was infidel ground. There is the specific statement attributed to Sīdī Maḥmūd in the *Qudwa*:

> The land of Aïr is in the land of the negroes! They said, 'We are in the land of the Sūdān. We now live in a place where the negroes used to live.' He [Sīdī Maḥmūd] said, 'It is the land of Hell Fire.' He used to say to the *fuqarā'*, 'Were you in the land of Islam you would attain the goal in the shortest time. As for this country, the *faqīr* spends the night on one stage/level, and awakes in one beneath it.'

The Aïr Records make it clear that Sīdī Maḥmūd was regarded as a Mujaddid by some, and a kind of Mahdī by others

The point is given emphasis in the way that al-Maghīlī is depicted as one who announces his imminent arrival. The Shehu would have found inspiration in this alongside the Ṣūfī role of the Baghdād Shaykh. The views expressed in the following passage from the

Shehu's *Sirāj al- ikhwān* (The Lamp of the Brethren) can be matched in a number of passages in the opening pages of the *Qudwa*:

And accordingly, it is related that at the beginning of every century God will send a learned man to the people to renew their faith, and the characteristics of this learned man in every century must be that he commands what is right and forbids what is disapproved of, and reforms the affairs of the people, and judges between them, and assists the truth against vanity, and the oppressed against the oppressors, in contrast to the characteristics of the other learned men of his age.[6]

What is curious about the *Qudwa* is the ambivalent attitude it adopts in regard to the status claimed for Sīdī Maḥmūd. Since his life and work followed so closely after the journeys and sojourns of al-Maghīlī in the southern Sahara and Hausaland, and al-Maghīlī himself was deemed by common consent to be a *mujaddid*, then what rôle did Sīdī Maḥmūd play in the divine scheme of things? Was he also a *mujaddid* or, if not, was he indeed more than this, a *mahdī* or *the Mahdī*? Was he, indeed, a man of promise and prophecy, or had the Saharan mystics misjudged his ultimate role and status? Should they be looking for another? All these problems are aired in the *Qudwa*. Nowhere is there any resolution to the question of his ultimate status. He is described as a mystic and as a martyr, a light in the darkness, and this light of divine mystical knowledge and illumination diverts the attention of the reader from these and other eschatological enigmas. The writings of Bello about him reveal the same viewpoint. They further underline the debt which he owed to Aïr sources, which furnished him with all the information he had.

The Chain of Initiation of the Shehu into the Maḥmūdiyya Ṭarīqa

There is now conclusive evidence that the Shehu, ᶜUthmān b. Fūdī, was initiated into the *Maḥmūdiyya ṭarīqa*. Probably this took place during his known stay in Agades.

The passage appears in a little studied work of the Shehu. It has recently been brought to our notice by Louis Brenner in his studies of the impact of Ṣūfism upon the leader of the *jihād*. The book is entitled *al-Salāsil al-dhahabiyya lil-sāda al-ṣūfiyya*, and it is undated.[7] In this treatise the Shehu begins by giving the *salāsil*, the chains of initiation, whereby he makes clear the authority which he has to recite the *shahāda* according to three specific *ṭuruq*, the *Qādiriyya*, the *Khalwatiyya*, and the *Maḥmūdiyya*. The last two *ṭuruq* are clearly distinguished. The latter part of the work contains several prayers which are designed to entreat the aid of the saints and they do not concern us here.

The *silsila* is furnished in the following passage (folios 7 and 8 of the *Salāsil*).

'Chapter Four'

'The chain of our ascription, by the inculcation of this confession, in the *Maḥmūdiyya Ṭarīqa*. As for the ascription, by the inculcation of this *Maḥmūdiyya* confession, I was instructed by Shaykh Muḥammad b. Ṣaddiq, known as Amaggadhar, in a manner where divine *baraka* was imparted. He was instructed by Shaykh Aḥmād, the Shaykh of the People of Yāfas, [Kel Afess], and he by the Shaykh who was known by his nickname, Āyyā, and he by Shaykh Abū Muḥammad al-Munīr Uways al-Qaranī, and he by the mighty and superior Shaykh Hārūn b. Muḥammad b. al-Ḥājj Aḥmad, and he by the Shaykh, possessor of mystic knowledge of Allāh, Sīdī ᶜAbd al-Qādir al-Kīlānī, who was the father of Shaykh Uways al-Qaranī, the aforementioned above. He was instructed by the scholar Shaykh, the saint, Muḥammad b. Muḥammad, known as Amezdennig, and he by the Shaykh and *Sharīf*, *Maḥmūd al-Baghdādī*.

He was instructed by Yūsuf b. ᶜAlī (al-) [al-Ḥumaydi] Muḥammad al-Marzafūnī al-Qusṭanṭīnī and he by Shaykh Jamāl al-Milla wa'l-Dīn al-Aqrānī. He was instructed by Shaykh Babā' al-Dīn ᶜUmar al-Azdanjānī [al-Arzinjānī] and he by Sayyid al-Ḥājj ᶜIzz al-Dīn [al-Khalwatī] and he by Muḥammad Mabrām [Mīram?] al-Khalwatī, and he by ᶜUmar al-Khalwatī, and he by Akh Muḥammad al-Khalwatī, and he by Ibrāhīm al-Zāhid al-Taklānī, and he by Sayyidī Jamāl al-Dīn al-Sarīrī, and he by Shihāb al-Dīn Muḥammad al-Shīrāzī, and he by Rukn al-Dīn Muḥammad al-Najāshī, and he by Quṭb al-Dīn al-Abharī, and he by Abū'l-Najīb al-Suhrawardī, and he by ᶜUmar al-Bakrī, and he by Wajīh al-Dīn al-Qāḍī, and he by Muḥammad al-Bakrī, and he by Muḥammad al-Dīnawarī, and he by Mimshādh al-Dīnawarī, and he by Sayyid al-Ṭā'ifa al-Junayd b. Muḥammad al-Baghdādī, and he by his Shaykh Sarī al-Saqaṭī, and he by his Shaykh Ḥabīb al-ᶜAjamī, and he by his Shaykh Ḥasan al-Baṣrī, and he by his Shaykh, the Commander of the Faithful, ᶜAli b. Abī Ṭālib, may Allāh be pleased with him. He was instructed by the Messenger of Allāh, His blessing and peace be upon him, and he was instructed by Gabriel, peace be upon him, and he was instructed by the Lord of Might, mighty is His majesty and his favour is universal.

The Biography of Sīdī Maḥmūd in Muḥammad Bello's Infāq al-maysūr

Bello introduces Sīdī Maḥmūd both as a mystic and as one amongst a number of scholars to whom much was owed for the spread of Arabic teaching and Islamic learning in the Sahara. He is also introduced as a martyr whose death is placed fairly and squarely on the shoulders of the Sulṭān of Agades. Nothing is said about Tuareg politics or religious fanatics as being in any way responsible for the sad events.

'Amongst them [the scholars and saints of Aïr] was the Shaykh and *Imām* al-Rabbānī, Sīdī Maḥmūd al-Baghdādī, who performed many acts of piety and remarkable and miraculous feats. He was the unique and unparalleled man of his age. He was its *Quṭb*, the revivifier of the *sunna* and the suppressor of heresy. He was the summoner to the Truth, his speech was that of the saints, he was the lord of the *ṭarīqa*, the proof of the *sharīᶜa*, and he spent all his time in worship and in devotion and in the recitation of the Ṣūfī *dhikr*. He entered the land of Aïr, enlightening and guiding. Men hastened to him in order to partake of his light and his guidance, such men as saw their need and their necessity in one who would save them from error, lead them into true guidance and deliver them from wrong doing's darkness into daylight, out of uncouth barbarism into knowledge ['light' in Whitting], and from heedlessness bring them to wakefulness, and from pre-occupation with things other than with Allāh to His sole preoccupation, from works of fancy to works of piety—Allāh have mercy upon all such (men) and grant them His pardon.

His companions studied with him, and many became Shaykhs on his account. Many Shaykhs partook of his light and the effects of his *baraka*, his divine blessing, and that of theirs, which were bestowed, endured. His companions exalted him and highly esteemed him to the extent that they gave him the title of the *Mahdī* who was awaited. They recounted [Prophetic] *ḥadīths* in regard to him [or citing him], all of which were close to being suprious! Allāh alone knows best. Be that as it may, he was a lordly scholar and an eternal succour. Allāh's saints declared him before he appeared and when he became famous in the country the jurists of the age took exception to him. They incited the Sulṭān against him so that warfare took place between them. They slew him at Aghalangha—may Allāh be pleased with him and may He withhold His pleasure from those who slew him.'[8]

The parallel passages in the Qudwa

A close resemblance to the above passage is to be read on the second folio at the very opening of the text of the *Qudwa*.

'Miraculous favour, in abundance, was manifested, and glad tidings, in abundance, were embellished by our lord the Shaykh, the *Imām* and scholar, the unique and unparalleled man of his age, our lord, the *Quṭb* of Islam, and of the Muslims, *Shaykh* of both worlds, the revivifier of the *Sunna* and the suppressor of heresy, the summoner to the Truth, whose speech was that of the saints, the lord of the *ṭarīqa*, the proof of the *sharīʿa*, the creator of realities, the abode of secrets, the fount of lights, the transmitter of *ḥadīths* of Allāh's Messenger, a master of command, who occupied his time in worship and devotion, praising Allāh in lonely meditation. During night-time and day-time he continued, beholding no bed [to sleep in] neither by night nor by day. Such was the Shaykh, the *Imām*, the lordly scholar, Maḥmūd al-Baghdādī—may Allāh be pleased with him and give him contentment and give us the benefit of his *baraka*—*Amen*, so be it. Many were the miracles which he accomplished in his land.

When he entered the land of Aïr . . . [men hastened to him?] in order to partake of his light and his guidance, such men as saw their need and their necessity in one who would save them from error, lead them into true guidance and deliver them from wrong doing's darkness into [day]light, and from ignorance to knowledge [Whitting's text has 'light'], and from heedlessness bring them to wakefulness, and from preoccupation with things other than with Allāh to preoccupation with Him alone, from works of fancy to works of piety—Allāh have mercy on all such [men] and grant them His pardon.'

At this point the *Qudwa* introduces details about these men, the leading saints and scholars of Aïr and Azawagh who became disciples of Sīdī Maḥmūd (see ch. 4).

A Comparison Between the Two Texts

Bello's biography in his *Infāq al-maysūr* is shorn of the detailed information about Aïr scholars which is a marked feature of the *Qudwa*. Nevertheless, there is sufficient evidence from the sentence structure and epithets of both passages in these works to show that Bello had access to a copy of the *Qudwa*, or a part of the latter, and that he drew from it only those statements, epithets, and laudatory remarks which he needed for his very brief entry. Bello made no attempt to fill in with further detail where the original text was unspecific. Thus, 'the lord of the *ṭariqa*' was left as it stood. He made no attempt to explain which Ṣūfī order it was. His passage above, which attributes the martyrdom to the jurists of Agades and to its Sulṭān at that time, whose name is omitted, is also a paraphrase of another passage in the *Qudwa*. Since his whole quotation is immediately followed by a survey of the illegal and un-Islamic practices of the people of Aïr and the uncanonic, matrilineal, manner by which its Sulṭāns were selected, it may be presumed that he wished to give some prominence to the evil role of the Sultanate in the martyrdom. Bello deals lightly with those who claimed that Sīdī Maḥmūd was some kind of *mahdī* or even the *Mahdī*. Bello's father, ʿUthmān, had disclaimed any such pretensions for himself, and neither father nor son could respect Sīdī Maḥmūd as anything more than a respected scholar and a saintly mystic. As for the popular reports that Sīdī Maḥmūd had been slain by religious fanatics amongst the Iberḳorăyăn Tuareg, these were either unknown to Bello, as they seem to have been to the author of the *Qudwa*, or else he had good reason for ignoring them, especially as the Iberḳoray *mahdī* of the Ayt Awari, Muḥammad al-Jaylānī, was amongst his allies.

In sum, Bello must have had access to a copy of the *Qudwa*, or part of a copy, or an abridgement of it, or the memory of a scholar who had read the *Qudwa*.

Conclusion

We have, as yet, no information which can help resolve the problem of Bello's sources, whether, for example, he had his own copy of the *Qudwa* or had access to one possessed by his father, or one or other of his relations, or whether, for example, the passage in his text relating to dubious *ḥadīths* in fact means this, or is a faulty citation of a passage in the *Qudwa*. The most likely person to have had access to a copy of the *Qudwa* would have been his father or Shaykh Jibrīl, himself from Agades. According to Aboubacar Adamou:

> The Dan Fodio mosque (Agades).
> This would be an ancient mosque where great masters once lived, masters such as Awgar al-Fullānī and his son the *Muqaddam* Awgar. During his stay in Agades, towards the end of the eighteenth century, 'Uthmān Dan Fodio remained in his mosque which was to later bear his name. In 1964 it was entirely rebuilt by Sarduna Ahmadu Bello, a descendant of ʿUthmān Dan Fodio.[9]

Awgar's son, Shaykh Aḥmad b. al-Faqīh Awgar, known as the *muqaddam*, who is buried at Imallag in the Aïr region, is mentioned in the *Qudwa* as being the leading Fullānī follower of Sīdī Maḥmūd (see ch. 4). It is hard to believe that at some point during his stay in this mosque Bello's father had not learnt, nor seen, the contents of the *Qudwa*, which spoke highly of Awgar and his son, but above all their master, Sīdī Maḥmūd.

II
Aïr Ṣūfism: Borno and the Kulumbardo *Zāwiya*

Although we have little evidence of any direct connection, it would appear that the first, and possibly the second, Kulumbardo Ṣūfī *Zāwiya*, located on the border betwixt Borno and the Sahara, owed some of their ideas, and some of their stimulus and fervour, to the *Maḥmūdiyya* and the sister Ṣūfī orders in Aïr. With the likelihood that it was favoured either by the Sultanate in Agades itself, or else by independent Tuareg zealots in the Aïr Massif, Kulumbardo appears to be an important example of the spread of Ṣūfism south-eastwards from the region of Aïr and the wider influence exerted by it.[10]

Almost all that is known in any detail about the first Kulumbardo movement is to be read, summarized, in a short description by Muḥammad Bello. It appears in a puzzling and chronologically uncertain passage in his *Infāq al-maysūr*. Variant names in the different editions complicate any interpretation.

The Fullānī Saint Waldīdu

'They have alleged that he chose to settle at Kulumbardo.[11] The Arabic letter *kāf* is vocalized with a *u* vowel (*ḍamma*), likewise the letter *lām* and the *bā'* is vocalized with an *a* vowel (*fatḥa*). This latter is assimilated to the latter *nūn* (which follows) and the latter *rā'* is unvocalized. It is in the district facing northwards from Birni Bornū.[12] He (Waldīdu) and the Shaykh and saint [Muḥammad] b. al-Jarmiyū, the Tuareg, began to revive the (Ṣūfī] "way [of truth]" (*ṭarīq*) and to teach the people the truth so that they rivalled one another in the contest to follow their example until there repented at their hands one/some? of the governors of the Amīr of Borno [Mai ᶜAlī b. ᶜUmar]. He/they? sent them both to the Sulṭān, Mai ᶜUmar, and he summoned them to attend his presence at court. He asked them about their business. The saint, (Muḥammad b.) al-Jarmiyū said, "Verily we have no wish to scatter your flock, but only to guide the people to the path of the truth (*ṭarīq al-ḥaqq*)." So he [the Sulṭān] slew him and his blood flowed upon utterance of the confession of faith.[13] He [the Sulṭān] set free Shaykh Waldīdu. He fled to Baghirmi[14] and he settled in it until he died.

They have alleged that he was born on the pilgrimage route. His mother went forth when she was pregnant. She strayed from the caravan and suffered from thirst. She gave birth to him and then died of thirst. For three days he lingered until another caravan came upon him as it passed by and they bore him to their country. He grew up, learnt the *Qur'ān*, and then he journeyed forth, seeking the path of knowledge [in the Islamic sciences] to Agades and to Timbuktu. Then he returned to his abode [in Kulumbardo] and then befell what happened [hitherto mentioned]. This Shaykh died a little after the close of the year 1000 AH/*c.*1595–1600? Allāh knows best.

They have alleged that he said to his (followers): "A time draws nigh unto you when one of Allāh's saints will appear in this country. He will renew the faith [as a *mujaddid*], he will revivify the *sunna*, and he will put to right the Muslim community (*milla*). Whosoever encounters him then let him follow him. His sign will be that at first he will wage the *jihād* with his tongue until most of those who are divinely helped will follow him. Then he will wage war with the point of the spear. He will possess this land and he will certainly eject the Amīr of Borno from his realm just as we have been ejected from our homes. He will rule it, Allāh be praised, he has already appeared and we have followed after him and we have aided him. May Allāh place us amongst those who are truly guided by him. May He grant success to the results of his labours, may He prolong his life and may he make the consequence a blessed favour." '[15]

A number of details in this passage deserve a fuller investigation. They may be prefaced by several comments which make reference to the movement of Sīdī Maḥmūd in Aïr and passages of a similar kind in the *Qudwa*.

(*a*) The date of Shaykh Waldīdu effectively fixes the *Zāwiya* at Kulumbardo in Borno as a foundation later than those in Aïr.

(*b*) The period of study in Agades makes it likely that Shaykh Waldīdu may have met Shaykh Muḥammad b. al-Jarmiyū while he was there. The latter could have studied under Shaykhs of the *Maḥmūdiyya*. We lack evidence however to prove this.

(*c*) Shaykh Muḥammad b. al-Jarmiyū was certainly a Tuareg. His place of origin could have been Jerma in the Fezzan, though I think it far more likely that he was one of the Aïr Tuareg. Rennell Rodd writes:

> Belkho's people, the Igermaden, are the parent stock of the Kel Tafidet, who not only became the most distinguished tribe in the Confederation, but also gave their name to the administrative ruler of the Kel Owi and the Confederation generally. They inherited the Tafidet mountains in the easternmost parts of Air and include an old 'I name' tribe, the Igademawen. The name Igermaden seems to associate them with Jerma or Garama in the Fezzan, but I am aware of no particular reasons for supposing that they came to Air from there, though it may once have been theirs in the remote past. There are, incidentally, numerous names of places in Air containing the root 'Germa' in their composition.[16]

Yet a third possibility is that Shaykh al-Jarmiyū was of mixed Tuareg and Djerma (Zerma) stock and that he may have had links with a region in south-west Niger, that is to say, with the area of Filingué, Tabla, or Dosso. Chronologically though this does not seem likely since at that time the Tuareg were only beginning to penetrate that region. At Tabla, some sixty-five miles to the east of Niamey, is located the alleged tomb of the Shaykh and Sharīf, Muḥammad al-Ḥājj (Khamadelkhaji), who lived at the end of the seventeenth century (or just after the second Kulumbardo), or at the beginning of the eighteenth. He was, by repute, a Ṣūfī disciple (*faqīr*). He allegedly came from the Ḥijāz, passed through Borno, stayed at Kulumbardo, then moved to Agades and Aïr, from whence he journeyed, via the region of Azawagh to Tadamakkat (as-Sūq) and there he married amongst the Tuareg *ineslemen*. He and his family settled in the part-Djerma (Zerma), part-Tuareg, inhabited plain at the entrance to the cliff-lined Dallol Boboya, at Sansani or Sabla, all within the Tuareg district of Teghazaret. The chief of Tabla, Aḥmad b. Ismāʿīl, who claims descent from Muḥammad al-Ḥājj, 'the man from Tabla' (*ales-n-Tabla*), has preserved a number of relics of the Shaykh and Sharīf, including several ancient Arabic manuscripts, on religious topics, including one in a seventeenth century Borno hand. It is at least feasible that at a later period the *ineslemen* of this south-west region were in touch with Ṣūfī centres in Borno, at Kulumbardo, and in Agades region. Besides the Hausa south towards Sokoto and Kano, Ṣūfī influences of the *Maḥmūdiyya* and Kulumbardo type also seem to have penetrated parts of Djerma (Zerma) country also.

(*d*) The alleged speech of Shaykh Waldīdu suggests that the movement did not eschew military methods to further its cause.

(*e*) The description of the death of al-Jarmiyū and the warning of Shaykh Waldīdu to the *Amīr* of Borno is very similar to passages in the *Qudwa*.

Spencer Trimingham dates these Ṣūfī activities to around the year 1600. He writes: 'About this time clerics who had caused trouble in Bornu took refuge in Bagirmi, among them Waladaidi (d. *c*.1600) who prophesied the advent of a *mujaddid* or reformer.'[17]

However, a date as early as this cannot be correct, since the martyrdom of Muḥammad b. al-Jarmiyū took place during the lifetime of the Mai, ᶜUmar b. Idrīs. Referring to these activities which began in Borno and which ended in Bagirmi, John Lavers remarks that their leader Mallam Dede is perhaps to be identified with the Shaykh Waldīdu mentioned in Muhammad Bello's *Infaq al-maysūr* as co-founder with Shaykh al-Jarmiyū, the Tuareg of the community of Kulumbardo. The latter was martyred by Mai ᶜUmar b. Idrīs of Borno (*c*.1620–1640) and it is known that Waldīdu then fled to Bagirmi. The chronology makes it more likely that it was his father who was the builder. He was no stranger to the country for according to tradition, an ancestor had founded Bidderi (in Bagirmi) and he had studied *tafsīr* there in his youth before travelling as far as Agades and Timbuktu 'in search of learning'. He was remembered as having foretold the coming of Shehu ᶜUthmān dan Fodio. Muḥammad Bello quoted from his writings:

> You are now under the shade of a saint from the saints of God who will appear in these lands and renew the religion; revive the *sunna* and establish the community, those that live in his time let them follow . . . he will declare a jihad with the spearhead and he shall rule these lands and expel the Amir of Borno from his own land—in the same way as we have been expelled—and rule it.

It is also possible that young ᶜAbd al-Karīm, later to found the Sultanate of Wadai, accompanied him for we know he studied in Bidderi. Other sources relate that ᶜAbd al-Karīm's master in theology was 'Mahammat al-Djirmi', and again to cite Palmer:

> According to another account the family were here before Abd ul Karim. Those who first came were Jami'u and his sons Ali and Alwa. Abd ul Karim was born here. Then he grew up he was very devout; sought knowledge, went to Bornu in pursuit of learning; and became the pupil of Sheikh Muhammad al Tarmiyu the Bornawi who was killed by the Jabarbara of

Bornu of the old dynasty, a crime which caused the loss of their ancient empire.[18]

Abd ul Karim returned from Bornu to Wadai, then went to Mecca the noble, and subsequently came back to Wadai with a large following.[19]

The Tribe of the Kel Yeti (Weti)

In a note, H. R. Palmer makes the interesting point of detail that 'Kulumbardu, or Kulumferdo, was the town of the "Koyam" or "Kel Etti" religious fraternity or *zawia*. It was associated with Mai ᶜUmr Idrismi in whose time Kulumbardu was said to have been founded (1625–1644 AD)'.[20]

Opinion is divided as to whether the Kanuriphone Kel Yeti were a separate Sahelian people, or are Tubu or Borno Tuareg. Rennell Rodd certainly favoured the latter view. Calling them Kel Yiti, or Kel Wati, he described them as a mercenary group, employed by the Mai of Borno, Idrīs Alawma, predecessor of ᶜUmar, to chasten and control the regions of the Agades Sultanate which came into subjection and were ruled by Borno during his lifetime.[21] It cannot therefore be excluded that Muḥammad al-Jarmiyū, if not of the Igermaden, was himself one of the Kel Yeti.

These people are specifically mentioned by the chronicler, the *Imām* Aḥmad b. Farṭūwa, where he describes the first twelve years of the reign of Mai Idrīs.[22] Borno launched three attacks on Aïr. The 'Kileti' took an important part in these attacks. Much of the population of Aïr was outside the fortified city of Agades itself, in the open desert between Teldas (the royal fortress of Tadeliẓa?) and Ahīr (the Aïr Massif proper). 'Before the fighting took place the Tuwareg including part of the Teluz and other big clans sent challenging the Sultan to come out and fight them.'[23] The Teluz would appear to be the family of the Sulṭān of Agades, Aḥmad b. Taluẓa, *c.*1541–1554/6, under whom Sīdī Maḥmūd allegedly met his death. Chronologically, these raids must have occurred in the 1570s, probably during the reign of the Agades Sulṭān, Muḥammad al-Ghudāla, immediately prior to the feuding and civil strife and anarchy in the Agades Sultanate, about 1601. Yūsuf b. al-Ḥājj Aḥmad b. al-Ḥājj Abashan the deposed Sulṭān strove to recover his throne, and indeed did so, against Muḥammad b. Mubārak b. al-Ghudāla who was helped militarily and politically by the ruler of Borno who regarded him as his puppet. It is presumably this civil war which has inspired stories of the retribution which the Sultanate of Agades had to suffer on account of the martyrdom of Sīdī Maḥmūd.

Counter attacks made against Borno by the Aïr Tuareg were

crushed. At Agalawa, in southern Aïr, they were routed and much booty fell into Borno hands. Aḥmad b. Farṭūwa says about this battle: 'They were in the midst of their rejoicing over their victory at this place, when, lo, their commander came, and ordered all the tribe of Kileti who were there, to make raids on the land of the Barbar constantly day and night, so that the latter would leave the land of Bornu and go far away into the desert.'[24] Many of the defeated Tuareg forsook the allegiance of Agades and became vassals of the Sulṭān of Borno.

All these campaigns in the region of Aïr meant that Borno took an active role in deciding the future orientation of the Agades Sultanate. Kulumbardo *Zāwiya*, via the Kel Yeti, established a closer relationship with Aïr and Agades and its religious leaders. Eventually Mai ᶜUmar b. Idrīs saw the *Zāwiya* as a threat. The fate of one of its leaders was remarkably similar to the martyrdom of Sīdī Maḥmūd.

III
The Relation of the *Maḥmūdiyya* to the *Khalwatiyya*

A substantial number of Aïr Tuareg, especially amongst the religious scholars, the *ineslemen*, maintain without question that Sīdī Maḥmūd was the founder of the *Khalwatiyya* in Aïr and that he was martyred at Aghalangha at the hands of the Iberḳorăyăn Tuareg fanatic, Ḥadāḥadā, who lived in the seventeenth century. This view is cited by Ghubayd, who has for long held this to be a historical record of the martyrdom. He writes:[25]

The Kél-Ăwăy dominated the Itésan and grave disaccords continued to stand in the way of the Iberḳorăyăn and the Kel Aïr. A *rezzou* (*ghazw*) of the Iberḳorăyăn attacked Talaq and seized livestock, however the principal encounter took place at Aghalangha (Agălăngha).

A man who called himself Khădakhăda (Ḥadāḥadā), who was a warrior hero and a scholar, came from amidst the Iberḳorăyăn and he became their *amenokal* . . .

The cause of the combat of Agălăngha was an Arab *faqīh*, who had come from Baghdād, who was called Sīdī Maḥmūd al-Baghdādī (Mekhmud Ălbăghdadi) and who converted the people to his doctrine. Many of the Kél-Ăwăy followed him; he built a mosque at Agălăngha and amongst the Kél-Ăwăy he increased hostility against the Iberḳorăyăn, because the latter refused the doctrine which he had brought, and because he learnt that they said that it was pure perdition. Now his doctrine was the *Khalwatiyya*, while certain of his adversaries professed the *Qādiriyya*, and others had no particular doctrine.

Khadăkhadă sent a message to the *amenokal* of Agades, Ăttăfrij ăg-Yusef, demanding that he should allow him a free hand in regard to the Kél-Ăwăy, and their religious master, Sīdī Maḥmūd; the *amenokal* replied that he would not intervene between them, so Khadăkhadă went to Agălăngha. Sīdī Maḥmūd and the Kél-Ăwăy heard word about him and rallied their forces to march against the enemy and a hard combat took place. After very heavy casualties the Kél-Ăwăy were vanquished, Sīdī Maḥmūd died, and Khadăkhadă seized herds of livestock and slaves. Certain of these slaves were free men of the Kél-Ăwăy, born from slave women.

The news of this battle and the booty captured in it reached the *amenokal* of Agades and he sent a message to Khadăkhadă asking him to set free the freemen who were made prisoner, even if they were negroes.[26]

Ghubayd concludes his presentation of this episode, which he dates to about 1655, with the statement that Ḥadāḥadā (Khadăkhadă) refused to relinquish his captives and that this act led to a serious disagreement between him and the *amenokal* of Agades. It was this dispute which decided the former's declaration of independence from the rulers of Agades.

Documentation is so scanty that the above story about the martyrdom of Sīdī Maḥmūd cannot be entirely rejected out of hand. The chronology is wildly inaccurate however. Some of the characters could not have taken part in the drama; other contexts of the story, for example, that the Kél-Ăwăy were involved in the *Maḥmūdiyya*, may contain some truth.

There is no question that the accounts above are incompatible, chronologically and in almost all the details, with the original text of the *Qudwa*. This was first written down following the alleged conflict between the Sulṭān of Agades and the fanatic, Ḥadāḥadā (Khadăkhadă). Nowhere in this text is the *Khalwatiyya* specifically mentioned as the Ṣūfī *ṭarīqa* promoted by Sīdī Maḥmūd. Nor does Bello support the assertion. The later *Qudwa* text lends some support for the view that the individual tradition of Sīdī Maḥmūd, at some stage, passed through some disciplines laid down by the founders of the *Khalwatiyya* order, and that it incorporated some of their teachings and rules. If it did so, then this must have been given emphasis at a date much later than the lifetime of Sīdī Maḥmūd himself. Evidence for this can be found in the *silsila*, the 'chain' of men of Ṣūfism, from whom he derived his spiritual initiation. This *silsila* is not only furnished in the existing *Qudwa*, and in the writings of ᶜUthmān b. Fūdī, but it is also quoted, almost verbatim, in the far later *Khalwatiyya* work, *Ṣifat al-wird*, which derives its inspiration from the later text of the *Qudwa*:

> This is the *silsila* of his Shaykhs, Praise be to Allāh who has made the hearts of those who possess mystic knowledge (*maᶜrifa*) to be the mines of

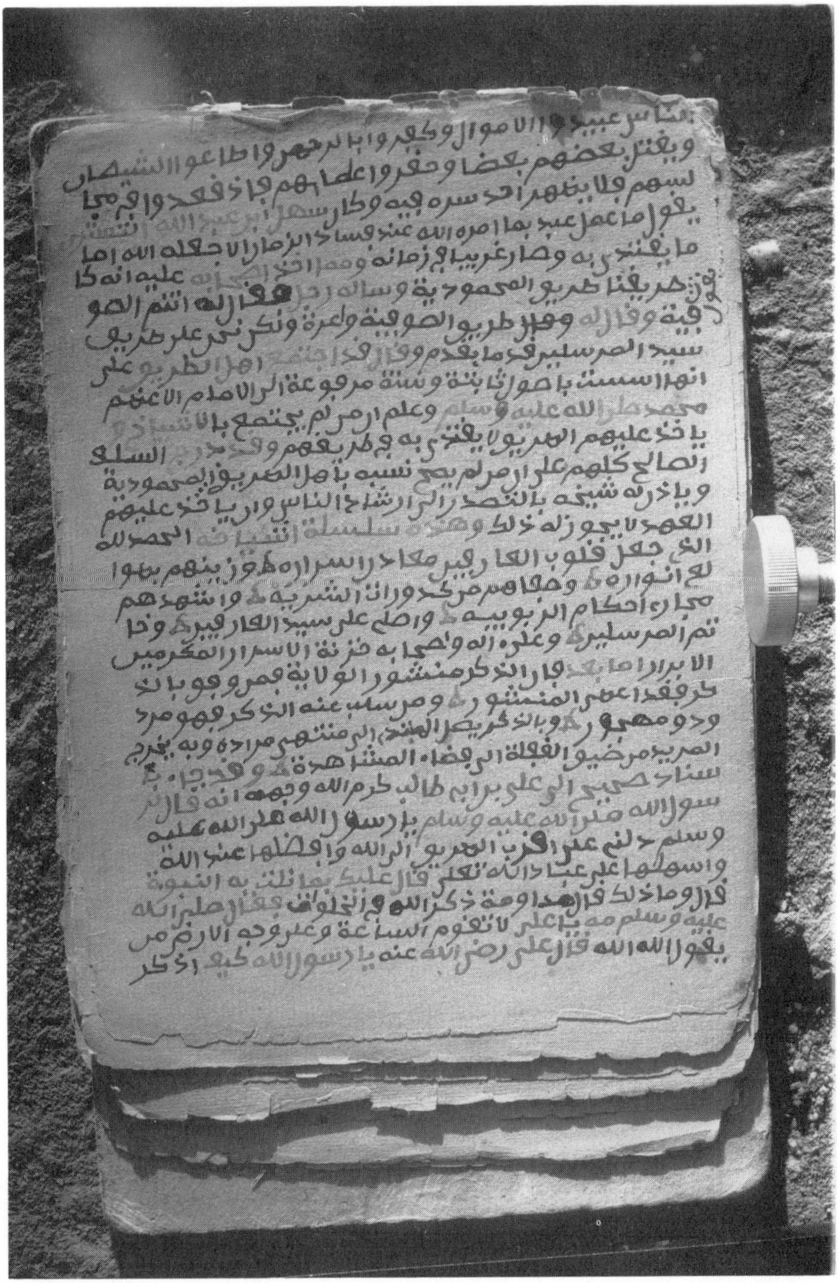

Pls. 23–5. The *silsila* of Sīdi Maḥmūd al-Baghdādī within the line of transmission and initiation going back to ᶜAlī and to the Prophet

قال غمض عينيك وانصت حتى اذكر ثلاث مرات وانت تسمع
ثم قل انت ثلاث مرات وانا اسمع منك فقال عليه السلام
لا اله الا الله ثلاث مرات ناحيا عن يمينه منتبئا الى شماله مغمضا
عينيه رافعا صوته وعلي يسمع ثم قال علي رضي الله عنه
لا اله الا الله ثلاث مرات ناحيا عن يمينه منتبئا الى شماله
مغمضا عينيه رافعا صوته والنبي صلى الله عليه وسلم

Plate 24

Plate 25

His secrets, and their adornment to be the rising of His lights in the heavens. He has purified them from the dross and filth of wickedness and has caused them to witness the streams of the rules of the divinity. I invoke blessings upon the lord of the mystics, the seal of those who were sent as messengers, upon his family and his Companions, the treasury of secrets, the noble ones and the pious. To proceed: verily the *dhikr* is sainthood made manifest. He who has been blessed in the *dhikr* has been granted the manifested and he from whom the *dhikr* has been removed is he who is denied and who is forsaken.

Through the *dhikr*, he who commences attains the goal he desires. By it the neophyte departs from the confinement of heedlessness to the vast space of awareness. It has been traced back, in a sound chain of authority, to ᶜAlī b. Abī Ṭālib, may Allāh honour his countenance. He said to the Messenger of Allāh, the blessing and peace of Allāh be upon him, 'O Messenger of Allāh, show me the nearest road to Allāh, and the one which He favours the most and the easiest of them for His servants.' He answered, 'You must follow the course whereby I attained the status of prophethood.' He said, 'What is it?' He said, 'Constant mention and recollection of Allāh in solitary retreats (*khalawāt*).' Then the Prophet said, 'O ᶜAlī, "The hour of Judgement will not take place when upon the face of the earth there are those who say, Allāh, Allāh." ' ᶜAlī said, may Allāh be pleased with him, 'O Messenger of Allāh, how shall I perform the *dhikr*?' He said, 'Shut your eyes and listen. I shall do it three times as you listen. Then you say it three times and I shall listen to you.' So he said, 'There is no god but Allāh' three times, discarding his [ᶜAlī's] right hand and fixing (his grasp) to his left, closing his eyes and raising his voice as ᶜAlī listened. Allāh opened his heart to him and he beheld what he [the Prophet] beheld. Umm Salama suckled him with the *baraka* of that.[27] He became wise.

Thus the Lord of Might instructed Gabriel. He instructed Muḥammad, peace be upon him, and he instructed ᶜAlī, may Allāh honour his countenance, and he instructed a company, including al-Ḥasan al-Baṣrī, whose father was called Yasār—may Allāh be pleased with them both. He instructed Ḥabīb al-ᶜAjam, may Allāh be pleased with him, and he instructed Dāwūd of Ṭayy'. He bore the agnomen Abū Sulaymān. He used to sit with Abū Ḥanīfa in order to study *ḥadīth* and *fiqh*. Then, after that, he became a Muᶜtazilite, may Allāh be pleased with him. He instructed Maᶜrūf al-Karkhī, may Allāh be pleased with him, and he instructed Sarī al-Saqaṭī,[28] may Allāh be pleased with him. He died in the year 251/866. He instructed his nephew, al-Shaykh, the 'lord of the party' al-Junayd[29] al-Baghdādī, may Allāh be pleased with him, the *muqaddam*[30] by general consent, Allāh show him mercy. He died in the year 297–8/910–11. He instructed Shaykh Mamshādh al-Dīnawarī,[31] may Allāh be pleased with him, who died in the year 299/914. He instructed Muḥammad al-Dīnawarī, may Allāh be pleased with him, and he instructed Muḥammad al-Bakrī, may Allāh be pleased with him, and he instructed Muḥyī al-Dīn al-Qāḍī, may Allāh be pleased with him, and he instructed ᶜUmar al-Bakrī, may Allāh be pleased with him.

He instructed Abū'l-Najīb al-Suhrawardī,[32] may Allāh be pleased with him and he instructed Quṭb al-Dīn al-Abharī, may Allāh be pleased with him. He instructed Rukn al-Dīn Muḥammad al-Najāshī, may Allāh be pleased with him, and he initiated Shihāb al-Dīn, may Allāh be pleased with him. He instructed Sīdī Jamāl al-Din, may Allāh be pleased with him, and he instructed Shaykh Ibrāhīm al-Zāhid, may Allāh be pleased with him. He instructed Akh Muḥammad, may Allāh be pleased with him and he instructed Shaykh ᶜUmar al-Khalwatī[33] may Allāh be pleased with him. He instructed Akh Mabram (Mīram?) [al-Khalwatī], may Allāh be pleased with him and he instructed Ḥājj ᶜIzz al-Dīn [al-Khalwatī], may Allāh be pleased with him. He instructed Shaykh Ṣadr al-Dīn [al-Khalwatī], may Allāh be pleased with him, and he instructed Sīdī Yaḥyā al-Bādkawī[34] may Allāh be pleased with him. He instructed Shaykh Arzinjānī, Shaykh ᶜUmar Arzinjānī (Rūshaniyya?), may Allāh be pleased with him, and he instructed Shaykh b. Jamāl al-Milla al-Aqrānī, may Allāh be pleased with him, and he instructed Shaykh Yūsuf b. ᶜAlī al-Ḥumayd(ī?) al-Marzafūnī al-Qusṭanṭanī, in the acquiring of science and in the mystic station, may Allāh be pleased with him. He it was who instructed Sīdī Maḥmūd al-Baghdādī,[35] may Allāh be pleased with him. He gave him permission to guide men, may Allāh give us and you success due to this companionship and repeat to us, and to you, the *baraka* of this lineal relationship, through the status of the Messenger of Allāh, His blessing be upon him and upon all the saints, and may He bestow favour which he bestowed upon them to us, likewise, for verily He is one who bestows bliss, favour and bounty and He is gracious and most merciful.

Despite a persistent claim in the *Qudwa* that the 'way' of Sīdī Maḥmūd was his own—the *Maḥmūdiyya*—that it was charismatic in appeal and that it set few obstacles in the path of those mystics of other 'Ways' who desired to share in the life of its retreats, it cannot be denied that association with the teaching of both Abū'l-Najīb al-Suhrawardī and Muḥammad Nūr al-Khalwatī imposed a decisive stamp on the early mysticism of Aïr as a whole. The *ṭarīqa* of Sīdī Maḥmūd can hardly be understood without reference to these two seminal 'Ways', the teachings of which through initiation (*talqīn*) became an integral part of Ṣūfism in Aïr. Hence, those who maintain that Sīdī Maḥmūd brought ideas of the *Khalwatiyya* to Aïr as well are not incorrect, however misleading their claim. What seems clear, however, is that the adoption of his teaching as an exclusive inheritance and privilege belonging to the *Khalwatiyya* alone is a quite recent phenomenon. This point has been brought out by Jean Louis Triaud in his studies of Ṣūfism in Aïr.[36]

The Khalwatiyya *Revival in Aïr*

Triaud has found that the first French reference to the presence of the *Khalwatyya* in Aïr is that of Nicolas in 1946, who claimed, without much evidence to support his case, that it had come there from the Anglo-Egyptian Sudan. To Nicolas, Sīdī Maḥmūd had brought the *Qādiriyya* to Aïr. However, Brouin[37] was nearer to the truth when he wrote that the *Khalwatiyya*, together with the *Shādhiliyya* and the *Qādiriyya*, was one of several early-established orders of Ṣūfism in Aïr. The life of Shaykh Jibrīl of Agades confirms this. The latter joined the *Khalwatiyya* in Egypt and he became a convinced, even fanatical, member of it. However, there is something puzzling about this. Why had he to go all the way to Cairo to be initiated? This indicates either that the *Khalwatiyya* was never established as such by Sīdī Maḥmūd, or else, after the lifetime of Aḥmad al-Ṣādiq (b.) al-Shaykh Uwāyis al-Lamtūnī (d. 1090/1679–80), who was not a professed Khalwatī himself, but a Suhrawardī, and who says in the *Qudwa* that the followers of Sīdī Maḥmūd were in decline in his days, nothing more was heard about *Khalwatiyya* activities in Aïr until Shaykh Jibrīl returned to Agades from Egypt, a gap of something like a century.

Once again the *Khalwatiyya* declined. It was given a prominent and privileged place in the Ṣūfī revival in Aïr which was the achievement of Mallam Mūsā of Abatūl (d. 1959) of Tabellot and Egandawel in the southern part of Aïr. He was the *muqaddam* of all three Ṣūfī orders mentioned above. The comments of J. Chapelle, who had a long interview with Mūsā, and whose views were cited extensively by Triaud,[38] are especially relevant:

> The religious affiliation to the *Qādiriyya*, introduced into Aïr by Sīdī Maḥmūd al-Baghdādī, a holy person venerated by the Kél Ǎwǎy. Mallam Mūsā explained to me that he belonged to the *Khalwatiyya* fraternity, of which I heard tell for the first time. He traced his affiliation to that fraternity as far as Sīdī Maḥmūd by a complicated chain. I had noted that Mallam Mūsā had studied in Nigeria and in the neighbourhood of Zinder, that he had only returned to Aïr some 10 to 15 years previously, and I had deduced from this that his affiliation to the *Khalwatiyya* was a result of this exile and that it was something personal to him. I thought that returning amongst his own and only being capable of putting himself in a setting of popular veneration, he had brought about the symbiosis of the two affiliations, rather than posing as an innovator. In fact, I have never been given a clear idea on this point. Remarkable is the material and spiritual success which he has achieved: wealth and visible influence, of these there are no grounds to doubt.[39]

Amongst a number of pertinent comments regarding Mūsā's true purpose, Triaud suggests that he may have drawn upon a perennial 'Baghdādiyya' tradition in the Massif, with an apt use made of the undoubted local obsession with the solitary retreat (*khalwa*). This may be the missing link with the *Khalwatiyya* in Aïr. He also points out the distinct *Shīʿite* flavour to parts of the martyrdom story. The suggestion is an interesting one since pious expressions about ʿAlī with the characteristic formula, 'may Allāh honour his countenance (*karrama Allāh wajhahu*)', punctuate the texts of parts of the *Qudwa*. The descendants of Mūsā at Egandawel insisted to Triaud that the *Khalwatiyya* in Aïr was ancient, that it had declined to the point of oblivion, but that Mūsā had revived it and had added things to it and had combined the *wird* of Aïr and the eastern *Khalwatiyya* and had made one *wird*.[40] Mūsā's success was marked by three noteworthy features:

(*a*) The development of agricultural production at Tabellot-Akririb.
(*b*) Contrary to the sentiment of many of the population, and especially amongst the *ineslemen*, he supported the French.
(*c*) The affirmation of an Islamic legitimacy founded on a double reference to the tradition of Sīdī Maḥmūd al-Baghdādī and the *Khalwatiyya ṭarīqa*.

Triaud points out, likewise, the literary sources of the men of Egandawel. This makes clear the ultimate source of Mūsā Abatūl's information:

The *silsila* put forward by Shaykh Mūsā and his heirs establishes a tie between Sīdī Maḥmūd al-Baghdādī and the founders of the *Khalwatiyya*, but it gives no information about the peculiar spiritual affiliation of Shaykh Mūsā himself. The *silsila* is recorded in his book called *Ṣifat al-wird*. According to the testimony of al-Ḥājj Muṣṭafā: 'The genealogy and the *silsila* of Sīdī Maḥmūd are extracted from the book written by Shaykh Mūsā, *Ṣifat al-wird*. The Shaykh has set out there all the things which are necessary for the practice of the *Khalwatiyya*. He has added or singled out many things in relation to an ancient book called *Qudwat al-Muʿtaqid*.'

This testimony is of special value. It confirms, openly, that *Ṣifat al-wird* is an updated or abridged and amended edition of the *Qudwa*. A brief sample of pages of the former work, seen in Agades, confirms this to be the case. The *silsila* of Sīdī Maḥmūd is taken, name for name, from the text of the *Qudwa*.

Triaud comments:

This *silsila*, such as we have gathered at Egandawel, appears as an appendix. It accords, to all intents and purposes, with the spiritual genealogy of the Egyptian *Khalwatiyya*, published by Bannerth. Only the terminus is different: according to the *silsila* from Niger, Sīdī Maḥmūd al-Baghdādī (who is unknown to Bannerth) would have received it from Jamāl al-Millatī al-Aqrānī, who seems to correspond with 'Jamāl al-Khalwatī', of

Bannerth and to 'Gemāl al-Dīn Chalvetī' of Kissling. This Jamāl would have died, according to Kissling, between 899/1493 and 912/1506. We are thus taken back to the 16th century: and that conforms with the presumed chronology of the saint of Aïr.[41]

Since this chronological fact is confirmed from the *Qudwa* as well as *Ṣifat al-wird*, then the tradition must predate Mallam Mūsā, possibly by several centuries.

Triaud sums up his feelings:

> Under the flag of the *Khalwatiyya*, Shaykh Mūsā presents himself as the revivifier and the sole skilled interpreter of the Ṣūfī traditions of the Massif. He makes himself out to be a disciple of a Sīdī Maḥmūd al-Baghdādī, about whom he knows the history, the *wird* and the *silsila*. In a region where the Islamic identity is constituted around this major saint, participation in the *baraka* of Baghdādī is, in the end, one of the most efficacious of titles of legitimacy.[42]

The political and social reasons for selecting the *Khalwatiyya* in particular may see worldly. However, in fairness to Mallam Mūsā, it could have been that his reasons were less obvious, less forced, and less calculated than at first appears. As has been shown, something of this self-same eclecticism is apparent in the existing text of the *Qudwa* itself, and in the viewpoint of its author or authors, three centuries perhaps before the revival of the *Khalwatiyya*.[43]

Notes

1. See J. L. Triaud, 'Hommes de Religion et *Ṭarīqāt* dans une société en crise, l'Aïr au XIXe et XXe siècles: Le cas *de la Khalwatiyya*', *Cahiers d'Études africaines*, 91, 23/3 (1983).
2. B. G. Martin, *Muslim Brotherhoods in Nineteenth-century Africa* (Cambridge, 1976), p. 18.
3. According to the *Khalwatiyya* genealogy of him, cited by Triaud.
4. Mervyn Hiskett, *The Sword of Truth* (Oxford, 1973), p. 65.
5. Mervyn Hiskett, 'The "Song of the Shaihu's Miracles", a Hausa Hagiography from Sokoto', *African Language Studies, 12* (1971), p. 81.
6. *The Sword of Truth*, p. 121.
7. University of Ibadan, Arabic MS no. 82/114. The significance of the content of this work has yet to be assessed. Discussion of some of its content has appeared in Louis Brenner, 'Muslim thought in eighteenth century West Africa: the case of Shaikh ᶜUthmān b. Fūdī (unpublished SOAS seminar paper, Islam in Africa).
8. Muhammad Bello, Sultan of Sokoto, *Infaku'l maisuri*, ed. by C. E. J. Whitting, (London, 1951), p. 16.
9. Aboubacar Adamou, *Etudes Nigériennes*, no. 44, (Niamey, 1979), p. 136. 'Agadez et sa région, Contribution à l'étude du Sahel et du Sahara nigériens'.
10. A detailed study has still to be made of the Kulumbardo Ṣūfī movements. The subject is central to John Lavers' 'Diversions on a journey, the travels of Shaykh Ahmad al-Yamani from Arbaji to Fez', *Proceedings of the Second Sudan Africa Conference* (Khartoum, 1978), (in press), and he has undertaken recent research on this topic. His latest findings

are to be read (eventually to be published in book form) in his paper, 'Two Sufi Communities in Seventeenth- and Eighteenth-Century Borno', which was discussed in the workshop on Ṣūfism in Africa in the 17th and 18th cents., 16–18 September, 1987.

The site of Kulumbardo is about three days' march to the north-west of the Maini Soroa, north of Geidam, according to Palmer. The name is also spelt and pronounced Kalumfardo. John Lavers cites an alternative name, Belbelec. This place he locates on the edge of the desert, some 80 km. north-east of the Borno capital, Birni Gazargamu. Kulumbardu, or Belbelec, is situated by some, in Niger, as lying 25 km. to the north of Gudumaria and 95 km. to the east of Guré. Kulumbardo *Zāwiya* was founded a second time during the reign of ᶜAlī b. ᶜUmar. It was visited and described by Aḥmad al-Yamanī in 1671. Kulumbardo, during this later period, had spiritual links with the eastern Sudan and also with Morocco, through Agades, especially through the family of Abū Aḥmad al-Ṣādiq (b?) al-Shaykh Uwāyis al-Lamtūnī, the author of the *Qudwa*.

John Lavers is of the opinion that Shaykh ᶜAbdallāh al-Burnawī was not of the Koyam, although this view is not shared by others. A scholar from the region in Niger, who has made a study in depth of the background to the Kulumbardo movement, is Dr Maïkoréma Zakari, of the University of Niamey, who discusses it *passim* in his *Contribution à l-Histoire des Populations du Sud-Est Nigérien, le cas du Mangari (XVI*[e]*–XIX*[e]*s.)*, Etudes Nigériennes no. 53 (Niamey, 1985). There are also references to the Kulumbardo movement in his *Traditions Orales du Mangari*, texts and French trans. publ. in typescript (Niamey, 1985), and available through Dioulde Laya, CELHTO (Centre for the Study of History by Oral Tradition), Niamey.

11. No date is given for this settlement but it probably took place between 1620 and 1625.
12. See n. 10. This would give the site an open stretch of traversed desert and communication routes towards Agades and Aïr, and towards Kawar and the Fezzan.
13. This passage has been translated by Palmer, *The Bornu Sahara and the Sudan* (London, 1936), p. 246, as 'his blood gushed out and traced on the ground the profession of Faith'. It is not certain that the literal spelling of the *shahāda* in Arabic letters, in human blood, is meant or whether the statement is intended to be merely figurative. The legend is probably inspired by the story of the martyrdom of the Caliph ᶜUthmān as he was reading the Qur'ān, and by other miraculous stories of God's saints.
14. On the history of Bagirmi, south-east of Lake Chad, see John E. Lavers, 'An Introduction to the History of Bagirmi c. 1500–1800', in *Annals of Borno*, University of Maiduguri, vol. i (1983), pp. 29–44.
15. *Infāq al-maysūr*, ed. by Whitting, pp. 6–7. The name of the Mais involved vary in other editions of the text. The *mujaddid* referred to by Waldīdu is sometimes held to be ᶜUthmān b. Fūdi, and this whole passage regarded as prophecy, or a later fabrication. If based on an authentic condemnation by Shaykh Waldīdu we have no notion as to who this *mujaddid*, who 'has already appeared', may have been. This passage resembles the *Qudwa* in its phraseology.
16. Rennell Rodd, *People of the Veil*, p. 306.
17. J. Spencer Trimingham, *A History of Islam in West Africa* (Oxford, 1962), p. 137.
18. *Jabābira*, Arabic for giants and tyrants.
19. John Lavers, 'An Introduction' (n. 14), p. 33, and H. R. Palmer, *Sudanese Memoirs* (Lagos, 1928), vol. ii, p. 26.
20. Palmer, *Bornu Sahara*, p. 245, n. 1.
21. Rennell Rodd, *People of the Veil*, pp. 412–3.
22. *History of the First Twelve Years of the Reign of Mai Idris Alooma of Bornu (1571–1583)*, by Ahmed b. Fartua, trans. by H. R. Palmer (Lagos, 1926), pp. 31–5.
23. Ibid. 34.
24. Ibid. 34.
25. *Histoire des Kel-Denneg* (Copenhagen, 1975), pp. 20–2. Another 'Khalwatiyya' view, which differs markedly in certain details from the above, is to be found in Aboubacar Adamou's book, *Agadez et sa Région (Études nigériennes*, 44; Niamey), p. 64, where he writes about Sīdī Maḥmūd as follows: 'Sīdī Maḥmūd al-Baghdādī, the introducer of the *Khalwatiyya ṭarīqah*. Sīdī Maḥmūd al-Baghdādī is a descendant of ᶜAbd al-Qādir al-Jīlānī. He arrived in Agades about the year 1512 where many *murābiṭs* saw him as "a *Mahdī*" (in

a note, Adamou adds that al-Maghīlī, Awgar and his son, Aḥmad *al-muqaddam* were likewise honoured with this title by some). But the Sulṭān, on the contrary, saw in him someone who sought to deprive him of his power. His successive sojourns were at Abatūl (three years), Teghzerin (three years), and Abatūl once more (seven years), from whence he was driven out by the Iberḳorăyăn Tuareg. Then he stayed for ten years in the mountain of Agallal from whence he was driven out by the Kél-Ăwăy Tuareg. He betook to Aghalangha as his haunt of refuge. He lived there for ten years before being killed by the Kél-Ăwăy. The goal of these conflicts was to propagate his brotherhood. Sīdī Maḥmūd al-Baghdādī is the figure behind the spiritual shaping of a certain number of masters who achieved wide fame in the entire region. He it was who founded the mosque at Aghalangha, which is still visited each year by numerous believers. His brotherhood, the *Khalwatiyya*, is predominant in the Aïr Massif and its present home is at Egandawel, sixty kilometres to the north of Agades.'

26. Regarding local traditions of an Iwillimmeden attack on Aïr directed against al-Maghīlī, who is sometimes confused with Sīdī Maḥmūd, see Rodd, *People of the Veil*, p. 292.
27. The exact sense of this passage is not especially clear. It appears to be a legendary elaboration of a passage in Ibn Isḥāq's *Sīrat Rasūl Allāh*, see A. Guillaume's trans. *The Life of Muhammad* (Oxford, 1955), p. 114, the first paragraph of the section entitled, "ᶜAlī b. Abū Tālib the first male to accept Islam.'
28. This name is unclear in our text. Maᶜrūf al-Karkhī died in 200/815–6 and he was a celebrated ascetic and mystic of the Baghdād school. Sarī al-Saqaṭī was his most famous pupil, who in turn became the master of al-Junayd, as our text says. Note that at this stage the *silsila*, as given here, is an ᶜAlīd one, and that after ᶜAlī's name, the expression 'may Allāh honour his countenance' (*karrama Allāhu wajhahu*) specifically appears. This chain to ᶜAlī, taken in conjunction with this formula, the liturgical singing and the ecstatic dancing in the *Maḥmūdiyya*, would appear to place it within the category of those *ṭuruq* which Irène Mélikoff has called 'heterodox' orders. The *silsila* is distinctly heterodox in part. Heterodox likewise is the substance of Aḥmad Bābā's severe criticism of the *Maḥmūdiyya*, see Conclusion (2). The point is to be found discussed in further detail in Irène Mélikoff, 'Ahmed Yesevi and Turkic popular Islam', *Utrecht Papers on Central Asia* (Utrecht Turkological Series, no. 2; 1987), pp. 83–94, especially pp. 84–5.
29. Abū'l-Qāsim b. Muḥammad b. al-Junayd al-Baghdādi, one of the greatest orthodox exponents of Ṣūfīsm.
30. *muqaddam* (see *Glossary*) in a Ṣūfī context denotes one who is authorized to teach the *wird*; the *wird khāṣṣ* (*dhikr sirrī*) is the secret name of God which a Shaykh only communicates to the initiate. A *muqaddam* may also grant a licence (*ijāza*) of affiliation to a *ṭarīqa*.
31. The name in the text is unclear. Triaud, on the basis of another name derived from *Ṣifat al-wird*, spells his name Mumāshīd al-Dīnawarī. He gives an alternative spelling Mamshādh al-Dīnawarī. This appears to be correct.
32. Abū'l-Najīb al-Suhrawardī, died 563/1168, was famous for his writings and teaching and as a founder of a *ribāṭ* on the western bank of the Tigris.
33. Key names in the *silsila* of the *Khalwatiyya* Ṣūfī order, see Hans Joachim Kissling: 'Aus der Geschichte des Chalvetijje-Ordens', *Zeitschrift der Deutschen Morgenlandischen Gesellschaft* 103/2 (1953), p. 283, and also his following notes. Akh Muḥammad should, I believe, read Aḥmad (al-Khalwatī), likewise Akh Mīram instead of Mabram.
34. Sīdī Yaḥyā al-Badakwī in the text of the *Qudwa*, Yaḥyā al-Bakūbī (also spelt Bakwī), of Baku in Azerbaijan, according to the *silsila* given by Triaud. This is in all likelihood the same person as Sayyid Yaḥyā al-Shirwānī/Shirvānī (d. 860/1464) in Kissling.
35. At this point in the *silsila* there is some lack of clarity in the spelling of names. ᶜUmar Arzinjānī [probably Dede ᶜUmar Rūshānī of Tabrīz (d. 892/1487)] may be explained by a confusion of Dede ᶜUmar Aydinī with Pīr Aḥmad (or Meḥmed) al-Arzinjānī, Mulla Pīrī, of Amasya in Anatolia, see B. G. Martin, 'A Short History of the Khalwati Order of Dervishes', in Nikkie R. Keddie (ed.), *Scholars, Saints and Sufis* (Berkeley, 1972), pp. 278–9. Ibn Jamāl al-Milla is clearly Jamāl al-Dīn al-Aqsaralī al-Khalwatī (Çelebi Efendi) who died in 903/1497 at Tābūt Qorosu. Shaykh Yūsuf b. ᶜAlī al-Ḥumaydī is a very uncertain identification, and his name, as the others named above, is confused. He may well be none

other than Yūsuf Sünbül Sinān al-Dīn (whose father however did *not* bear the name of ᶜAlī) who died in 936/1529 in Istanbul, and who was the head of the *tekke* of Qoja Muṣṭafā Pasha in Istanbul, hence the *nisba*, al-Qusṭanaṭanī, in the *Qudwa*. The *nisba* of Yūsuf b. ᶜAlī relating to the town of Merzifon may also be significant in regard to the type of mystical background and example which greatly influenced Sīdī Maḥmūd when he was himself a novice. F. W. Hasluck in his *Christianity and Islam under the Sultans* (Oxford, 1929), vol. ii, p. 512, draws attention to a Shīᶜite presence in this area of Asia Minor and around Amasya, though the latter was *Sunnī*. Merzifon itself contains the tomb of Piri Dede, who was a companion of Ḥājjī Bektāsh. In the time of Evliyā Çelebī, the town housed some two hundred dervishes and the convent in question was supported by the revenues of 366 villages.

36. See the arguments of Triaud in 'Hommes de religion', pp. 265–7.
37. E. Brouin, *Rapport de tournée dans l'Est de l'Aïr, cercle d'Agadès, Mai–Juin, 1947*, *AN/SGG*, Archives du Niger: Secrétériat Général du Gouvernement (unpublished report, Niamey).
38. Triaud, 'Hommes de religion', pp. 250–1.
39. Note the confusion between the *Qādiriyya* and the *Khalwatiyya.*
40. This is explained in *Ṣifat al-wird*. However, the only passages from this work which are known to me do not deal with this particular subject. On the subject of Shīᶜite influences see B. G. Martin, 'A Short History', p. 284.
41. Triaud, 'Hommes de religion', p. 266.
42. Ibid. 273.
43. See in particular pp. 85 (n. 31) and 95 (n. 65).

Conclusion

Sīdī Maḥmūd in history and myth

Mention has been made throughout this book of the miraculous acts of Sīdī Maḥmūd. It would have been surprising indeed if he had not gathered about him, or if there had not grown around his name, a corpus of the miraculous and of the mythological, a thaumaturgical narrative which was felt to be appropriate for a major regional saint and mystic. Such is to be found in all religious traditions. The miraculous is more especially associated with his luminosity and with his knowledge of the unseen world. Yet, in a number of respects, the life and works of Sīdī Maḥmūd, as revealed in the text of the *Qudwa*, and in the Aïr tradition, are bereft of the excessively hagiographical and cluttered biographical detail which marks some Maghribī writings of this kind and even some of the alleged feats of his Aïr contemporaries.

Djibo Hamani of the University of Niamey, who has researched extensively into Aïr history, has noted the fact that the heart of the Aïr Massif, and the desert regions that surround it, are cut off from the city of Agades and from much of the religious life led within it. This is true in respect to the allegiance which is shown to holy men. Whilst the Tuareg of the Massif, amongst certain 'maraboutic groups', and amongst the Kél Åwăy, revere the memory and the holy sites which are associated with the life and death of Sīdī Maḥmūd and of his followers, the citizens of Agades revere the memory of other scholars and men of faith who were near contemporaries of Sīdī Maḥmūd.

One example is Muḥammad Shambaki (who may, in fact, be cited in the *Qudwa*). He composed an ode, in verse, known as *Yā Mawlā* (Aya Maoula). It is described as a eulogy of the saints and as a satire of tyrannical power. It is said that when Muḥammad Shambaki built his Agades mosque, about 1550, the men of piety, who taught the faith, remarked that its structure was poorly designed for prayer. Shambaki invited them to enter it. He showed them a small hole or aperture placed within the wall. Through it they could behold the whole of Mecca and its Kaᶜba.

Abū Yazīd, whose squat and slightly domed mausoleum dominates the Tanibéré cemetery in Agades, was the patron saint of the Imourdan-n-Afalla quarter. After he died, his body disappeared, once it had been ceremoniously washed. Only traces left by a camel were to be found in its place. The damp earth which had been used to wash his corpse was placed in a shroud which was buried in that spot which has become his official tomb.

Other miracles were performed in Agades by Aḥmad (Nisla-n-Katigué) Ūzūrūk, like Abū Yazīd born in Aïr itself, who preserved the city from an enemy attack by casting his sandal in the path of their advance and he routed them. Mention has already been made of al-Najīb Muḥammad, nicknamed '*al-sayf*' (ch. 2) who, or his son, is the one leading Agades figure (excluding Awgar and his son, who were of much lesser status) to be specifically associated with the movement of Sīdī Maḥmūd and to have received a special mention in the *Qudwa*.

Foremost amongst the scholar saints in Agades city was Zakariyyā', who in all accounts is credited with building the principal mosques, more especially the great mosque (possibly founded in 1515) with its unforgettable minaret, which still dominates the skyline, although the existing minaret was largely restored in the nineteenth century.[1] He allegedly entered Aïr from the Fezzan about 1530. Discovered by herdsmen in his grotto, or *khalwa* of meditation, at Inabamba (in Abanbarey),[2] whilst he rang his metal ablutions cup, his presence was reported to the Sulṭān, who experienced great initial difficulty in persuading him to leave his retreat and take up residence in Agades. According to Djibo Hamani, Zakariyyā' and Sīdī Maḥmūd have now become the two focal-points of saintly life and belief, the former in the city, the latter in the Massif and in the desert. It is indeed a fact that nowhere in the *Qudwa* is mention made of Zakariyyā', yet other men of piety in Agades are mentioned. Nowhere does he figure amongst noteworthy men of Ṣūfism. The writings of the scholars of the Kel Es-Sūq remain silent, though as we have seen (ch. 2) Sīdī Maḥmūd is known to them, and likewise those disciples of his who were men of the Kel Es-Sūq, for example Abū'l-Hudā, for whom Sīdī Maḥmūd became the supreme, even the exclusive, guide to the 'Way'.

The Historicity of Sīdī Maḥmūd

Sīdī Maḥmūd was a historical figure in Aïr. His life and role there in the early half of the sixteenth century may be authenticated from the following documentary evidence, outside the *Qudwa* itself:

1. A reference to the existence of *khalwas* in the general area of Aïr and Azawagh, amongst those questions sent by the scholar,

Muḥammad b. Muḥammad b. ᶜAlī al-Lamtūnī to al-Suyūṭī in August 1493. This scholar specifically remarks: 'Section (30). Some have no other work but reciting the Qur'ān and *ḥadīth*, worship, solitude (*khalwa*), reading the *Risāla* and *al-Shihāb* and the like.'

Al-Suyūṭī, in his reply, expressed the view that these were wholly praiseworthy practices.[3]

The presence of cells of retreat in the region of Aïr, seemingly prior to the mission of Sīdī Maḥmūd, is specifically referred to in the *Qudwa*. Furthermore, it is an Aïr tradition that Ṣūfī centres at Agallal and elsewhere were already in existence in the fifteenth century.

2. A brief, but extremely important, reference to Sīdī Maḥmūd, though not by name, in the writings of the Timbuktu scholar, Aḥmad Bābā.[4] The short work in question (some nine pages in all) was originally composed in Timbuktu on 11 Shawwāl 1024/4 November 1616. It is a set of replies on four questions which had been put to him and bears the title, *al-Lamᶜ fī ajwibat al-as'ila al-arbaᶜa*. The specific question is the third and it relates to the *dhikr* of a certain religious brotherhood during which they join together to sing and to dance until they lose control of their functions and are totally exhausted. At the same time, they refuse to observe, or ignore, the prayer and the fast and they abstain from learning and studying the *Qur'ān* and *ḥadīth* and they consider as heretics all those others who do not follow in their 'Way'.

Sīdī Maḥmūd is the schismatic, 'al-Baghdādī', and he is branded as an innovator by Aḥmad Bābā. Apart from confirming the killing of Sīdī Maḥmūd, this reference indicates that seemingly Oriental and Ottoman Ṣūfī practices of his followers were beginning to have an influence in the entire southern Sahara region, more particularly his *ādāb*, *dhikr*, and *dawarān*, and that the nature of these latter were something new, strange, and wholly unacceptable to many of the pious in that region.

As for the third question, [it is] in regard to the students who assemble in order to perform the *dhikr* until they foam at the mouth, some faint in their midst, and they allege, furthermore, that neither the recitation of the *Qur'ān*, nor the knowledge of scripture, nor the doctrine of the divine unity, nor fasting during *Ramaḍān*, nor the statutory prayer—none of these, together with [that status of] those who are not members of their Ṣūfī 'Way', are allowable, they are irrelevant and are not in any way lawful.

As for the answers [to this question and their claim], if it be correct indeed that they are in such a wicked circumstance and that they firmly and truly believe it to be so, then they are in no sense Muslims. Rather, they are infidels, men who are in sad and grievous error. They are evil livers, they have no portion in the faith of Islam, and this on account of their denial of

Pl. 26. A specific reference to the heretical and schismatical 'dervish' from Baghdād who was slain in Agades and his followers dispersed (Aḥmad Bāba, *Al-Lam*ᶜ *fī ajwibat al-as'ila al-arba*ᶜ*a*)

that which is knowingly demanded in the faith, that is to say the statutory prayer, the *Ramaḍān* fast, and the recitation of the *Qur'ān*. If they say, as you so report, that the same is not laid down in the canonic law, then Allāh has said [in *Sūra* 73, *al-Muzammil*, verse 20] 'recite thereof of the *Qur'ān* as much as ye may,' and, in regard to the *Qur'ān*, He has said [in *Sūra* 73, *al-Muzammil*, verse 4] 'recite the *Qur'ān* in slow and measured rhythmic tones.' He has said so in many verses. It is said [in *Sūra* 29, *al-ᶜAnkabūt*, verse 45] 'for prayer restrains from shameful and unjust deeds.' Such is the verse. The Muslim are in a consensus, all of them, on that.

Hence it is imperative to chide and scold them over their perverse belief. Should they continue to pursue it, then they are apostates. If it be known that they were already Muslims prior to this, then they should repent and amend their ways. If they refuse to return [to the true path] then they should be fought and slain. To wage a *jihād* against them will earn a greater reward than against those who were already infidels, this due to the manifest error of their ways and the leading of others into their error. This is clear and explicit. There is no doubt about it. Any difference of view amongst scholars is in regard to the performance of the *dhikr* itself, whether it be in accordance with the *sunna* and whether those who take part in it bear all the hall-marks of orthodox *sunnite* practice, and are of a true doctrinal belief and that they are free of any kind of heresy. In respect of all this the scholars do hold differing views as to whether it be sound and proper and meet to be rewarded, or whether it be a heresy (*bidᶜa*) that is eschewed, strongly disapproved of, and, indeed, prohibited, for such was not the act of the pious Muslim in the earliest times. What they have said about this is very extensive and is to be read in many books.

As for these persons [whom you describe], there is no doubt that they are in error and that there is a duty to chide them and to fight them, should they persist in their erroneous ways. It may well be that they are from the remnants of the 'companies of the Baghdādī heretic,' who was killed in the further regions of Agades, at the commencement of the tenth [sixteenth] century, and of the man who was called Saᶜīd. He it was who dissipated and scattered their writing (*qirṭās*). If Allāh so wills, then happy will he be. May Allāh make him and us all happy men, although for him it is most meet that it be so. Consult that edict, so that witnesses may testify against them, and if it be established amongst those who wield the power of authority, they may thereby be enabled to deal with the matter and to effect the same.[4]

The most valuable piece of information in this reference, in Aḥmad Bābā's writings, is that it specifically dates the movement of the heretical and innovatory 'Baghdādī', who was killed in the suburbs of, or at some distance from, Agades, to the earlier years of the sixteenth century. Once this date is accepted, indeed with pleasure, the rest of Aḥmad Bābā's response would appear to raise more problems than are solved in regard to the entire purpose of the Ṣūfī movement. Among the many questions which could be posed one might include the following:

(*a*) How is it to be explained that Sīdī Maḥmūd, a vile heretic, even 'infidel', in the opinion of Aḥmad Bābā (based on hearsay) came to be accepted as a saintly example of the divine light by Muḥammad Bello, especially since Aḥmad Bābā, and his writings, were a major source of guidance to Muḥammad Bello and to his father?

(*b*) Aḥmad Bābā was a contemporary of Shams al-Dīn al-Najīb b. Muḥammad al-Anūṣammanī. The latter was still alive in 1005/1597, when the *Nayl*, written by the former, was completed. In 1616, Aḥmad Bāba condemned the movement of Sīdī Maḥmūd. However, in the *Qudwa*, al-Najīb (*al-sayf*?), or his son, is listed amongst the devoted followers of Sīdī Maḥmūd.

(*c*) Is this text of Aḥmad Bābā a *carte blanche* for the destruction of the Ṣūfī lodges of the Adrar, Azawagh, and Aïr undertaken by the Iberḳorăyăn fanatic, Ḥadāḥadā? Could the target of the latter's wrath be a descendant of Sīdī Maḥmūd, his alleged son Aḥmad or another 'Baghdādī' even with the same name, hence a confused chronology in the Aïr oral traditions?

(*d*) By what channel did this report reach Aḥmad Bābā and who is the Saᶜīd to whom he refers? No mention of this name occurs anywhere in the *Qudwa*, only a general mention of the counsellors of the Sulṭān of Agades and of the book (*qirṭās*?) of Sīdī Maḥmūd.

(*e*) Are fragments of the *qirṭās* to be found in the *Qudwa*?

(*f*) Aḥmad Bābā accuses the Ṣūfīs of excess, uncontrolled ecstatic rituals, neglect and indifference to other Muslim duties in religion and an intolerance of all other 'Ways'. Nothing at all of this is advocated in the *Qudwa*, other than a toleration of charismatic emotional expression and the claim that Sīdī Maḥmūd preached a superior 'Way'; namely that one, it was believed, laid down by the Prophet himself.

(*g*) The fact that Agades appears in Aḥmad Bābā's text may not be unconnected with a report amongst the Kel Es-Sūq that Karidenna, the first *amenokal* of the Iwillimmeden Tuareg, was invested in office and took the *bayᶜa* of allegiance from the Sulṭān of Agades, Muḥammad al-Ghudāla, when it would appear that links between this new Tuareg power of the Iwillimmeden, in the region of Timbuktu, and the Aïr Sultanate were being encouraged and strengthened. This was a time when the Agades Sultanate enjoyed esteem and status following the reign of Ahmad b. Talyaṭ (Taluẓa). Muḥammad al-Ghudāla was a brother of the latter and it would have been politic to have depicted the activities of Sīdī Maḥmūd in the least favourite light at that time.

3. The *silsila* of the *Maḥmūdiyya*, subsequent to Sīdī Maḥmūd himself, is to be read in the pages of a work by Shehu ᶜUthmān Dan

Fodio which is entitled *al-Salāsil al-dhahabiyya lil-sāda al-Ṣūfiyya*. The *silsila* is given in Fig. 2, together with comments on the personalities who appear within it by reference to the *Qudwa* and to other sources which make mention of these Aïr personalities.

FIG. 2

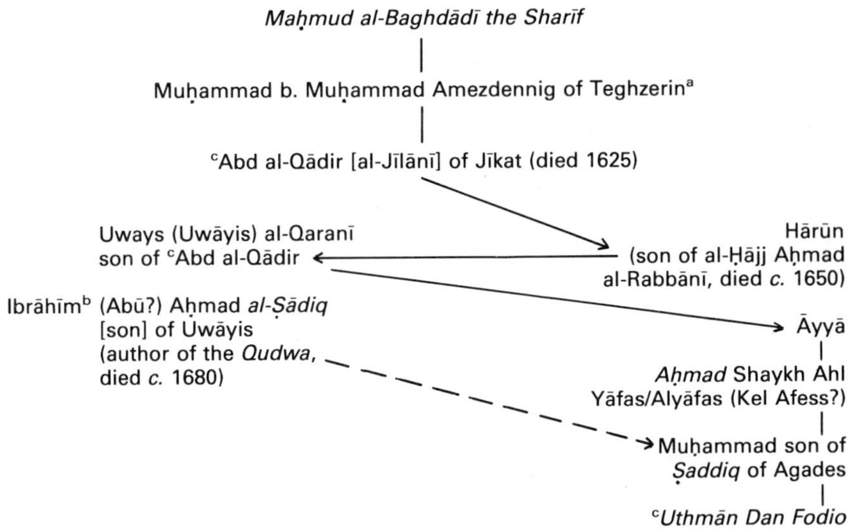

[a] Teghzerin, spelt also Ciggazaren, is a locality which lies to the east of Timia in the Aïr Massif.

[b] It is possible that the copyist of Muḥammad b. Tighna's famous ode against Ḥadāḥadā and Ḥamidtu, Ibrāhīm b. Uwāyis of Jīkat, was a brother of the author of the *Qudwa*.

The Tuareg names which follow are known from the information provided in the *Qudwa* (pp. 49–52). The *Qudwa* furnishes no names in a specific *Maḥmūdiyya silsila*, as such, after Sīdī Maḥmūd himself.

(*a*) *Muḥammad b. Muḥammad (Amezdennig) of Teghzerin*[5]

He was initiated by Sīdī Maḥmūd as his successor. A Tuareg possibly connected with the Iwillimmeden Kel Denneg or Kel-Innek, a sub-tribe of the Itesen. His nickname 'Amezdennig', means 'of the East'. He was the son of Inzakrīn.[6] Like Sīdī Maḥmūd, he believed in the 'gnostic, illuminatory and emanatory principle of the divinity' (*nūrāniyya*). He had a vision of al-Khaḍir and Elias.[7] He settled in Assodé (Asūṭay) which, together with Agalāl, Teghzerin, Abatūl, and Jikāt, seems to have become a headquarters for the *Maḥmūdiyya* in the late sixteenth century. He was buried at Teghzerin. He initiated novices into the *ṭarīqa*.

(*b*) *ᶜAbd al-Qādir [al-Jīlanī] of Jīkat* (*d. 1625*)
The son of Shaykh Abū Yaḥyā who was a close associate of (*a*). To him was attributed knowledge of the 'divine secret'. He established his *khalwa* called 'sandhill of the oath or the right hand' (*rabwat al-yamīn*) at Jīkat and he was buried there. It became the most important south-westerly settlement in the Massif of the *Maḥmūdiyya*. He was the father of Shaykh Uways (Uwāyis) al-Qaranī, (*d*) below.

(*c*) *Shaykh Hārūn b. Muḥammad b. al-Ḥājj Aḥmad, also of Jīkat*
The companion of (*b*) and his 'milk brother', brought up with him in the Aïr home of Sīdī Maḥmūd. He initiated novices for (*b*).

(*d*) *Shaykh Abū Muḥammad al-Munīr Uways (Uwāyis) al-Qaranī*
A son of (*b*) above, and the father of (*e*), below. It is also possible that he was the father of [Abū] Aḥmad al-Ṣādiq (b.) Uwāyis al-Lamtūnī, the author of the *Qudwa*, who died *c.*1680, or the name, Aḥmad, could be a misreading of Muḥammad and the name we have here is that of the author of the *Qudwa* himself.

(*e*) *Āyyā*
An unknown Shaykh. Āyyā is a Tuareg name that is common amongst the Kel Es-Sūq.

(*f*) *Shaykh Aḥmad, Shaykh of the people of Yāfas/Alyāfas or Alefas—Kel Afess*
An unknown Shaykh about whom no details are furnished. Yafās could also be read as Tafās, Tīfīs, and this name associated with holy families from Fez in Morocco. Rodd records a major Arab inscription on a tomb at Afis (Afess),[8] and it is possible—though I have not seen it—that this Shaykh Aḥmad is the person in question.

(*g*) *Muḥammad b. Ṣaddiq, known as Amaggadhar* (possibly Amaggadhaz, = from Agades)
An unknown Shaykh (though just possibly a son of someone who bore a relationship to the author of the *Qudwa* had he lived to be a very great age), who initiated the Shehu ᶜUthmān Dan Fodio into the *Maḥmūdiyya*.

The influence of the *Maḥmūdiyya* on the Shehu and his sons can be further demonstrated from the vocabulary and, indeed, whole passages from *Infāq al-maysūr*, which, in its chapter dealing with the Sultanate of Aïr, and the life of Sīdī Maḥmūd al-Baghdādī, without doubt draws upon the opening of the *Qudwa* for almost all of its essential biographical material. The Shehu must have obtained, or have possessed, or have seen, a copy. Muḥammad b. Ibrāhīm was buried at Tīfīs (Tefis). Muḥammad b. Aḥmad Inzikrān (who perhaps is related to (*a*) above), lies buried between Tahoua and In Gall. Another scholar is also mentioned in *al-I*ᶜ*lān*. He is the *faqīh*, Muḥammad Adaïday, the 'father of orphans', Abū'l-Yatāmā. He was buried at Tintagassane.

On pp. 22–3 of the texts in Boubou Hama, *Recherches sur l'histoire des Toureg Sahariens et Soudanais* (Niamey, 1967), the author associates Aïr and the Tagedda region with the territory of the Bardāma, a tribe mentioned by the Arab geographer, Ibn Baṭṭūṭa, who says that they were a Berber people in the Mali Adrār between Walāta and Tegidda. Aïr itself is referred to as 'the waterless tracts' (*al-falawāt*), a term which, if applied to the Massif itself, is by no means accurate. As regards the desert zones to the south and west of Aïr the term was known, since the district lying between Agades city and Tadeliẓa, just within the Massif, is referred to in the accounts of the wars of Mai Idrīs Alooma of Borno as the 'wide desert tract', *al-falāh al-wāsi*ᶜ*a*. The author of *al-I*ᶜ*lān* gives as his reasons for associating Elias with the Aïr Massif several passages in the 'Tales of the Prophets', *Qiṣaṣ al-Anbiyā*'. According to its author, Muḥammad b. ᶜAbdallāh al-Kisā'ī (Leiden ed., 1923, pp. 243–50) Elias burnt alive some of the Banū Isrāᶜīl, in the *falawāt*, these men bent on doing him harm in revenge for the death of one of their fellows. The *falawāt* of Aïr around Azeru were believed to be the abode of Elias after these events. This story would explain the promixity of his presence to the saints, and especially to certain of the disciples of Sīdī Maḥmūd, in particular Shaykh Muḥammad b. Muḥammad (Amezdennig) of Teghzerin.

Chronological Difficulties in regard to the Date of the Martyrdom

It is not possible to assign a specific date for the martyrdom of Sīdī Maḥmūd, since we cannot be certain which of the Sulṭāns of Agades he offended. Besides, the so-called Agades chronicles, which tell us of these Sulṭāns, are not in themselves consistent historical documents which can be verified from non-Aïr sources during this particular period. The mission of Sīdī Maḥmūd without question is now seen to be placed at the beginning of the sixteenth century. The written accounts which we have (as opposed to the oral traditions amongst the Aïr Tuareg, which are generally a century too late), the *Qudwa* and the chronicles of the Kel Es-Sūq, agree that this Sulṭān was named Aḥmad b. Taluẓa/Talẓa/Talāzāy, with variants of spelling. Muḥammad is very occasionally given as a variant of Aḥmad. One source maintains that the *Qāḍī* of this Sulṭān was al-Najīb, nicknamed *al-sayf*. Allegedly misled and misinformed by his jurists about the true status and true mission of Sīdī Maḥmūd, and apparently frightened by reports that the Ṣūfī movement led by him was a threat to his throne, the Sulṭān sent a military force to crush the movement. All the accounts, whether written or oral, concur that this Ṣūfī movement was not one which condemned militant resistance, rather that is maintained that use of force was, if need arose, a legitimate part of its activities. A saying current in Aïr, attributed to Sīdī Maḥmūd, 'He who slays one of the Iberḳorăyăn will enter Paradise' (*man qatala Ibarkuray dakhala'l-janna*) is in all likelihood apocryphal.

Who was this Sulṭān Aḥmad b. Taluẓa? No light is shed on these events in the Agades 'chronicles' in any way. No dynastic rupture is recorded which suggests that the martyrdom was its cause or had any long-term effect on the Sultanate whatsoever. Djibo Hamani, in his as yet unpublished thesis, defended in the Sorbonne in March 1985, entitled 'Au carrefour du Soudan, et de la Berberie, le Sultanat Touareg de l'Ayar', has studied three possible Sulṭāns who could be Aḥmad b. Taluẓa.

1. Muḥammad b. ᶜAbd al-Raḥmān. He was nicknamed Ṭalẓi Ṭanaṭ and he reigned between 899/1493–4 and 908/1502–3. His nine year reign ended with his assassination following conflicts with his maternal uncles and sister's son. Chronologically, this Sulṭān's reign is unlikely to be relevant. It cannot be squared with the life of al-Maghīlī, who predated Sīdī Maḥmūd, and who died either in 909/1503–4 or 910/1505–6.

2. Muḥammad b. Talādha or Taluẓa, 922/1516 to 924/1518, whose allegedly two year reign, and lack of importance, make him also an unlikely ruler. Yet part of his name, Taluẓa, is undoubtedly close to the spelling of the Sulṭān's name in the *Qudwa*.

By no means all the sources citing names of the Agades Sulṭāns reduce his reign so drastically. A reign of twenty-five years is also given to him. Elsewhere it is given to Ibrāhīm b. Muḥammad Ṣeṭṭefen. According to J. Hunwick, 'The conflicting versions appear to reflect a power struggle involving a son of Muḥammad Ṣeṭṭefen (who, in Tuareg traditions, could not normally inherit power) and Muḥammad Shala/Talẓa.'[9] Some involvement of the *Maḥmūdiyya* in this struggle cannot be excluded; furthermore, this reign fits best the chronology of Aḥmad Bāba.

3. Aḥmad b. Talyaṭ (Taluẓa in one source at least) who reigned between 948/1541–2 and 961/1553–4. His lengthy reign, fourteen years, together with those events which took place with Borno during

the reigns of his successors, might suggest that it was during his rule that a major conflict with the *Maḥmūdiyya* in the Massif took place. The Aïr sources concur that dire distress later befell the Sultanate and none was more grave than the attacks launched against it by Idrīs Alawma, Mai of Borno. The latter reigned between 971–2/1564–5 and 1005/1596, and punitive expeditions were made against the Aïr Sultanate.

The Borno version of events is to be read in Ibn Farṭūwa's account of the wars of the Sulṭān Idrīs Alawma of Borno, as translated by Dierk Lange, in *A Sudanic Chronicle*.[10]

In his translation and comment on the raids launched against the region of Aïr, Lange refrains from identifying Tādus as Tadelīẓa or indeed any other locality, remaining sceptical of the view that Tadelīẓa was a residential centre for the Sultanate at that time. Rodd mentions a locality called Tadesa, on the southern edge of the Aïr Massif. There is therefore justification for his reticence. Lange (pages 162–4) also discusses the problem of the identification of the confederation of Talaẓ, who are mentioned as the defeated enemy of the ruler of Borno. He draws attention to the spelling of this name in the *Ta'rīkh al-Sūdān* as Talẓa, thus closely conforming to the spelling of the Aïr Sulṭān's surname in the *Qudwa*. However, in the context of this Timbuktu text, so too in the *Ta'rīkh al-Fattāsh*, from the same provenance, the context of this name is that of a couple of expeditions, launched in 1499/1500 and 1514/15 by Askia Muḥammad against the Aïr Sulṭān, al-ᶜAdala, who allegedly reigned between Sulṭāns (1) and (2) above. Lange concludes that a tribal confederation must be indicated by this recurrent name, though not necessarily the Itesen.

It is apparent from this Aïr campaign that the 'Taluz clan' (Taluẓ) were the principal foe and the principal object of punishment in the Mai's campaign. The reverses suffered then by the Sultanate could certainly explain a subsequent view of the pious that such a memorable retribution was divine response to the slaying of Sīdī Maḥmūd. This said, however, the campaign did not take place during the reign of Aḥmad b. Talyaṭ, but during that of his brother and successor, Muḥammad al-Ghudāla (al-ᶜAddāla), who probably had deposed him. He allegedly reigned from 964/1556 and he held the office of Sulṭān for some forty years. Nor is there any evidence to suggest that his rule, or that of his predecessor, was marked by any special impiety that justified a Borno *jihād*. It is noteworthy that the Tuareg oral traditions of Aïr ignore him altogether. They chronologically adjust the local events so as to establish the martyrdom of Sīdī Maḥmūd within the reign of

Muḥammad al-Tafrīja, who commenced his reign towards the close of the sixteenth century. His long rule was broken in two by the enthronement of the Itesen-backed Sulṭān, Awgar b. Talyaṭ, a relative of Aḥmad b. Talyaṭ. The length of Awgar's reign is not recorded. ʿUmar b. Idrīs, Mai of Borno, reigned between 1029/1619 and 1048/1639. He would have been a contemporary of Muḥammad al-Tafrīja. Aïr oral tradition, in the main, describes the martyrdom of Sīdī Maḥmūd as an act involving the Sulṭān, al-Tafrīja, at the same period when ʿUmar b. Idrīs was engaged in suppressing the Kulumbardo Ṣūfī movement, further south, and ordering the assassination of the Ṣūfī Muḥammad b. al-Jarmiyū, for very similar reasons, and with a similar description of the contemporary circumstances in the sources. There may well be shared hagiographical details in both accounts which became incorporated into a martyrdom story as late as the lifetime of the author of the *Qudwa*. Chronologically, therefore, the life and death of Sīdī Maḥmūd in Aïr took place in the first half of the sixteenth century. Hagiographically, however, much of the substance of the story about the circumstances of his martyrdom, despite, or even by virtue of, their inconsistency, may be later. This makes it rash to accept as historical any of the Aïr traditions which tell of the exact circumstances where Sīdī Maḥmūd met his death.

The Element of the Miraculous in the Personality of Sīdi Maḥmūd

The life of Sīdī Maḥmūd, both in the *Qudwa* and in those sources and writings which are derived from it, together with the oral traditions of the Tuareg of Aïr and Azawagh, conforms to patterns of sanctity within the Saharan, and indeed the Maghribī, Islamic tradition. The Ṣūfī saints are clearly portrayed in this tradition. Some were physicians, others great scholars, some were martyrs, others itinerant dervishes and sojourners, whose final resting-place was either an empty tomb or else a sudden departure heavenwards upon a prayer-rug, or on the sea, or in some other manner, leaving behind a small body of men who were to continue the 'Way' that was set forth in the teachings and in the practices of their founder, while he lived with them.

Thomas Mann in his great work, *Joseph and His Brothers*, has most effectively portrayed this 'man of light' whose nature was to bring to mankind some inkling of that light which could be rekindled, again and again, by initiation into a brotherhood, or by the performance of movements of ecstasy in the *dhikr*, or by a silent communion in a *khalwa* retreat, or through communion with departed saints. He writes:

A very ancient tradition of human thought, based upon man's truest knowledge of himself and going back to exceeding early days whence it has become incorporated into the succession of religions, prophecies and doctrines of the East, into Avesta, Islam, Manichaeanism, Gnosticism and Hellenism, deals with the figure of the first or first completely human man, the Hebraic *Adam qadmon*; conceived as a youthful being made out of pure light, formed before the beginning of the world as prototype and abstract of humanity. To this conception others have attached themselves, varying to some extent, yet in essentials the same. Thus, and accordingly, primitive man was at his very beginning God's chosen champion in the struggle against that evil which penetrated into the new creation; yet harm befell him, he was fettered by demons, imprisoned in the flesh, estranged from his origins, and only freed from the darkness of earthly and fleshly existence by a second emissary of the deity, who in some mysterious way was the same as himself, his own higher self, and restored to the world of light, leaving behind him, however, some portions of his light, which then were utilized for the creation of the material world and earthly creatures. (Trans. H. T. Lowe-Porter in Penguin Modern Classics).

This 'cosmic' personality, in Saharan tradition, from the Shāṭirī lad in Shinjīṭ, or Shaykh Ḥamallāh in Mauritania, back to Sīdī Maḥmūd in the Aïr Massif, was personified as youthful, as the embodiment of light, a lively man of learning and of authority, a person who drew men to follow him, usually a *sharīf* who was directly descended, through Fāṭima, from the Prophet, who came from Fez in Morocco, or who at least passed through Fez, who wandered through many lands and who usually came from the west.[11] But such a saint and divine figure was arrayed in the clothing of his time. Sīdī Maḥmūd lived in the age of the greatest Ottoman Sulṭāns. He was initiated by a master, whose identity is far from certain, but whose name, Yūsuf b. ᶜAlī, together with his home town of Merzifon in Asia Minor, and his association with Ṣūfism in Constantinople, are together indicative of an Ottoman background to Maḥmūd, the 'man from Baghdād'.

There are similarities in Ṣūfī background, in status and in deeds, between Sīdī Maḥmūd and Gül-Baba, the Bektāshī of Budapest, who is buried there. L. Fekete remarks that Gül-Baba was a half-historical, half-legendary character.[12] He was born in Merzifon, that important centre of the *Khalwatiyya* and the *Bektāshiyya*. He was a dervish and he came from the Prophet's family. He lived during the reigns of Sulṭāns Bajazet, Selim, and Sulayman. He was a contemporary of Sīdī Maḥmūd.

Fekete notes that the seventeenth-century Turkish traveller, Evliyā Çelebi, was the first to furnish details about this latter dervish and his life. He mentioned that Merzifon was his birth-place, that he was a Bektāshī, and that he was a descendant in the Prophet's household. Following the death of Mehmet II (died 1481), and during the reigns of Bajazet, Selim, and Sulayman, he took part in all their expeditions. Like Sīdī Maḥmūd, Gül-Baba wandered widely in the earth and he slept out of doors, yet he was spotlessly clean in his habits.

At this time, holy men of valour were sent from Baghdād. The great scholar, Veliyyuddin, in that city, sent his two sons, both 'ghazis', Seyyid Cafer or Güldede, and Esseyyid Hüsein or Sünbüldede to the court of Sulayman at the latter's formal invitation. Then, in 1541, the year when the Turks captured Buda, Güldede died an honoured martyr there and Sünbüldede died in Romania. Sulṭān Sulayman himself was present at their funeral.

Some of the biographical material in the *Qudwa* dates from the time of Evliyā Çelebi. The *Qudwa* is about Ṣūfī happenings in the Ottoman age.

Khalwa, *Dhikr*, and *Nūrāniyya* (Luminosity), the Legacy of Sīdī Maḥmūd

Only two Ṣūfī *ṭuruq* are relevant to the *Qudwa*. On the one hand, the *Maḥmūdiyya*, founded by Sīdī Maḥmūd himself, and related by its chain of transmission to leading figures in the *Khalwatiyya* and the Ṣūfī movement in Merzifon which was both *Khalwatiyya* and *Bektāshiyya*, and, on the other hand, the *Suhrawardiyya*, which we are told was the order of the author of *Qudwa*, though nothing is said of this in the heart of the work itself. Retreats were to be found in the Aïr Massif as a feature of mysticism, and elsewhere in those regions, prior to the arrival of Sīdī Maḥmūd. The *khalwa*, in itself, does not mean that the *ṭarīqa* was *Khalwatiyya*. This monopoly is a late development in the history of Ṣūfism in Aïr. Secondly, the originality of the message of Sīdī Maḥmūd is to be found in other innovations. He encouraged a formal brotherhood with acknowledged strata of initiates. He made the *dhikr* an uninhibited central act of corporate worship, and he promoted the *dawarān*, the revolving movements of circles of men, as a ritual followed by adepts during their ceremonies. All this seems to have been a controversial matter in Saharan Ṣūfism at that time, and it is perhaps best illustrated by the description of the Kulumbardo ritual, which was very similar to the practice in Aïr.

The following comments suggest that similarities too close to be explained by coincidence existed with the *Maḥmūdiyya* not only in the commercial, agricultural, and educational goals of the movements but also in *dhikr*, *samāᶜ*, and *dawarān*, in an annual *khalwa* of forty days (as in the *Khalwatiyya* although also in individual retreat on the lines suggested by al-Suhrawardī in his *ᶜAwārif*).

Autrefois, les *mokaddems* des Koyams étaient de véritables *soufis* ou ascètes mystiques. Une de leurs pratiques religieuses caractéristiques était la suivante: tous les jeudis soirs, les disciples se mettaient en cercle autour du *mokaddem* et tournaient autour de lui pendant de longues heures en répétant: "*la ilaha ill allah Mohammed rassoul allah* (il n'y a de Dieu que Dieu et Mahomet est son prophète)", frappant en même temps leurs mains en cadence sur les cuisses. Ils avaient coutume aussi de faire chaque année une sorte de retraite religieuse pendant laquelle ils ne mangeaient qu'une fois par jour et ne sortaient de leur case (chacun d'eux ayant la sienne autour de celle du cheikh) que pour les prières. Cette retraite durait quarante jours; elle était supprimée pendant les années de famine. Autrefois, tous les Koyams observaient ces deux pratiques religieuses; actuellement, les *Talems* seuls les observent.[13]

The third legacy of Sīdī Maḥmūd to the Ṣūfism of the southern Saharan regions is far more difficult to assess. The *Qudwa* includes a passing reference to it, although it never discloses all its meaning to those whom it addresses on its pages. This is the doctrine of the 'light' of the Prophet Muḥammad, the *Nūr Muḥammadī*, the *ḥaqīqa Muḥammadiyya* of Ibn ᶜArabī. Sīdī Maḥmūd was the embodiment of such light and because of this his lineal descent, his status as a *sharīf*, is endowed with a special sanctity throughout the work, even more so in the popular belief of the devout in the Massif and in the desert of Azawagh. What he had to disclose in this doctrine was something quite new in those districts amongst its practising Ṣūfīs. Furthermore, it seems to have survived the demise of the *Maḥmūdiyya* and to have become an essential element in mystical life until recent times in the Niger desert.

An illustration of it, with a compelling simplicity, is to be seen and read in an Arabic inscription raised in the ruins of In Taduq. It is nameless, though the Tuareg *ineslemen* maintain that it is placed above the tomb of Abū'l-Hudā al-Sūqī, or another of the closest companions of Sīdī Maḥmūd.

In the name of Allāh, the Compassionate and Most Merciful. The blessing and peace of Allāh be upon our Lord, Muḥammad, upon his family and his companions. I bear witness that there is no god but Allāh. This is the tomb of the lordly Shaykh who wandered in the earth. His hand gave a [divine] light, bestowing happiness. His Ṣūfī 'Way' was that of Muḥammad and his spiritual states, together with his Shaykhs [who initiated him] were those of the 'Men of the Way', of a continuous chain of unbroken initiation. He was a summoner and a 'renewer of the "Way" ' of his Shaykhs, after their departure [to a better abode], until he, likewise, died therein. [Allāh] have mercy upon him and pardon him. O Lord, cause him to be with them in their loftiest of stations, O Lord, as Thou appointed him to be the one whose concern was Thy religion and to be a protector of it, be to him a keeper and a helper by Thy mercy. O Most Merciful of the merciful, O Lord of the worlds, most certainly, Lord, cause him to abide for ever, like unto the Prophets and the saints where'er they be in the blissful enjoyment of the contemplation of Thy countenance. By Allāh, O Allāh, verily Thou art the great Giver. O Lord, be to us the creative power of the religion after the Prophets and the saints.[14]

Notes

1. The life, building activities, and scholastic achievements of Zakariyyā' b. ᶜAbdallāh b. Ibrāhīm are to be read in the following book and articles: Aboubacar Adamou, *Agadez et sa Région* (Études Nigériennes n. 44; 1979), pp. 60–4; Patrice Cressier and Suzanne Bernus, 'La Grande Mosquée, Architecture et Histoire', *Journal des Africanistes* 54 (1/2); *Ta'rīkh masjid madīnat Akdas* (LRSH, Collection of Arabic Mss., Niamey, n. 57; 1986).
2. In Abanbary, 9 km. to the west of Agades; see the article by Cressier and Bernus, 'La Grande Mosquée', p. 6, n. 5.
3. John Hunwick, 'Notes on a late fifteenth-century document concerning "al-Takrūr" ', from C. H. Allen and R. W. Johnson (eds.), *African Perspectives* (Cambridge, 1970), p. 19.
4. I am indebted to Dr M. Zoubeir, to Dr Shammari, and to Mohamed Ben Madani for tracing this reference and for acquiring a copy of the passage for me from the Bibliothèque Nationale in Algiers, Ms. no. 532 (9°), fos. 150–3. It is dated 1158/1750 (or 1152, since the dating in the colophon is far from clear). Mr Paul Fox has kindly processed the microfiche. To him I am indebted for all the photos of the pages of the *Qudwa* which were taken by me in the house of Shaykh Muḥammad Ibrāhīm in Abalagh (Tahoua).
5. On Teghzerin, and this 'adopted' son of Sīdī Maḥmūd, see F. Nicolas, 'Etude sur l'Islam, les confréries et les centres maraboutiques chez les Twareg du Sud', in *Contribution à l'étude de l'Aïr* (Paris, 1950), pp. 480–91.
6. The name of his father was Muḥammad Wa-n-Ezekran (Inzakrīn), who came from Assodé (Asūṭay).
7. Elias, Ilyās b. Asāsiyā, with whom, in the *Maḥmūdiyya*, spiritual communion could be attained, so too with Jesus, receives special mention in the Agades text, *al-Iᶜlān*, attributed to Yūsuf al-Nabhānī. The passages in question are quoted in a collection of Aïr histories, assembled together by al-Sayyid Amanna b. Aḥmad Bugunū. The Arabic texts so collected were edited in 1968–9 by the late Boubou Hama. The passage in *al-Iᶜlān* would suggest that the scholar al-Najīb, who was the follower of Sīdī Maḥmūd, was a son of al-Najīb, who bore the nickname '*al-sayf*'. It confirms that the Sulṭān at that time was Aḥmad b. Talāzāy (Taluẓa) and it maintains that Abū'l-Hudā al-Sūqī was buried at In Taduq. It would therefore agree with *Ṣifat al-wird* on this point although not with the *Qudwa* as we have it. In *al-Iᶜlān*, Abū Ruways is described as an Algerian, and it is stated that he lies buried at Sanbaba. It is also stated that he himself became a disciple of Sīdī Maḥmūd, having trained a number of novices. Shaykh Muḥammad al-Amīn, it is maintained, was buried at Ṭawāz.
8. Rennell Rodd, *People of the Veil* (London, 1926), p. 260.

9. J. Hunwick, 'The Dynastic Chronologies of the Central Sudan States in the Sixteenth Century: Some Reinterpretations', *Kano Studies*, vol. i, no. 1 (1973), pp. 38–9.
10. Dierk Lange, *A Sudanic Chronicle: The Borno Expeditions of Idris Alauma (1564–1576)* (Wiesbaden, 1987), pp. 31–6 of the Arabic text, *al-faṣl al-khāmis, al-ghazawāt ᶜalā'l-Tawāriq*, pp. 70–5 of the English translation.
11. See J. R. Willis, *Studies in West African History*, vol. i, *The Cultivators of Islam* (London, 1979), pp. 148–9, and Constant Hamès, 'Cheikh Hamallah, ou qu'est ce qu'une confrèrie islamique (Ṭarīqa)?', *Archives des Sciences Sociales des Religions*, 55/1 (1983), pp. 73, 79–81.
12. L. Fekete, 'Gül-Baba et le *Bektasi Derk'ah* de Buda', *Acta Orientalia*, vol. iv (Budapest, 1954).
13. *Documents Scientifiques de la Mission Tilho (1906–1909)*, vol. ii (Paris, 1911), p. 397, n. 1.
14. I am grateful to Suzanne and Edmund Bernus for a copy of this inscription. Their initial report on In Taduq (*Programme Vallée de l'Azawagh*, Campagne Nov.–Déc., 1984), ch. 11, 'La Tradition' (by E. Bernus, pp. 31–2), cites Boubou Hama for the presence of the tomb there of another scholar, besides Abū'l-Hudā and Mawhūb b. Afalāwas, namely the *faqīh* ᶜAbd al-Raḥmān b. Takarsha al-Kuntī. This latter, about whom little or nothing is known, would appear to be later than the Tuareg *ineslemen*, though this suggests a continuing importance of In Taduq in Saharan Islam.

    In regard to the background to this illuminatory mysticism, see Edward Jabra Jurji, *Illumination in Islamic Mysticism*, (Princeton, 1938), more especially pp. 12–14. The term *maqtūl*, as opposed to *shahīd*, martyr, was applied to Yaḥyā al-Suhrawardī, and the same description, *al-Baghdādī al-maqtūl*, with its deprecatory connotation, is applied by Aḥmad Bābā to Sīdī Maḥmūd.

Glossary

Ṣūfī terms used by the Tuareg and non-Tuareg of Aïr, and which also appear in the *Qudwat al-muᶜtaqid fī siyar al-ajwād* by Shaykh (Abū'l-ᶜAbbās) Aḥmad al-Ṣādiq b. al-Shaykh Uwāyis al-Lamtūnī al-Tārikī.

abărăqqa/ibărăqqan Temajeq term, cf. Ghubăyd ăgg-Ălăwjeli, *Lexique Touareg-Français*, (Copenhagen, 1980), path, way or road (*chemin*), p. 10. According to F. Nicolas, 'Étude sur l'Islam, les confréries et les centres maraboutiques, chez les Twareg du Sud', *Contribution a l'étude de l'Aïr*, (*Mémoire de l'IFAN*, 10; Paris, 1950), this word is synonymous with *ṭarīqa* (see below with Ghubayd's comments).

abdāl (term appears in the *Qudwa*), the hierarchy of Ṣūfī saints, see R. A. Nicholson, *The Mystics of Islam* (London, 1914), pp. 123 ff. In the *Qudwa* this term normally means dervishes in general, compare John Kingsley Birge, *The Bektashi Order of Dervishes* (London, 1937), p. 251.

ādāb (term means in the *Qudwa*), rules of conduct, ethics, rules of 'the discipline to be observed in the prosecution of study, by the disciple with respect to the preceptor, and by the preceptor with respect to the disciple' (Lane, *Lexicon*). It indicates all the rules laid down in the *Maḥmūdiyya*.

ajwād (var. *ajāwīd*) term appears in the title of the *Qudwa*), the body of 'noble men' to whom, or about whom, the *Qudwa* is addressed. The sense in which it is used is by no means clear. It may well mean members of the *Maḥmūdiyya*, or the pupils of Shaykh Aḥmad, the author of the *Qudwa*, or it may embrace a much wider Tuareg group in Aïr. According to Issa Hassan Khayar, *Tchad, Regards sur les élites Ouaddaïennes*, (Paris, 1984), p. 204, '*Adjawīd* (sing. *adjwadi*): Au Ouaddai ce mot signifie également les nobles, les membres de la noblesse d'épée, et par extension les détenteurs du pouvoir . . .'

baraka divine blessing or 'grace' bestowed upon Ṣūfīs in holy places, in their communal meals, in prayer from a specific and revered Shaykh, and also from the discarded *khirqa* worn in the *samāᶜ* (see below).

dhikr (term appears frequently in the *Qudwa*), see *EI*. Both 'remembrance' and 'audible mention' are contained in its sense. More especially, an assembly of Ṣūfīs who are dedicated to the recitation of Allāh's name. In the *Maḥmūdiyya* the ritual is mainly confined to the repetition of divine names and phrases without musical accompaniment or ritual dancing, although the latter may also have been practised on some occasions.

al-faqīh (term employed frequently in the *Qudwa*), plural *fuqahā'*. This denotes a jurist and scholar without any pejorative sense. It also indicates the legalistic scholar who was opposed to the teachings of Sīdī Maḥmūd and who advised the Sulṭān of Agades to oppose him and finally to put him to death and disperse his movement. The term is known in the Temajeq of Aïr; *elfeqqĭy* is used specifically to indicate Sīdī Mahmūd himself in Ghubăyd,

Histoire des Kel Denneg (Copenhagen, 1975), pp. 21–2, 'La cause du combat d'Agǎlǎngha, était un Arabe *faquih* (*arab eyyǎn n-elfeqqǐy*) qui était venu de Baghdad et s'appelait Sidi Mekhmud Ǎlbǎghdadi.'

al-faqīr (plural *fuqarā'*) (both singular and plural are employed throughout the *Qudwa*). Sīdī Maḥmūd himself used the term to describe his followers, lay members as well as those dervishes who observed the rules of poverty. According to the *Qudwa*, 'The people repented at his hand. Amongst them were the *ʿulamā'* and the *ṭalaba*, whilst others were the ignorant common folk. Their number rose until it totalled almost one hundred. They were called the *fuqarā'* in this country. They joined together in order to perform the *dhikr* of Allāh Almighty.'

al-fātiḥa the opening *sūra* of the Qur'ān. This was frequently recited by Sīdī Maḥmūd, when he ascended the Aïr mountains, when he visited graveyards, and when he recited the *dhikr*. This *sūra* was likewise recited at various points of the ceremony of initiation (*talqīn*) into the *ṭarīqa* (see below).

al-ḥaqq according to Martin Lings, *A Sufi Saint of the Twentieth Century*, (London, 1971), p. 122, 'behind the illusory veil of created plurality there lies the one Divine Truth—not that God is made up of parts, but that underlying each apparently separate feature of the created universe there is the One Infinite Plenitude of God in His Indivisible Totality.'

ikhwān the 'brotherhood' or 'brethren', the fellow members of a Ṣūfī order or a religious sect. This expression very rarely appears in the *Qudwa*.

al-khādim (term used in parts of the *Qudwa* which refer to the history and the organization of the *ṭarīqa*). It specifically denotes a steward of a Ṣūfī brotherhood. In the *Maḥmūdiyya* it would appear to denote a subordinate, occasionally a deputy, of the *Shaykh*, who is responsible for advising, tutoring and channelling the wishes, complaints, and personal confessions of the *fuqarā'*.

khalwa (term which appears on numerous pages of the *Qudwa* and which is described in great detail both as a rite to be observed and as a physical cell or private hermitage wherein a prolonged retreat is to be practised). The term has specific meanings in the *Qudwa*: (*a*) the cell of retreat based on the tradition of the Prophet's retreat in the Hirā' cave, (*b*) the recommendations of al-Suhrawardī in this regard (the author of the *Qudwa* was a Suhrawardī), (*c*) entry into *khalwa* after the *ʿishā'* prayer on a Tuesday night and exit from it after the sunset prayer on Friday night, (*d*) retreat during *Ramaḍān* and exit to celebrate *ʿĪd al-Fiṭr*, (*e*) gathering during a period of *khalwa* to obtain the correction of the Shaykh, followed by the recitation of the *fātiḥa* (see above) followed by a *dhikr*, (*f*) a cell of specific dimensions, without aperture, niche, or cellar, located on the outskirts of a village in an unfrequented spot. A privy should be half a mile distant, likewise a supply of water, (*g*) whilst in the *khalwa*, sleep should be avoided, similarly any harm or injury to any living creature. (see ch. 6). Nowhere is the *Khalwatiyya ṭarīqa* mentioned specifically in the *Qudwa*.

khirqa the standard term for the Ṣūfī mantle worn during the *dhikr* or *samā*ᶜ and an important ritual in the *Maḥmūdiyya*. It is often a coarse woollen garment, occasionally decorated. If such a *khirqa*, filled with *baraka* (see above), is thrown off during the *samā*ᶜ it is 'divided' amongst the participants. The redemption of the *khirqa* by some pecuniary payment, before it is returned to the Ṣūfī, or Ṣūfīs, is conditionally justified by al-Suhrawardī. His view is quoted by the author of the *Qudwa*.

al-kull the attainment of the Universal and the passing away of human attributes to God. This is the highest level of experience attainable in the *samā*ᶜ.

al-Mahdī the guided one, see *EI*. In the *Qudwa* discussion revolves around the signs of the eschatological Mahdī who will appear at the end of time and, on the other hand, a disclaimer that Sīdī Maḥmūd was the *Mahdī* foretold, a claim made by his enemies. On the other hand it is probable that, during his lifetime, some of the supporters of the *Maḥmūdiyya* did make claims of an excessive kind and that this could have led to alarm and suspicion amongst the *ᶜulamā'* of Aïr in the sixteenth century.

al-mashāyikh the company of Ṣūfī Shaykhs. In the *Qudwa* this term is specifically used to mean those whose words and lives conformed to the words and example of Sīdī Maḥmūd himself.

al-muqaddam an overseer in a Ṣūfī *ṭarīqa*, the one who is specifically authorized to teach the *wird* (see below) of the *ṭarīqa* and to grant the *ijāza* of affiliation to it. (The term appears frequently in the *Qudwa* and was clearly well known and highly regarded in the *Maḥmūdiyya*.) Awgar Aḥmad, nicknamed the *muqaddam*, was the first of the Ṣūfī disciples of Sīdī Maḥmūd, following, it is said, a description of him by the Algerian reformist, al-Maghīlī. The *muqaddam* played a major part in the disciplining of the *murīdūn*, (see *murīd*, below). Interestingly, in a question sent to al-Suyūṭī from Aïr, it is the Sulṭān of Agades himself who is called the '*muqaddam* of Aïr'.

al-murīd a Ṣūfī novice. The *murīd* is initiated into a *ṭarīqa* by a special *rite de passage* which will vary in detail from one *ṭarīqa* to another.

al-naqīb a superintendent and overseer who is responsible for the maintenance of discipline amongst the *murīdūn* (see above) (the term appears only rarely in the *Qudwa*; only one *naqīb* of Sīdī Maḥmūd is mentioned, Shaykh Tibardudāz).

al-nūrāniyya the belief in the Divine 'Light', see *Nūr* in the *EI*. (The term is found rarely in the *Qudwa* though it is prominent in the teachings of the *Maḥmūdiyya* to whom Sīdī Maḥmūd himself was a living manifestation of the Divine Light.) This doctrine and belief was also prominent in the teachings of his successor, Muḥammad b. Muḥammad Amezdennig, who, to cite the *Qudwa* (see ch. 4), 'was a scholar and pious saint, the pillar of Islam and the *Imām* of the chosen elect and of the masses. In his doctrine and his belief he was a follower in his (Sīdī Maḥmūd's) belief in the gnostic emanatory and illuminatory principle of the divinity (*al-nūrāniyya*).'

ribāṭ see *EI*. The word appears only once in the *Qudwa*. The sense there seems to be a stronghold, or headquarters of the *Maḥmūdiyya* in the Aïr Massif, or else a community of members from whose grace and fellowship a disobedient novice or lay member could be banished. If such a member refused repentance, pay out of his wealth, the undertaking of some service, or retirement into a retreat, then they would cut him off from the *ṭarīqa*. 'Whosoever is not an established member amongst them, him they banish from their *ribāṭ*.' (See ch. 6, under 'Following the Way'.)

*samā*ᶜ a ritual and communal form of divine service introduced into Aïr by Sīdī Maḥmūd himself (the term receives much mention in the *Qudwa*, and how and when it is held is explained in some detail). The *samā*ᶜ of the *Maḥmūdiyya* seems to have principally included recited prayers, *dhikr* (see above), 'speaking in tongues', dancing, long breathing exclamations of the divine name, clapping, and ecstatic cries (*shaṭḥiyyāt*).

al-ṣawm (fasting of various kinds is recommended as a discipline in several parts of the *Qudwa*), see Ghubayd, p. 222, '*uẓam*, jeûner, *eẓum*/*iẓămmăm*, jeûne, carême, jeûne du Ramadan.' The special fasts which are specified for *fuqarā'* in the *Maḥmūdiyya* include: Monday, Thursday, *Rajab*, nine days in *Dhū'l-Ḥijja*, and voluntary fasting by individual members, in addition to the month of *Ramaḍān*.

*sharī*ᶜ*a* (mentioned throughout the *Qudwa* in various contexts). See the *EI*. The canonic law of Islam. Sīdī Maḥmūd's teaching saw no conflict between Ṣūfism and the *sharī*ᶜ*a*, 'Shaykh (Sīdī Maḥmūd)—may Allāh be pleased with him—used to say, "the *fuqarā'* are upon the scales of the *sharī*ᶜ*a* (*mīzān al-sharī*ᶜ*a*)" ' (see p. 59). In Temajeq, see Ghubayd, p. 185, '*eshregh*, juger, *ăsshărigha*/*ăsshărighatăn*, droit musulman, judgement, legislation (quelconque).'

sharīf (a title given to several Shaykhs in the *Qudwa*, but especially to Sīdī Maḥmūd himself). Descent from the Prophet, to cite Mūsā Abatūl, gives Sīdī Maḥmūd a pedigree, both through Ṣūfī Shaykhs and a Ḥasanid genealogy, to ᶜAlī b. Abī Ṭālib, (see Jean-Louis Triaud, 'Hommes de religion', *Cahiers d'Études Africaines*, 23/3, 91, (1983), pp. 275–6). *F. Nicolas, 'Étude sur l'Islam . . .', Contribution a l'étude de l'Aïr* (Paris, 1950), mentions several of the Shaykhs of the *Maḥmūdiyya* as being *shurafā'* from the Kel Es-Sūq of the Mali Adrār. Ghubayd, p. 185, gives the Temajeq, '*essherif*/*essherifăn*, descendant du Prophète,' and '*oshrăf*/*oshrăfăn*, honneur, dignite, noblesse, fait d'être *essherif*.

shaykh (title given to all the leading religious figures of the *Maḥmūdiyya* who receive a mention in the *Qudwa*). The Temajeq form, see Ghubayd, p. 184, takes a form known also in the Western Sahara, '*esshikh*/*ęsshikhăn*, maître d'études religieuses (quelconque), supérieur, chef religieux, saint, personne sainte (vivant ou mort).'

silsila the spiritual chain of initiation and descent within a specific Ṣūfī *ṭarīqa* (see below). The latter part of the *Qudwa* sets forth the *silsila* of the *Maḥmūdiyya*, which includes the names of several leading figures of the

Khalwatiyya. There is some evidence to suggest that the author of the *Qudwa* was himself a figure of importance in the *silsila* of the *Maḥmūdiyya* during the period between the death of its founder and the virtual extinction of the *ṭarīqa* before its reconstruction by Shaykh Mūsā Abatūl.

Snbl (Sanbaba?) these radicals indicate a locality in the Aïr Massif, mentioned in both the *Qudwa* and *Ṣifat al-wird* (by Shaykh Mūsā) as a centre for the followers of Sīdī Maḥmūd and as a burial place. While some connection with the Ottomon *Sünbüliyya ṭarīqa*, possibly the 'mother order' for the *Maḥmūdiyya*, cannot be wholly discounted, it seems far more likely that the Temajeq, '*enḅel/senḅel*, enterrer', (see Ghubayd, p. 138) accounts for this name.

taleqqî a term which is not found in the *Qudwa* but which would appear to be connected with *al-faqīr* (see above), the conventional term for the followers of Sīdī Maḥmūd. According to F. Nicolas, 'Étude sur l'Islam. . .', *Constitution a l'étude de l'Aïr* (Paris, 1950), p. 48: 'Auprès, sont toujours des nécropoles, avec petites mosquées-annexes, bâtisses-magasin, reposoirs de plein air dans lesquels le marabout prie à longueur de journée, et où le fidèle, l'*Humble* (*Taleqqî*) vient, derrière lui, imiter son *Rite* après sa tâche.'

According to Ghubayd, p. 111, '*taleqqe/tileqqawen*, pauvre, *taleqqăy*, membre d'une famille/tribu pauvre/client (protégé)/sujet (d'une autorité quelconque)'. This would correspond to the *fuqarā'* in the *Qudwa*.

temezgedda Temajeq for any form of mosque, loan-word from the Arabic word *masjid*.

ṭarīqa sometimes *ṭarīq*, the mystical 'way' and also the specific term used for a Ṣūfī Order or 'Way', e.g. *al-ṭarīqa al-Maḥmūdiyya*. (The term *ṭarīq* is used more frequently in the *Qudwa*). The form *ṭarīqa* has also come into Temajeq in Aïr, see Ghubayd, pp. 20–3, 'La cause du combat d'Agălăngha était un Arabe *faquih* qui était venu de Baghdad et s'appelait Sidi Mekhmud Ălbăghdadi, et qui, convertissait les gens à sa doctrine (*etteriqăt-net*). Beaucoup de Kél-Ăwăy le suivirent, il construisit une mosquée (*temezgedda*) à Agălăngha, et augmenta chez les Kél-Ăwăy l'hostilité envers les Iberḳorăyăn, parce que ceux-ci refusèrent la doctrine qu'il avait apportée, et parce qu'il apprit qu'ils disaient qu'elle était pure perdition. Or sa doctrine (*etteriqăt-net*) était la *Khalwatiyya (ălkhălutĭyya)*, alors que certains de ses adversaires professaient la *Qâdiriyya* (*elqaderĭyya*), et que d'autres *n'avaient aucune doctrine particulière* (*weyyaḍ wer-elen etteriqăt welĭyyăt*).

al-taṣliya the phrase 'the blessing and peace of God be upon the Prophet'. This term throughout the *Qudwa* is particularly associated with the *wird* (see below) of the *Maḥmūdiyya*.

tayammum ablutions made with sand before prayer where water is lacking. This figured prominently in the *Maḥmūdiyya*. According to the *Qudwa*, 'Amongst their rules is constant purity. As one of them said, "I hate to be impure." When a brother arises in the daytime and he finds no water, he will strike his hands upon the walls and will perform the dry ablutions (*tayammum*), guarding his purity, until he finds water.' (see ch. 6).

al-tawba 'repentance' (term used frequently in the *Qudwa*). Repentance and penitence are enforced for misdemeanours, slight or grave, which are committed by novices. This Arabic word is also used in the Temajeq of Aïr, see Ghubayd, p. 187, '*utab*, avoir le regret de (un péché commis) avec la ferme décision de ne plus le commettre, se repentir de.'

tékotâwin see F. Nicolas, 'Étude sur l'Islam . . .', *Contribution à l'étude de l'Aïr* (Paris, 1950), p. 483, (term not used in the *Qudwa*) which relates to the practice of almsgiving during the prayer on the day when the fast is broken (*amûd*). The term is found in Aïr Temajeq, see Ghubayd, p. 102, '*takuteltikutawen*, aumône.' The word may be related to Arabic *ṣadaqa*, likewise *izdag*, p. 209.

wārid al-dhikr term mentioned in the *Qudwa* as part of the *dhikr* (see above), a sudden inspiration which comes to the participant, a prompting of some mystical state, a sudden inspiration of the divine influence which 'may enliven his presence in an instant in such a way that is not to be achieved by religious exercises and by strenuous efforts for over thirty years'. *Wārid* also means 'the revelation of hidden meanings in the heart of the Ṣūfī, and the *wāridāt*, a more general term, for mystical revelations. This term, as several others in the *Qudwa* in regard to the Divine Light (see *al-nūrāniyya* above) and 'the Truth', (*al-ḥaqq*, see above), discloses an influence of the teachings of Ibn al-ᶜArabī within the *Maḥmūdiyya*.

al-wird the specific series of invocations or prayer (litany?) which are determined by the founder of a specific *ṭarīqa* (see above). These are recited during the *dhikr* and *samāᶜ* (see above) and during the ceremony of initiation (*talqīn*) into the *ṭarīqa*. According to De Jong, in his article on the *Khalwatiyya* in the *EI*, all branches of it have the *wird al-Sattār* of Yaḥyā al-Shirwānī (Shirvānī) of Baku, whose name appears in the *silsila* of the *Maḥmūdiyya*. Designed to preserve the faithful from sins, it includes praises of God, the Prophet, the Companions, and a request for a blessing. An entire section of the *Qudwa* is concerned with the *wird* of the *Maḥmūdiyya*. 'As for their *wird*, it is the prayer which prays for blessings upon the Prophet (the *taṣliya*), and it is one thousand of such prayers every Friday night, and one hundred every night coupled to the *wird* of the sunset prayer' (see ch. 6, under 'A chapter concerning their *wird*'). A few verses of the *ᶜIshrīniyyāt* of al-Fāzāzī and the *Witriyyāt*(?) by Muḥammad b. Abī Bakr al-Baghdādī (?) are also recited.

Bibliography

Adamou, A., *Agadez et sa région: Contribution à l'étude du Sahel et du Sahara nigériens* (Institut de recherches en sciences humaines, Études nigériennes, 44; Niamey, 1979).

ăgg-Ălăwjeli, Ghubăyd, *Ăttarikh en-Kel-Denneg/Histoire des Kel-Denneg*, ed. & trad. par K.-G. Prasse (Akademisk Forlag; Copenhagen, 1975).

Arberry, A. J., *Muslim Saints and Mystics* (London, 1966).

Bannerth, E., 'La Khalwatiyya en Égypte: Quelques aspects de la vie d'une confrérie', *Mélanges de l'Institut Dominicain d'Études Orientales du Caire*, 8, 1964–66, 1–74.

Bataillon, P., *L'Islam et l'organisation politique des Touaregs du Niger* ('Mémoire du CHEAM, 937; Paris, 1946).

Batrān, 'A. 'A., A Contribution to the Biography of Shaikh Muḥammad Ibn 'Abd-al-Karīm Ibn Muḥammad ('Umar-A'mar) al-Maghīlī, Al-Tilimsānī', *Journal of African History*, 14/3, 1973, 381–94.

Bello, M., *Infāq al-maysur*, (Cairo, 1964).

Bernus, E., 'Aïr (techniques agricoles)', *Encyclopédie berbère* (Aix-en-Provence, Université de Provence, Laboratoire d'anthropologie et de préhistoire des pays de la Méditerranée occidentale, 1973, 3).

—— 'Les Palmeraies de l'Aïr', *Revue de l'Occident musulman et de la Méditerranée*, 2, 1972, 37–50.

Bernus, E., Bernus, S., and Cressier, P., *Programme Vallée de l'Azawagh, Campagne Novembre–Decembre, 1984* (Documents provisoires, Equipe ORSTOM-CNRS (UR B22), Paris, 1985).

Bernus, S. (ed. and trans.), *Henri Barth chez les Touaregs de l'Aïr: extraits du Journal de Barth dans l'Aïr, juillet–décembre 1850* (Niamey, Centre nigérien de recherche en sciences humaines, 'Études nigériennes', 1972, 28).

Birge, J. K., *The Bektashi Order of Dervishes* (London, 1937).

Bisson, J., 'Eleveurs-caravaniers et vieux sédentaires de l'Aïr sud-oriental', *Travaux de l'Institut de Recherches sahariennes* (Alger), 23, 1964, 95–110.

Corpus of Early Arabic Sources for West African History, trans. by J. F. P. Hopkins, ed. and annotated by N. Levtzion and J. F. P. Hopkins (Cambridge, 1981).

Cressier, P., and Bernus, S. 'La grande mosquée d'Agadez: Architecture et Histoire', *Journal des Africanistes*, 54 (1/2), 1986.

Daumas, E., and Chancel, A. de, *Le Grand Désert, ou Itinéraire d'une caravane du Sahara au pays des Nègres (royaume Haoussa)*, (Paris, 1848).

De Jong, F., 'Khalwatiyya, in *Encyclopedia of Islam*, new English edn., Leide, vol. iv, 1978, 1023–6, pp. 991–3.

DEPONT. O. and X. COPPOLANI *Les Confréries religieuses musulmanes*, (Algiers, 1897).

DRESCH, J., 'Notes de géographie humaine sur l'Aïr', *Annales de Géographie*, 367, 1959, 257–63.

GAUBERT, M., *Les Kel Owëy, groupement touareg de l'Aër* (Paris; Mémoire du CHEAM, 1948, 1315).

HAMA, BOUBOU, *Recherches sur l'Histoire des Touareg Sahariens et Soudanais*, (Publication de la Republique du Niger, Presence Africaine, Niamey, 1967).

HISKETT, M., 'The "Song of the Shehu's Miracles": A Hausa Hagiography from Sokoto', *African Language Studies*, xii, 1971.

—— *The Sword of Truth* (Oxford, 1973).

—— *The Development of Islam in West Africa*, (London, 1984).

HUNWICK, J. O., 'Notes on a Late Fifteenth-Century Document concerning "al-Takrûr" ', in C. Allen and R. W. Johnson (eds.), *Africa Perspectives: Papers in the History, Politics and Economics of Africa Presented to Thomas Hodgkin* (Cambridge, 1970), 7–33.

—— 'Songhay, Bornu and Hausaland in the Sixteenth Century', in J. F. A. Ajayi and M. Crowder (eds.), *History of West Africa*, (London, 1975), vol. i, 202–39.

—— Sharīʿa in Songhay: *The Replies of al-Maghīlī to ten questions of Askia al-Ḥājj Muhammad*, ed. and trans. with an introduction and commentary (Fontes Historiae Africanae, Series Arabica V; Oxford, 1985).

JEAN, C., *Les Touareg du Sud-Est: l'Aïr; leur rôle dans la politique saharienne* (Paris, 1909).

KHAYAR, ISSA HASSAN, *Tchad, Regards sur le élites Ouaddaïennes* (Editions du Centre National de la Recherche Scientifique, Paris, 1984).

KHUSHAIM, DR. ALI FAHMI, *Zarrūq the Ṣūfī*, General Company for Publication, Tripoli, and Robert Hale and Co, London, 1967 (especially Chapter IV, the Ṣūfī Way according to Zarrūq, in view of the alleged link between the pupils of Aḥmad b. Aḥmad Zarrūq and the early membership of the *Maḥmūdiyya* (see page 45)).

KISSLING, H. J., 'Aus der Geschichte des Chalvetijje-Ordens', *Zeitschrift der Deutschen Morgenländischen Gesellschaft*, 1032/2, 1953, 233–89.

LANGE, D., *A Sudanic Chronicle: The Borno Expeditions of Idrīs Alauma (1954–1576) according to the Account of Aḥmad B. Furtu*, Arabic text, English translation, commentary and geographical gazeteer, (Studien zur Kulturkunde, 86; Wiesbaden / Stuttgart, 1987).

LAURENT, C., *L'Aïr et ses gens* (Memoire du CHEAM, 4236; Paris, 1966).

MADELUNG, WILFERD, The Sufyānī between tradition and history, *Studia Islamica*, LXIII, 1986, pp. 5–48.

MARTIN, B. G., 'Notes sur l'origine de la *tarīqa* des Tiğāniyya, et sur les débuts d'al-Hāğğ ʿUmar', *Revue des Études islamiques*, 37/2, 1969, 267–90.

—— 'A Short History of the Khalwati Order of Dervishes', in N. R. Keddie (ed.), *Scholars, Saints and Sufis: Muslim Religious Institutions in the Middle East since 1500* (Berkeley, 1972), 275–305.

—— 'ᶜMaî Idrîs of Bornu and the Ottoman Turks, 1576–78', *International Journal of Middle East Studies*, vol. 3, 1972, 470–90.

—— *Muslim Brotherhoods in Nineteenth-Century Africa* (Cambridge, 1976).

MARTY, P., 'L'Islam et les tribus dans la colonie du Niger', *Revue des Études islamiques*, 2nd ser., 5/2, 1931, 139–240.

MILSON, M., *A Sufi Rule for Novices*, Kitāb Ādāb al-Murīdīn of Abū'l Najīb al-Suhrawardī (Harvard Middle Eastern Studies; Cambridge, Mass., 1975).

NICOLAISEN, J., *Ecology and Culture of the Pastoral Tuareg of Ayr and Ahaggar* (Ethnografisk Raekke', 9; Copenhagen, 1963).

NICOLAS, F., 'L'Islam en Aër (colonie du Niger)', in *Questions sahariennes* ('Mémoire du CHEAM', 1009; Paris, 1046), 122–34.

—— 'Contribution à l'étude des Twareg de l'Aïr', in *Contribution à l'étude de l'Aïr* ('Mémoire de l'IFAN', 10; Paris, 1950), 459–80.

—— 'Étude sur l'Islam, les confréries et les centres maraboutiques chez les Twareg du Sud', in *Contribution á l'étude de l'Aïr* ('Mémoire de l'IFAN', 10; Paris, 1950), 480–91.

NORRIS, H. T., *The Tuaregs: Their Islamic Legacy and its Diffusion in the Sahel*, (Warminster, 1975).

—— 'Sīdī Mahmūd al-Baghdādī: His Life and Teachings', in *Fontes Historiae Africanae: Bulletin d'Information / Bulletin of Information* (Evanston, 1982–3), 59–62.

—— 'À la recherche de Sîdî Mahmûd al-Baghdâdî: The *Silsila of the Mahmûdiyya Tarîqa in the "Qudwa"* ', *Islam et Sociétés au Sud du Sahara* (Paris, 1989), no. 3, pp. 128–58.

NWYIA, P., *Ibn 'Ata' Allāh (m. 709/1309) et la naissance de la confrérie shādhilite*, ed. and trans. with an Introduction and Notes (Beirut, 1972).

PALMER, H. R., 'Notes on Some Asben Records', *Journal of the Royal African Society*, 9/36, 1910, 388–400.

—— *History of the First Twelve Years of the Reign of Mai Idris Alooma of Bornu (1571–1583)*, by Ahmed ibn Fartua, trans. Palmer, (Lagos, 1926), 31–5.

—— 'An Asben Record', in id., *The Bornu, Sahara and Sudan*, (London, 1936).

REIBELL, E., *L'Épopée Saharienne: Carnet de route de la mission saharienne Foureau-Lamy (1898–1900)* (Paris, 1931).

RICHARDSON, J., *Travels in the Great Desert of Sahara in 1845 and 1846* . . . , (London, 1848). 2 vols.

—— *Narrative of a Mission to Central Africa Performed in the Years 1850–51* (London, 1853), 2 vols.

RINN, L., *Marabouts et Khouan, Etude sur l'Islam en Algérie* (Algiers, 1884).

ROBINSON, F., 'Islamic History as the History of Learned and Holy Men', *La Transmission du savoir dans le monde musulman périphérique* (CNRS, Jeune Equipe, no. 42.004, Lettre d'information, no. 5, Paris, 1986), 1–10.

Rodd, F. J. Rennell, *People of the Veil: Being an Account of the Habits, Organisation and History of the Wandering Tuareg Tribes Which Inhabit the Mountains of Air or Asben in the Central Sahara*, (London, 1926).

Saad, Elias, N., *Social History of Timbuktu: the role of Muslim Scholars and Notables, 1400–1900*, (Cambridge, 1983).

Schimmel, A., *Mystical Dimensions of Islam*, (Chapel Hill, 1975).

Stewart, C. C., 'Southern Saharan Scholarship and the *Bilad al-Sudan*', *Journal of African History*, 17, 1 1976, 73–93.

Tawfīq al-Ṭawīl, *al-Taṣawwuf fī Miṣr ibbāna'l- ^{c}aṣr al- ^{c}Uthmānī, Ṣūfīsm in Egypt during the Ottoman age, al-Silsila al-falsafiyya al-ijtimā^{c}iyya*, No. 3, Cairo, 1946.

Triaud, J.-L., 'L'Islam et l'État en République du Niger', *Le Mois en Afrique*, 192–3, 1981, 9–26; 194–5, 1982, 35–48.

—— 'Hommes de religion et confrériers islamiques dans une société en crise, L'Aïr aux XIXe et XXe siècles, Le cas de la Khalwatiyya', *Cahiers d'Études africaines*, 91, 23/3, 1983, 239–80.

Trimingham, J. S., *A History of Islam in West Africa* (Oxford, 1962).

—— *The Sufi Orders in Islam* (Oxford, 1971).

Urvoy, Y. 'Chronique d'Agadès', *Journal de la Société des Africanistes*, 4/2, 1934, 145–77.

Indices

I. Index of Qur'an references in the text of the *Qudwa* by Shaykh Aḥmad al-Ṣādiq [b] al-Shaykh Uwāyis al-Lamtūnī and in *al-Lam*[c] *fī ajwibat al-as'ila al-arba*[c]*a* by Shaykh Aḥmad Bābā al-Tinbuktī

II. Index of Proper Names and Saharan Tribes

III. Geographical Index

IV. Index of Islamic and Ṣūfī terms and of Arabic literary works